THE CLASSICAL DEBT

THE CLASSICAL DEBT

GREEK ANTIQUITY IN AN
ERA OF AUSTERITY

JOHANNA HANINK

THE BELKNAP PRESS OF
HARVARD UNIVERSITY PRESS

Cambridge, Massachusetts
London, England

2017

First printing

Library of Congress Cataloging-in-Publication Data
Names: Hanink, Johanna, 1982– author.
Title: The classical debt : Greek antiquity in an era of austerity /
Johanna Hanink.
Description: Cambridge, Massachusetts : The Belknap Press
of Harvard University Press, 2017. | Includes bibliographical
references and index.
Identifiers: LCCN 2016044934 | ISBN 9780674971547 (alk. paper)
Subjects: LCSH: Hellenism. | Greece—Civilization—To 146 B.C. |
Debt—Greece. | Greece—Relations—Western countries. |
Western countries—Relations—Greece.
Classification: LCC DF77 .H3423 2017 | DDC 938—dc23
LC record available at https://lccn.loc.gov/2016044934

To Costas Efimeros and Konstantinos Poulis,
who reminded me to look ahead at my lighted candles

CONTENTS

PREFACE

A 2016 ILLUSTRATION BY GREECE'S most famous cartoonist, Arkas, depicts ancient Athenians standing in front of the Acropolis. In the cartoon, an orator stands atop a speaking platform and is berating his fellow citizens: "It was a crime for us to create such a civilization! Just think of the economic crises and memoranda the foreigners will inflict on our descendants out of jealousy!" This book was prompted by the Greek economic crisis, but it is not a book about the Greek economic crisis. It is, essentially, an attempt to explain that cartoon.

The seed of this book was nevertheless planted when I found myself, somewhat unexpectedly, a front-row spectator of the crisis. From February 2014 to June 2015, thanks to a research sabbatical and certain personal developments, I lived partially in Greece. During those months, I became outraged at the international media's coverage of the crisis— at all the cheap "Greek tragedy" puns, cartoons of Greek banks "in ruins," and think pieces about what Greeks today might learn by, say, brushing up on ancient Stoicism. That lightheartedness seemed to stand in sinister contrast to a reality that I was, even from Greece, only glimpsing.

Ever since the global financial crisis crossed Greek borders, rates of unemployment, poverty, and even suicide have been staggering. Even friends of mine who have jobs have not been paid in months and live with the constant prospect of being evicted from their homes. Colleagues struggle to continue their research without access to basic resources. In the summer of 2015, when capital controls restricted the amount of money that could leave the country or its ATMs on any given day, a friend confessed to me how worried he was about whether his father would be able to continue with chemotherapy. Over the year and a half during which I spent so much of my time in Greece, I felt increasingly helpless as I watched people close to me suffer, and I could only fume over how the media seemed to find the whole situation deliciously ironic. Inspired by the great international esteem for ancient Greek civilization, they were painting the crisis as something of a giant practical joke that the Greeks of today had decided to play on the world.

On June 25, 2015, the life that I was half living in Greece came, at least temporarily, to an end. About twenty-four hours after my flight touched down in Boston, in the early hours of June 27, Prime Minister Alexis Tsipras announced that he would hold his bailout referendum.

Not long before I had left, I had met Konstantinos Poulis on the island of Icaria. Poulis is a brilliant author; he is also one of Greece's most esteemed political analysts and the host of the popular satirical show *Anaskopisi* (he also holds a doctorate in Classics). Meeting him was one of the most providential things that has ever happened to me. When I got back to the United States, I wrote to Konstantinos, who is a regular contributor to the Greek news outlet *ThePressProject,* to say that I would be happy to help edit English versions of articles for the site's international edition. He put me in contact with Costas Efimeros, the editor in chief, and within hours I was frantically translating articles for the site's English-language feed. I was still numb from the circumstances that had caused me to leave Greece, but work for *ThePressProject*—depressing work, of course, given the nature of the news rolling in—allowed me to feel at last that I was helping, even if just a tiny bit. During some of the most difficult months that Greece has seen in decades, Costas and Konstantinos both stayed in hourly contact with me. Their friendship and encouragement—and the inspiration of their examples—brought me back to life. That is why I dedicate this book to them; no one else knows so well all the stories between its lines.

As I worked for *ThePressProject* and kept glued to the news about Greece, the cartoons and op-eds with classical clichés only came thicker and faster. A few days into July, I decided that I was ready to write about it. I reached out to Donna Zuckerberg, who had recently started an on-line journal called *Eidolon* ("a modern way to write about the ancient world," Eidolon.pub), to ask whether she would be interested in a piece about antiquity's role in representations of the crisis. She told me that she was, and without that first green light this book would not have been written. With Donna's guidance, the article I was writing quickly transformed into a critique of how classicists, of all people, were actually contributing to the problem by dredging up ancient economic advice and comparing the Greeks to the hapless characters of ancient comedy. The piece was published on July 20, 2015, as "Ode on a Grecian Crisis: What Can Classicists Really Say about the Greek Economy?" Small parts of it have been integrated into the text of Chapter 6 here.

The piece got more reaction than I expected. Friends and strangers alike began sending me link after link to articles whose headlines and authors brought Greek antiquity to bear on the financial crisis and soon on the refugee one as well. After a few weeks, I decided that there was more than enough material for a book. Tim Whitmarsh put me in contact with George Lucas of Inkwell Management, who guided me through writing the book proposal and helped me turn a hodgepodge of thoughts and observations into a coherent argument. Felipe Rojas, Kevin McLaughlin, and Mark Blyth all generously commented on drafts of that proposal. (It was, I admit, no small encouragement to hear

Mark tell me, with what I think was a touch of surprise, that he thought I was on to something.)

A few months later, I was overjoyed to hear that Sharmila Sen at Harvard University Press was willing to take a chance on the project. She retaught me to write and pushed me hard to widen the scope of my argument and deepen the argumentation. At the press, I am also grateful to Heather Hughes, as well as to Louise Robbins, whose careful comments showed me how the first draft of this book could be rethought and reworked. I am also deeply in debt to the manuscript's two anonymous readers, whose detailed and challenging reports pushed me to rethink my assumptions and voice.

Throughout the entire process, colleagues at Brown University were unfailingly generous with their time and insight. I am especially grateful to Andrew Laird, Graham Oliver, Jay Reed, and Ken Sacks. Charles Larmore put me on to Rémi Brague and his notion of *secondarité*. I also benefited enormously from the generosity of Yannis Hamilakis, my new colleague at Brown, whose work on so many aspects of the Greek "nation and its ruins" has been foundational for this book.

Other friends and colleagues provided essential and much-appreciated intellectual and psychological support. After every conversation I had about this project with Nancy Khalek, I went home and wrote down notes. Felipe Rojas read and commented on many late drafts of chapters, and I was inspired largely by his own work to write Chapter 3's section on Evliya Çelebi. Vangelis Calotychos, unsurprisingly, turned out to be a bottomless well of knowledge and insight. Trigg Settle and Matt Wellenbach read and commented on various phases of every chapter. Their notes and suggestions strengthened my arguments, saved me from factual mistakes, and greatly improved my prose. I am also grateful to two undergraduate students, Kathleen Larkin and Kutay Onayli, for their comments, conversation, and general enthusiasm. Kathleen was my research assistant in the spring of 2015 and wrote a beautiful undergraduate honors thesis about how Greek myths have been used (and often misused) in coverage of the crisis.

Ilias Papagiannopoulos and Yanis Varoufakis were both gracious enough to allow me to interview them. Ilias, like Yannis Hamilakis, also kindly shared forthcoming work. Josh Pugh Ginn, Vassilis Varouhakis (aka Punx Minoica), and "Byzantine Justice" (@ByzantJustice) were lively and insightful correspondents. In April 2016, Sarah Thomas and I organized a miniconference at Brown, "Crash Culture: Humanities Engagements with Economic Crisis," which introduced me to a whole new set of inspiring scholars: Sebastian Faaber, Alex Gourevitch, Despina Lalaki, and Luis Moreno Caballud. That conference, rounded off by comments from the inimitable Cornel Ban, was generously funded by Brown's Office of the Dean of the Faculty, the Watson Institute for International and Public Affairs, the Cogut Center for Humanities, and the Department of Hispanic Studies. Sarah herself, along with Daniel Blanco, has been a boundless source of cheerfulness and general positive thinking over the past few years. Many ideas presented here began to take shape at the Thomas-Blanco Alehouse.

Two other friends deserve special mention. Anna Uhlig supported me and this book at every phase and read every word in its last one. I still consider her my intellectual better half. Elsa Amanatidou, now the director of Brown's Program in Modern Greek Studies, also provided encouragement and insight at every step. I once heard someone describe Elsa as "made of magic," and over the past six years I have had countless opportunities to confirm that this is true.

I would also like to thank Artemis Leontis, the scholar so often cited for her important observation that the Greek people, too, have experienced "colonization of the mind." In my last semester as an undergraduate at the University of Michigan, I took her course in modern Greek history. Ten summers ago, when I visited Athens for the first time, she showed me the city and made sure that I got a metro map and a SIM card. When I graduated from the University of Michigan, she gave me a copy of Henry Miller's *The Colossus of Maroussi*. Now, many years later, I think that I better appreciate what that book meant to her, and what she thought it might mean to me.

My family was, as ever, enormously supportive throughout. My father, Dean Hanink, a professor of geography, read and commented on everything that I wrote, from the initial proposal to the last draft of the book's Epilogue. When I was young, his father, the legendary John Hanink, used to send him monthly batches of issues of the *Economist*. Today, my father sometimes leaves an issue or two behind when he visits me in Rhode Island. I am proud to count myself in the third generation of Haninks to read, admire, and grow exasperated at that magazine, whose coverage of the Greek crisis both inspired and shaped this book's arguments. I also have to mention that a sweet pup named Nova arrived in my life at the end of January 2015. She and our daily beach walks at the Rhode Island School of Design's Tillinghast Farm did a great deal to lift my spirits and urge me on as I worked both to write this book and to come to terms with everything—in the world and in my own life—that had prompted it.

CHAPTER ONE

Champions of the West

ON THE EVENING OF June 11, 2012, a public debate took place in London. It was sponsored by Intelligence Squared, an organization that regularly sells out prestigious venues for events that showcase experts—politicians, journalists, artists, and others—debating "the issues that matter."[1] In this case, the issue that mattered was a very old question: should the British Museum return its collection of Parthenon Marbles to Greece?

The controversy began more than two hundred years ago, when the British ambassador to the Ottoman court, Thomas Bruce, 7th Earl of Elgin, oversaw the removal of nearly half the sculpted marbles from the ancient temple of Athena Parthenos—the Parthenon—on the Acropolis in Athens, then part of the Ottoman Empire. Elgin shipped the stones back to England, where debate broke out even before the last of his ships arrived from Greece. Soon, drowning in debt after a messy divorce, he tried to sell off the sculptures, the so-called Elgin Marbles, to the British government. After a parliamentary inquiry into the lawfulness of his acquisitions and their artistic merits, Britain purchased the artifacts in 1816 for the then-enormous sum of £35,000. For two centuries, they have been the pride of the British Museum's permanent collection; today only the Rosetta Stone seems to enjoy more popularity as a backdrop for visitors' selfies.

On February 19, 2008, a few years before the public debate in London, a motion to repatriate the Elgin Marbles had also been the subject of a formal debate at the Cambridge Union, the debating society at the University of Cambridge. Anthony Snodgrass, then chairman of the British Committee for the Reunification of the Parthenon Marbles, took the floor to argue in favor of the sculptures' return. Snodgrass is one of Britain's greatest living archeologists, a tall and distinguished man who, for all his gentle demeanor, cuts an intimidating figure. He mesmerized the audience as he explained that those who opposed returning the marbles to Greece—the trustees of the British Museum and certain members of Parliament—had for decades been performing "a sort of Dance of the Seven Veils, in which a whole series of transparent arguments has been tried and jettisoned, one after another, as each one's inadequacy has been revealed."[2] He then spent his allotted minutes reviewing and refuting seven of the opposition's "inadequate" arguments. Each time he dismantled one of those arguments, he made a dramatic gesture of stripping away a veil.

I was present at that debate, and the intensity in the room—many audience members were students from Greece—was piercing. Yet, as heady as that evening was, the air must have been even thicker at the Oxford Union more than twenty years earlier when, on June 12, 1986,

2

Boris Johnson and Melina Mercouri in Oxford on the occasion of the 1986
Oxford Union debate about the Elgin Marbles.

Boris Johnson presided over an Elgin Marbles debate. That year
Johnson, now Britain's secretary of state for foreign and Commonwealth affairs, was a twenty-one-year-old undergraduate who, as president of the Oxford Union, was just starting his political career. The
headline speaker, by contrast, was an international star: actress Melina
Mercouri, Greece's minister of culture and architect of the modern
campaign for the reunification of the Parthenon Marbles in Athens. As
she concluded her speech, she gave this impassioned appraisal of the
marbles' significance to the Greek people: "They are our pride. They
are our sacrifices. They are our noblest symbol of excellence. They are
a tribute to the democratic philosophy. They are our aspirations and
our name. They are the essence of Greekness."[3]

Elgin Marbles debates are something of a British institution, but
at the more recent June 2012 Intelligence Squared event in London,

something was different. In 1986, when Melina Mercouri argued for her people's rights to the marbles, and in early 2008, when Anthony Snodgrass championed the cause, the Greek economy was running strong. Greece had been fully admitted to the European Communities (forerunner of the European Union) in 1981 and in those earlier years was thriving as a poster child of a new Europe and a success story of Western modernization. When the financial crisis erupted in the United States in September 2008, Greece's newfound prosperity as a member of the Eurozone monetary union led many to be hopeful that the trouble would never cross its borders. By the close of 2009, however, the country's credit rating had been downgraded across the board. On May 9, 2010, a bailout of 110 billion euros by the International Monetary Fund was announced. A new era of austerity, hardship, and pessimism was beginning, although few could then grasp the severity of the situation. That same May, on the bustling island of Mykonos, things seemed nearly normal as everyone prepared for a busy summer season. The only hints that something was wrong were handwritten signs taped to the doors of a few shops. They advertised "crisis prices."

By June 2012, the situation in Greece had severely deteriorated. On the evening of the debate in London, speakers on both sides nevertheless ran through the typical arguments—many as old as the controversy itself—for and against the marbles' return. The panel against the motion to return the sculptures emphasized that Lord Elgin had bought them fair and square and insisted that artifacts of such undisputed significance for world history ought to be housed in a true world museum; the British Museum is just such a museum, they maintained, but Athens's New Acropolis Museum is not. Speakers in favor of the marbles' repatriation insisted that even if Elgin had "legally" acquired them from the Ottomans, who, after all, were Greece's occupiers, he had stolen them from Greece and its people: Athens was and will always be their rightful home.

But this particular debate also featured a new twist. In his remarks in favor of handing over the marbles, British actor and author Stephen Fry openly confronted the elephant in the room: the Greek financial crisis. He contrasted the Greeks' outstanding loans with a far greater, more abstract kind of debt at play, namely, the debt that "we" owe the ancient Greeks, who built the Parthenon and created the masterpieces of sculpture under discussion. Speaking with classical Athens in mind, he reminded the hall how "that period saw the rise of everything that our culture now depends on. Philosophy. Logic. Euclidean mathematics. Empiricism. A refusal to take on trust everything that is told to you— Socrates died by that principle. History. Algebra. Astronomy. Justice." Fry was primarily addressing the British public, but his remarks implied that everyone who believes that his or her culture owes something to ancient Greece is indebted to modern Greece, too. He finished by balancing the Greeks' present financial ruin—their piles of outstanding loans to Europe and the world's financial institutions—against their staggering ancestral achievements. By repatriating the marbles, he declared, "We can show them that no matter how much the sovereign debt crisis means they owe us" (the audience nervously chuckled at that), "we will never repay the debt that we owe Greece."[4] At the end, the motion to return the sculptures carried the evening: the audience's vote tallied at 384 in favor and 125 against.

Ever since 2010, Greece's debt has been widely publicized international news. Today most people have some sense that Greece has immense sovereign debt: it owes its creditors (other countries, institutions, and individuals) an unfathomable amount of money. That kind of debt, though, makes for only one part of the story. As Fry's comments vividly illustrate, the crisis in Greece has also prompted a great deal of discussion and reflection about the deeply entrenched idea that "we"—not just Britain, but Europe and the whole of the Western world—owe the Greeks, whose ancestors supposedly, by some accounts even nearly consciously, sowed the seeds of Western civilization. Among the Greek public, too, a sense that the country is owed a debt has been predictably strong. As early as February 2010, when news outlets were still using the words "emerging" and "mounting" to describe the crisis, a Greek civil servant told the *New York Times,* "We feel humiliated and we understand that things cannot remain the same as they did before . . . but we gave the world democracy, and we expect the European Union to support us."[5] This alternative account of Greek debt, an account that champions culture over capital, enjoys a great deal of international sympathy, especially in Britain and the United States. But where and how did the idea originate? Why is it still so powerful today, in a globalized era remote in so many ways from the debt's imagined origins? Should—and could—such an abstract debt ever be repaid?

These questions are at the heart of this book, which traces two intertwined stories. The first is the story of how the West, particularly the Anglophone secular West, came to invent the idea of its symbolic debt to Greece. The second is the story of the consequences that the idea has had for the rocky course of modern Greek history. Throughout that history, Greece has been locked in an elaborate dance with Western powers over the concept of debt. Britain, France, Germany, and the United States have all had their fair share of devotees of Greek antiquity. Citizens of those countries have also used an imagined stake in that distant past to justify intervention in contemporary Greek affairs. On the other hand, ever since Greece declared independence from the Ottoman Empire in 1821, it has struggled to manage obligations to pay off staggering loans. In most cases, this literal debt has been owed to the same countries that take such pride in touting their "indebtedness" to the ancient Greeks. It is a complex push-and-pull that constantly interweaves—without ever truly defining—the relative values of money, history, and culture.

The recent financial crisis in Greece has proved to be a particularly harsh reminder of the country's captivity in the golden prison of a classical ideal. Political cartoons about the Greek economy nearly always feature a broken marble column or two, and journalists can rarely resist the temptation to contrast the country's current sorry state with its celebrated past. Droves of op-ed writers have mined the pages of ancient Greek literature for clues about how the Greeks of today (or even their creditors) might escape from, or at least better cope with, the mess. Yet, although Socrates, Plato, and Aristotle might have been influential and wide-ranging thinkers, at the end of the day none of them had anything to say about housing-market bubbles or bank failures, quantitative easing or credit-default swaps.

Greek antiquity's insistent presence in this very modern story is a testament to the enduring symbolic power of the classical past, but it is also used to conceal anxieties, conflicts, and questions about the modern world. Greece has recently found itself at the center of two global crises—a financial crisis and a refugee crisis—that have served to expose deep cracks in the edifice, however illusory, of Western identity. These kinds of cracks, only made deeper when Britain voted in 2016 to leave the European Union (the so-called Brexit), were already becoming conspicuous in the summer of 2015 as the prospect of a "Grexit" served to resuscitate a number of old and delicate questions. Can Europe claim the legacy of ancient Greece if the country of Greece is not part of Europe? To what extent do Greeks get to claim that legacy as their own? How much does the Western world continue to owe the Greek people for things that their ancestors did thousands of years ago?

Is the idea that Greek antiquity is the root of the modern West just a mirage, or has Brexit proved that an admiration of ancient Greece is actually a stronger bond among Western nations, especially in Europe, than fragile modern political coalitions such as the European Union and NATO? Finally, if the twenty-first century is proving that we are not all Greeks after all, then who are we?

These knotty questions do not have simple answers. The aim of this book is to contribute to discussion of them by showing how they arose and why they are so urgent today.

OLD NEWS

Antiquity in general, not just Greek antiquity, is often exploited to influence how we perceive current events. Ancient buildings, artworks, and artifacts, along with spectacles of their violent destruction, have received an enormous amount of publicity in news stories about major and ongoing political, economic, and humanitarian crises. The year 2015 was a rich case in point. In March, the Islamic State released carefully produced footage of militants toppling and smashing ancient artifacts at Mosul Museum, the second-largest museum in Iraq, and exploding ancient monuments in the ancient Assyrian city of Nimrud. A few months later, it committed a series of orchestrated atrocities at the site of ancient Palmyra in modern-day Syria. With chilling theatricality that evoked the horror of ancient gladiatorial games, members staged mass executions atop the ruins of the Roman-era amphitheater. The prominent local archeologist Khaled al-Asaad was beheaded, allegedly for refusing to reveal the locations of the city's ancient treasures. In short, the media-savvy Islamic State made the staged destruction and desecration of antiquities a vital cog in its terror machine.

The horrifying events at Palmyra contrasted with a show in defense of heritage that had been orchestrated earlier the same summer. Back in March 2001, the Taliban had begun a slow, multistage, and highly deliberate process of destroying the so-called Buddhas of Bamiyan, two enormous statues of the Buddha that had been carved in the sixth century CE into sandstone cliffs in central Afghanistan. As in the case of the Islamic State's actions at Palmyra, for many Western commentators the Taliban leaders' destruction of the Buddhas seemed to confirm "the status of that country as out of time with Western modernity."[6] Yet, as some scholars have pointed out, that same modernity's tendency to see all such acts as fitting within a single history of Islamic iconoclasm is dangerously simplistic: both the Taliban and the Islamic State destroyed these artifacts in part because they knew that the "art-loving" West would take notice and be appalled.

In June 2015, the Buddhas of Bamiyan were temporarily brought back to life when Zhang Xinyu and Liang Hong, a millionaire couple from China, produced a laser projection in the hollows of the cliffs where they had stood. These laser-light Buddhas were received in Western media with general, though not universal, enthusiasm. Academics and activists continued to express indignation that so many people seemed to react with more disgust and outrage at the destruction of antiquities than at related efforts to annihilate and degrade human lives. That critique raises a set of difficult questions. Just what about antiquity and its physical artifacts makes it so compelling? Why do some people see those artifacts as such a powerful symbol of humanity—so powerful that in some cases they are more worth saving than human beings?

Antiquity's part in depictions of the Greek economic crisis is vastly different from the role that it has recently been made to play in actual war zones. Nevertheless, events that unfolded in Greece in the summer of 2015 also made for bracing reminders that ideas about the ancient past shape understandings of the modern world. On June 27, 2015, a couple of weeks after the Buddhas' resurrection in Afghanistan, Prime Minister Alexis Tsipras of Greece announced a snap national referendum. Coverage of the story consistently framed the referendum (as Tsipras himself often did) as a modern chapter in the long story of Greek democracy. The question that the referendum posed to the Greek people was essentially whether they would be willing to continue living under the harsh austerity measures demanded by the country's creditors as conditions of further bailouts and aid. On July 5, 2015, the day after the Islamic State released its footage of the Palmyra executions, the people of Greece went to the polls. Despite their overwhelming "no" vote against austerity (a vote that made *ohi,* the Greek word for "no," the word of the summer), Tsipras caved in to the unwavering demands of his country's creditors and signed a new bailout agreement for Greece. That memorandum of understanding, the third in a series, demanded even harsher measures than the ones the Greek people had just voted to reject.

During the first half of 2015, when Tsipras and his new government regularly made international news, the Greek public relations machine shared one characteristic with the Islamic State: both manipulated images of antiquity to affect public opinion. Just a few months before the referendum, televisions in the thirty-five Athens metro stations had started to run a fifty-second spot for a new Greek campaign demanding reparations to the tune of 303 billion euros for the Nazi occupation of Greece from 1941 to 1944 during World War II. The video, produced by the Greek Ministry of Defense, showed footage of atrocities committed during that occupation and used a series of statistics (for example, 40,000 executed, 300,000 dead from starvation, and 63,000 Greek Jewish victims) to caption images of its brutality. The last photograph in the

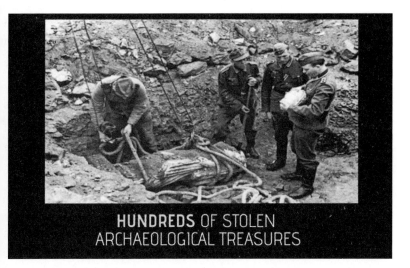

HUNDREDS OF STOLEN
ARCHAEOLOGICAL TREASURES

Still from a Greek Ministry of Defense video shown in Athenian metro stations in May 2015, part of a campaign calling on Germany to pay reparations for the Nazi occupation of Greece during World War II.

sequence was of uniformed soldiers removing an ancient statue from the ground with the accompanying text, "Hundreds of stolen archaeological treasures." The video ended with the declaration, "We claim what Germany owes us." Under that statement, the details were spelled out in these bullet points:

- War reparations
- Repayment of the occupation loan
- Compensation to the victims
- Return of archeological treasures

Ever since the Greek financial crisis began, German leaders have largely assumed the bad-cop role at financial negotiations. In the summer of the bailout referendum, Prime Minister Angela Merkel and Finance

Minister Wolfgang Schäuble secured particular legacies as national villains in Greece. It is no coincidence, then, that during those negotiations Greece became far more vocal about a point it has long maintained: that Germany owes it reparations.

Germany, meanwhile, has claimed that the matter was closed in 1990 with the "Two plus Four Agreement" (officially the Treaty on the Final Settlement with Respect to Germany). This was the treaty that paved the way for German unification in 1991 (West and East Germany were the "Two"), but it was also signed by the United States, the United Kingdom, France, and the then Soviet Union (the "Four"). As part of the treaty's terms, the old Allied powers renounced all future World War II–based rights and claims on Germany. Greece, however, was not one of the allies to which Germany officially surrendered, which meant that it was not included as a signatory to the 1990 agreement. Many Greek leaders, like many members of the Greek public more broadly, therefore feel justified in claiming that reparations are yet another form of debt that Europe owes to Greece. In April 2016, members of a new Greek political party called Course of Freedom, formed by leaders who parted ways with Tsipras and his party, Syriza, after the referendum debacle, announced that demands for reparations from Germany would be a pillar of their party's platform.

In the reparations-campaign video, the image of desecrated antiquity is meant to be equally, or nearly equally, horrifying as the other images that document torture and death. The Greek government made this video to bring to the world's attention—or at least to foreign tourists' attention (the video's text is in English)—how Germans have committed yet other shocking crimes against Greeks, and not so long ago. In the summer in which the video ran on a loop in the Athens subway, the Islamic State's publicity campaign was also coupling the same kinds of combinations of images: of annihilation of human life, on the one hand, and desecration of heritage on the other. Thus, while the Greek government used the strategy to underscore the cruelty of Germany during World War II (but also, no doubt, in the context of the financial crisis), the Islamic State did so to terrorize the world into fearing its capacity for violence. Both authorities were keenly aware of the power that images of antiquity have to rouse public sympathy, and both exploited public beliefs about the pricelessness of ancient artifacts to enhance the horror of other gruesome deeds.

IT'S ALL GREEK TO SOME

In the autumn of that year, on November 13, 2015, the Islamic State led a series of coordinated attacks on Paris that left 130 people dead. Two weeks later, on November 27, the American edition of *The Week* magazine ran a cover depicting a cloudy Paris skyline dominated by an illuminated Eiffel Tower, but with a faint image of the Islamic State's emblem in the night sky. The image was accompanied by an ominous headline: "Heart of Darkness: ISIS Brings Its Barbarism to the West." The words *barbarism, barbarian,* and *barbaric* are persistently sprinkled across articles about Islamist terrorist and insurgent organizations (al-Qaeda, the Islamic State, the Taliban, and others). *Medieval* is another word that often appears in these contexts. In response to repeated media characterizations of the Islamic State, its tactics, and ideology as medieval, in February 2016 a medieval historian published a piece in *Slate* defending the good name of the Middle Ages and arguing that medieval conquest tactics were nowhere near as brutal as is generally assumed.[7] The conceptual opposite of *barbarism* is *civilization,* and the Middle Ages—Europe's "Dark Age"—are still often imagined as a gloomy antithesis of more luminous, more enlightened ancient civilizations. The Renaissance, after all, is largely understood as a rebirth of learning through the rediscovery of ancient Greek and Roman literature, knowledge, and thought.

More than half a century ago, Mircea Eliade, one of the greatest twentieth-century scholars of religion, observed that "traditional societies" tend to view the world in terms of "cosmos" and "chaos." The cosmos is the familiar world, the world of civilization that "we" inhabit and control. Beyond the borders of that world exists chaos: "a sort of 'other world,' a foreign, chaotic space, peopled by ghosts, demons, 'foreigners' (who are assimilated to demons and souls of the dead)."[8] Today few people who self-identify as members of Western society would be eager to characterize it as particularly "traditional," at least in the sense that Eliade meant. Yet the text and image of Paris on that cover of *The Week* served as a perfect illustration of his point: in the Western mind the Islamic State represents chaos, barbarism, and the peril of encroaching night. The West, by contrast, is civilized and luminous—and terrified of the dark.

Less than four months after the Paris attacks, *The Week* ran another provocative cover calling attention to a very different new threat to the West: U.S. presidential candidate Donald Trump. The cover's imagery makes a telling assumption about readers' ability to recognize ancient Greece as shorthand for Western civilization. It paints Trump sitting astride a massive wrecking ball, crashing through Washington, DC, where the Capitol is faintly visible in the background. Otherwise the cover depicts no specific monuments; the space is simply crowded with plain, toppled white columns and broken buildings that look like ruins of ancient Greek temples. All these fractured structures evoke the actual neoclassical buildings of the American capital, but their unmistakable aura of "Greekness," with all of Greece's resonances of democracy and rational thought, is also enough to suggest that Donald Trump

"Heart of Darkness": cover of the November 27, 2015, American edition of *The Week*.

has emerged as a danger to civilization—Western civilization—as the magazine's readers know it.

There is, of course, no such thing as the monolithic "West" or a self-contained "Western civilization." But ever since those concepts emerged in the late nineteenth century, the idea of the West—like other powerful constructs, such as race and gender—has had very real consequences. It has been used to justify wars and colonization, calibrate stereotypes, and structure narratives of white supremacy; its roots and nature also continue to be the subject of countless lesson plans, debates, and articles. And when "Westerners" set out to describe and account for the West, they typically identify ancient Greece—especially classical Athens—as its revered wellspring.

In his 1996 *Clash of Civilizations and the Remaking of the World Order,* the American political scientist Samuel P. Huntington famously defined the West as "Europe, North America, plus other European settler countries such as Australia and New Zealand" (with the important exclusion of Latin America).[9] He also outlined eight "distinguishing features" that "may legitimately be identified as the core of Western civilization." These included principles—for example, individualism, rule of law, and separation of church and state—that many children are taught from a very young age to value as the hallmarks of society. But the very first feature on the list was rooted in history rather than values: Western Christendom, Huntington argued, had always been united by its common roots in classical civilization. "Islamic and Orthodox civilizations also inherited from Classical civilization," he allowed, "but nowhere near to the same degree the West did."[10]

The twentieth century saw many and varied manifestations of this belief that the West has long held about itself, namely, that a "classical" inheritance is one of its touchstones. And on many points it is Greece rather than Rome that is taken for granted as classical civilization's

"Unstoppable Force?" Donald Trump on the cover of the March 4, 2016,
American edition of *The Week*.

better half. As the Danish historian David Gress has shown, the standard "Grand Narrative" of Western identity has long "defined liberty as an abstract, philosophical principle, which it then traced through a series of great books and great ideas divorced from passions and politics back to classical Greece."[11] I will say more about the origins of that narrative in Chapter 2, but a single example will be helpful here. In December 1940, when Britain was already deeply embroiled in World War II, the British classicist Gilbert Murray broadcast a lecture titled "Greece and Her Tradition" for the BBC Home Service. During the talk, Murray clarified the importance of ancient Greek values for British civilization when he declared that "the thing called Hellenism—I apologize for the rather highbrow word—almost covers the cause we are now fighting for." For Murray, ancient Greece offered a glimpse at "what sort of society, what attempt at a better world, we can dare aim at after the war."[12] This is much the same point that Stephen Fry would insist on at the Elgin Marbles debate in London more than seventy years later, namely, that everything that is best about Western civilization (democracy, rationality, progress, industry, philosophy, and art) was dreamed up by the Greeks.

Academics and others have nevertheless worked, since at least the mid-twentieth century, to question and even dismantle this picture. In his landmark 1954 book *Stolen Legacy: Greek Philosophy Is Stolen Egyptian Philosophy,* George James, a historian from Guyana, opened a new direction in historical scholarship when he argued that Europe's greatest crime against Africa had been the ancient Greeks' theft and appropriation of African philosophy and civilization via the ancient Egyptians. James's premise became a pillar of twentieth-century Afrocentrism and had an especially large influence on African thinkers, including the Senegalese historian, anthropologist, and politician Cheikh Anta Diop (after whom Dakar's premier university is named). In the 1980s, James's premise was also taken up by Martin Bernal, then a professor of Near Eastern studies at Cornell University. In a three-volume series of books titled *Black Athena: The Afroasiatic Roots of Classical Civilization,* Bernal claimed that European intellectual developments of the eighteenth century had radically skewed the West's understanding of Greek antiquity. For reasons of pure chauvinism, he argued, white classical scholars crafted a narrative that saw all of the ancient Greeks' achievements—all those reasons for which the West allegedly owes Greece a symbolic debt—as practically sui generis. Like George James, Bernal maintained that much of ancient Greek civilization (as many ancient Greeks themselves acknowledged) was owed to the ancient Egyptians and Phoenicians. In the early nineteenth century, however, the endemic racism and anti-Semitism of the European intellectual establishment began to recast the ancient Greeks as descendants of a mixture of Aegean-basin natives and northern, "Aryan" invaders. A handful of classicists received Bernal's work with passionate indignation.[13] They dismissed his scholarly methods and decried his allegedly shaky grasp of linguistics and his naïve willingness to read ancient myth as evidence of history. In both academia and the media—*Black Athena* quickly became the most famous work of late twentieth-century classical scholarship—these kinds of theories were bitterly chalked up to flimsy attempts to boost African and African American self-esteem.

Since then, many classical scholars—though certainly not all of them—have moderated the kinds of claims they make for the uniqueness of the Greek achievement. New generations better appreciate and strive harder to understand the multicultural complexities of "ancient Greek civilization." The mass media, on the other hand, have been—understandably if not forgivably—slow to catch up. When a National Geographic Society three-part documentary titled *The Greeks* premiered on PBS in June 2016, the first episode introduced the series' subject with the voice-over line "They rose from nothing . . . and changed everything."[14] Even museum displays and textbooks that place human civilization's first grand stirrings in the "Near East" (i.e., in Mesopotamia and Egypt) tend to locate the beginning of civilization, as we know it today, in Greece. An issue of the popular French magazine *Philosophie* proudly makes this very case. The week of July 7, 2016, its cover featured an image by French photographer Léo Caillard of a statue of a Greek god dressed as a modern-day hipster (the statue provided a convenient beard), accompanied by the headline "The Greek Miracle: In the 5th Century BC They Invented Everything." The cover also printed a teaser list of some of those inventions: democracy, ethics, history, mathematics, mythology, philosophy, and tragedy.

The ancient Greeks hardly "invented" all these things, and they certainly did not do so out of thin air. What both Fry and the editors at *Philosophie* presumably meant—and what most people who make these kinds of claims probably assume—is that the Greeks were the first to mold them into recognizably "modern" forms. This logic was spelled out memorably by the Cambridge mathematician G. H. Hardy in a passage of his 1940 essay *A Mathematician's Apology*: "The Greeks were the first mathematicians who are still 'real' to us to-day. Oriental mathematics may be an interesting curiosity, but Greek mathematics is the real thing. The Greeks first spoke a language which modern mathematicians can understand: as [J. E.] Littlewood said to me once, they are not clever schoolboys or 'scholarship candidates,' but 'Fellows of another college.'"[15] Hardy's observation might now sound dated, but it is still a good illustration of what, in the Western imagination, seems to separate the Greeks from the earlier civilizations of the Near East and the later civilization of the Romans. As influential as the Roman Empire may have been for the emergence of Western and European identities, the Romans' admiration for Greek culture has been taken as proof that the ancient Greeks did everything first. Greek civilization, the thinking goes, was wholly original, unpolluted by a sense of what French philosopher Rémi Brague has called *secondarité*—of "secondariness" and of owing something (and being inferior) to a prior culture.[16] The Romans suffered acute anxiety over their *secondarité* to the Greeks; the Greeks, by contrast, felt secondary to no one. This picture, too, conceals mountains of complicating and contradictory evidence. It is nonetheless the prevailing one.

All of this means that for the illustrator, cartoonist, or graphic designer, images of white columns are an easy shorthand for a whole bundle of received ideas about Western civilization and the role that the ancient Greeks are thought to have played in "inventing" it. Even when classical Athens is not explicitly mentioned or depicted, its presence can often be felt as an implied counterweight to barbarism: the Athens of Pericles and Socrates stands for everything we in the West value but they do not. The case of Greece is thus both representative of antiquity's general enduring fascination and profoundly unique. Every modern country has an ancient past, but, as one anthropologist has cannily put it, "Greece is unusual in having a past that is almost as highly valued internationally as it is nationally."[17] This is in part because Greece's ancient past is often made to stand for the West's, and sometimes even the entire world's, past as a whole. The logo of the United Nations' heritage organization, UNESCO, is an outline of the Athenian Parthenon, the building that Adolf Hitler once called the "symbol of human culture."[18]

Even in the United States, a country that places less obvious stock than, say, Britain or Germany or France in an imagined classical inheritance, popular culture is filled with images that allude to ancient Greece. For reasons rooted in everything from Hollywood marketing to Cold War politics, most Americans, regardless of their level of formal education, have a sense that democracy was invented in Athens, Aphrodite was a literal sex goddess, Leonidas and his band of three hundred Spartans bravely fought the Persians at the Battle of Thermopylae, and (Eric Bana's) Hector was no match for (Brad Pitt's) Achilles in the Trojan War. References to classical Greece appear on television, in ads, and in hip-hop lyrics; Jay-Z's "No Church in the Wild," for example, imagines a dialogue between Socrates and Plato.[19] (The popular music industry more generally is no stranger to Greek myth: on the September 2013 cover of the British *GQ*, the pop-star diva Rihanna posed as the snake-haired Greek monster Medusa; when Lady Gaga made a grand entrance at the Athens airport in September 2014, she did so as Aphrodite.) The architecture of many government and university buildings has been designed to evoke the solemn grandeur of Greek temples. The enduring cachet of the Greek classics is the reason that so many of those same universities still cling to versions of great-books curricula, which almost invariably begin with Homer and wind their way through Herodotus, Thucydides, and the greatest hits of ancient Athenian drama.

The media also revel in pieces that interpret the significance of modern events with reference to ancient Greek myth and literature. When American swimming champion Michael Phelps won his fourteenth individual-event Olympic gold medal at the 2016 Summer Olympic Games in Rio de Janeiro, commentators were quick to point out that he had broken a record for individual Olympic wins set by the second-century-BCE athlete Leonidas of Rhodes (the American satirical paper *The Onion* reacted with a story underscoring Phelps's status as "Olympian" in all senses: "Michael Phelps Spots Estranged Father Poseidon in Stands").[20] Greek classical references are also regularly pressed into analysis of graver events. When, for example, many Boston-area cemetery directors refused to accept the body of Tamerlan Tsarnaev (one of the brothers who bombed the Boston Marathon on April 15, 2013), the critic and classicist Daniel Mendelsohn wrote a piece in the *New Yorker* reminding readers of the lessons of Sophocles's *Antigone*. Antigone, a teenager, defied a prohibition against burying bodies of traitors by scattering dust over the corpse of her brother. Mendelsohn's reading of why she did so—because she believed "that to not bury her brother, to not treat the war criminal like a human being, would ultimately have been to forfeit her own humanity"—lent gravitas to his position on the need to bury Tsarnaev.[21]

English-language books about the legacy of ancient Greece also appear in publishers' catalogs on both sides of the Atlantic year after year. The past few years alone have seen Adam Nicolson's *Why Homer Matters* (2014), Armand Marie Leroi's *The Lagoon: How Aristotle Invented Science* (2014), Edith Hall's *Introducing the Ancient Greeks: From Bronze-Age Seafarers to Navigators of the Western Mind* (2014), and Paul Cartledge's *Democracy: A Life* (2016). All these books set out, each in its own way, to convince the general public that what the ancient Greeks did, thought, and wrote is still important today.

The mode of understanding "Greece" through the filter of ideas about its antiquity perhaps made it unavoidable that the same filter would be applied to the crises the country has experienced in recent years. The understanding it yields, however, is misleading. For example, middle-school students are often taught to rattle off inaccurate or at least distorted "facts" about classical Athens. Take this paragraph from the field-test version of a lesson plan designed for "gifted and talented" sixth-graders in New York City public schools:

> The existence today of the United States is a result of our
> forefathers following the Ancient Greeks' debates about the

best form of government, their ideas about citizenship and their philosophical discussions.[22]

The architects of the American Constitution hardly relied wholesale on the political or philosophical debates of "the ancient Greeks"; the reputation that Athens enjoys today as the seedbed of liberal democracy is, as we will see in Chapter 5, largely an inheritance of Anglo-American Cold War propaganda. Today the idea that a straight line can be drawn between Western democracies and the Athenian political system might rank among general knowledge, but many American and British university students (at least in my experience) have never heard of the Byzantine or Ottoman Empires. The persistent cultural ubiquity of ancient Greece thus means that the public has a much more vivid, if distorted, idea of "Greece" than of other financially unstable countries that have recently suffered economic crises. However famous Wagner's Ring Cycle and Marvel's superhero Thor may be among certain demographics, the cast of Old Norse mythology did not grace nearly as many headlines when Iceland's three largest private banks defaulted in 2008.

Greek antiquity—especially the antiquity of Pericles, Sophocles, and Socrates—does matter a great deal for current events in Greece, but not in the ways that the media like to claim and imply. It is not important because a precise link can be made between Western systems of government and Athenian democracy (it cannot) or between the management of the Greek economy and the plots of ancient tragedies or comedies. It matters because ideas about what antiquity really means—and controversies over who owns its legacy—have played an enormous role in shaping the West's sense of its civilizational roots. Those ideas also mold the public's understanding of what is happening in Greece today and why. Long-standing points of tension in the fraught triangle of relationships among the European West, modern Greece, and Greece's classical past have even appeared to influence how some of the main players in the economic crisis (especially leaders and lenders) view Greece, and ultimately how they make practical policy decisions. One camp insists that thanks to the many gifts of the Greeks—the kinds of achievements recited by Stephen Fry at the 2012 Elgin Marbles debate—it is the world's duty to save the country at any literal cost. Another seems to believe that the Greeks should be punished by tighter and tighter austerity measures for their endemic corruption and laziness—the very qualities that prove them to be undeserving heirs of their classical ancestors or, still worse, not heirs at all. In chapters to come, we will see that neither of these positions is anything new.

GREECE AT EUROPE'S ENDS

There is a striking irony to Greece's considerable role in the grand narratives—the origin stories—of Europe and the West. Until the nineteenth century, relatively recently in the scheme of things, the land of Greece faced primarily east. In the Bronze Age, highly developed trade networks connected Greece to Egypt, Asia, and Cyprus. Early Greek myth and literature were richly influenced by contact with the peoples of the ancient Near East: Assyrians, Babylonians, Persians, and others. The Trojan War—the conflict at the heart of the *Iliad* and the *Odyssey*, many ancient Greek tragedies, and much of Greek mythology—was fought on a plain on the northwest coast of Asia Minor, in modern-day Turkey. Mainland Greece marked the westernmost boundary of the empire of Alexander the Great, who carried the Greek language and culture as far east as the Himalayas.

The Romans later conquered Greece in an effort to expand their empire vastly eastward. The Roman Empire's successor, Byzantium, stretched across Greece, Asia Minor, and part of the Middle East and North Africa. When the Byzantine Empire collapsed in the fifteenth century, its Ottoman conquerors gained sway over Greece, Egypt, and parts of the Arabian Peninsula but never penetrated Europe as far as Venice or Vienna. But when Greece became independent in the early nineteenth century, its entire geographic orientation began to shift. The new country abruptly found itself positioned as the eastern frontier of a European civilization that, by way of the Renaissance and the Enlightenment, had come to attribute its intellectual origins and aesthetic ideals to ancient Greece. Historian Pierre Briant has detailed, for example, how, in a twist of history, thinkers of the European Enlightenment came to cast Alexander the Great as the first European: the original bearer of civilization to "backward" peoples of the East.[23] For millennia, then, Greece was the western edge of an Eastern cosmos that stretched from Delphi to Delhi and beyond, but for the last two centuries it has played the relatively new role of the eastern edge of a Western cosmos seen as stretching from Delphi to Denver and beyond.[24]

In the 1990s, Huntington nonetheless classified Greece as part not of Western but of "Orthodox civilization," where it supposedly keeps company with Russia, the civilization's "core state," together with the rest of the former Soviet Union and Yugoslavia, as well as Romania, Bulgaria, and Cyprus. Like others who had made a similar distinction, Huntington saw this set of countries as sharing a common culture that is "an offspring of Byzantine civilization."[25] The earlier generations of Orthodox civilization have long been cast as "Eastern": the Eastern Roman Empire, which became the Byzantine Empire, the source of the Eastern Orthodox Church. When in the early decades of independence

Greek intellectuals questioned whether Greece was "West or East," by "East" they meant the Christian Orthodox world. Until the end of the Cold War, the Soviet Union and other Communist countries of Central and Eastern Europe belonged to what NATO—which has counted Greece as a member since 1952—called the Eastern bloc. Old Greek ties to Russia, rooted in both religion and politics (the Greek Communist Party is still relatively robust), have found renewed vitality in the present financial crisis. In 2015, Greece's newly elected leftist leaders even appeared ready—to Europe and the United States' great irritation—to play the Russian card by courting aid from Russian president Vladimir Putin. That March, a few months before the referendum, a Greek supermarket worker told the BBC, "It is clear that Germany wants to impoverish our people. . . . Our response should be to turn to Moscow, even if it means they kick us out of the EU."[26]

Today, though, Greece is also regarded as Eastern for reasons beyond its tradition of Russian sympathies and its overwhelming Christian Orthodox majority. This is due in part to relatively recent shifts in the geopolitical landscape. In the early 1990s, as Huntington was refining his ideas, common notions about the "East" were altering to reflect a changing of the guard among the West's enemies as the apparent threat of (Soviet) Orthodoxy was giving way to the threat of Islam(ism). On December 25, 1991, the Soviet Union formally dissolved. Fourteen months later, on February 27, 1993, a group of terrorists financed by Khalid Sheikh Mohammed, the man the 9/11 Commission would later identify as the principal architect of the September 11, 2001, attacks, detonated a truck bomb underneath the North Tower of the World Trade Center. This was the first major terrorist attack on U.S. soil to be ascribed to "Islamic fundamentalism." With the Communist threat apparently eliminated, militant Islamism became the new dark specter on the Western horizon: in Mircea Eliade's terms, the chaos beyond the cosmos.

Huntington himself notoriously declared that "Europe ends where Western Christianity ends and Islam and Orthodoxy begin."[27] This is precisely the three-way crossroads at which Greece is imagined to stand. In whichever way the West decides to define the threatening East—as preserve of communism or training ground of terrorists—Greece remains an object of suspicion. Nowadays Greece's European credentials are often undermined less by insinuations of Russian allegiances than by suspicions that the country's culture is too (Middle) Eastern, too "Oriental." As early as the late eighteenth century, Western Europeans began to see Byzantium as a "medieval version of the Ottoman Empire";[28] the first edition of the *Cambridge Medieval History*, from 1923, coolly pronounces, "In many ways the Byzantine was an Oriental."[29] Today, Greece's Ottoman legacy is a staple of analyses about just what has gone wrong. One oft-repeated theory about the origins of the Greek crisis accepts the premise that corruption is inherent in Greek culture but defends the Greeks by arguing that this flaw is rooted in the centuries Greece spent under Ottoman rule, when tax evasion came to be seen as an act of resistance and even a patriotic duty.

Some European leaders have openly expressed apprehension that this Ottoman inheritance is too great to surmount. In an interview published in English on the website of the German magazine *Der Spiegel,* Valéry Giscard d'Estaing, president of France from 1974 to 1981, confessed his belief that the Eurozone had simply expanded too far. Referring to Greece's entry into the common currency in 2011, he remarked, "To be perfectly frank, it was a mistake to accept Greece. Greece simply wasn't ready. Greece is basically an Oriental country."[30] Giscard d'Estaing's observation hints at more of those old but enduring questions: Does today's Greece have the classical soul that would make it part of the

Western European cosmos? Or did the Byzantine and Ottoman Empires draw it too far into what the West perceives as chaos?

In 1996, the year in which Huntington's *Clash of Civilizations* appeared, the American author Patricia Storace published *Dinner with Persephone,* an account of a year she had recently spent in Greece. Writing, like Huntington, shortly after the breakup of the Soviet Union, Storace was fascinated by Greece's struggle to sort out the question of its Europeanness. At that time, a new version of Europe was just starting to find its feet: the Treaty of Maastricht that gave birth to the European Union had been signed by member states on February 7, 1992, and had gone into effect on November 1 of the next year. Not long afterward, Storace observed that in Greece, "the simultaneous rejection and embrace of Europe shifts and collides still, like tectonic plates, under the surface of the country."[31] *Dinner with Persephone* was well received by the English-speaking public, but when it was issued in Greek translation, it was widely criticized for reinforcing cultural stereotypes of Greeks (for example, that they are lazy, evade taxes, and are prone to exaggeration, moralizing, and nationalism). This was a valid critique, but Storace's geophysical metaphor is still a useful one. It also applies just as well to Europe's relationship with Greece: Europe's "simultaneous rejection and embrace" of Greece resembles, perhaps now more than ever, two tectonic plates in friction. When, in the second decade of the twenty-first century, the country suddenly found itself at the epicenter of two major international crises, that friction only intensified.

The controversial British historian Niall Ferguson has nevertheless seen the balance of the debt Greece owes against the debt it is supposedly owed as precisely what holds the plates together. For him, the combination of abstract and literal debt both grants and guarantees the country its status as an *"ex officio* member" of the West. That membership is valid, he argues, "thanks to our enduring debt to ancient Hellenic philosophy and the Greeks' more recent debts to the European Union."[32] Even if some European leaders have expressed second thoughts about Greece's place in Europe, ancient Greece's immense significance for European and Western identity means that a failure to keep Greece in Europe would mark a (further) failure of Europe itself.

The following chapters will examine how the notion of abstract debt to Greece formed and evolved. The idea has been present at many points in history that, like the current era, saw Greece (or ancient Greek city-states) burdened by great monetary debt or other forms of financial obligation. This book, to be clear, does not appraise the validity of claims about the existence of a Western "classical debt" to Greece, nor does it proffer accounts of what Greek, European, or Western identity "really is." Rather, it attempts to chart how and why the notion of a symbolic debt to Greece arose, and how that concept has served as a battleground for the bigger related questions. Its historical survey will take us through two and a half millennia of Greek history. We will have to leap over many parts of it, but we will also retrace our steps, sometimes more than once, through other parts.

The story begins in Chapter 2 with classical Athens, where we will watch the Athenians develop the enduring messages of their "national brand" and, in doing so, lay—though certainly not intentionally— foundations for the West's fantasy of itself as the bulwark against barbarism and the enlightened steward of the arts. In Chapter 3, we will then fast-forward through two millennia to meet up with a whole host of early modern travelers to Greece. Those travelers played a critical role in Europe's "colonization" of Greece—not of the modern land, but of the abstract and imaginary terrain of Greek antiquity. In the accounts they left of their journeys, many of those visitors registered disappointment and even dismay at just how different the place was from the Greece of their dreams. Chapter 4 will bring us into the era of Greek independence and attempt to account for the seismic shift that caused Greece's gaze to shift from east to west. This dramatic about-face was owed in large part to the rise of European philhellenism, which more than any other intellectual movement set the terms of the tense and ambivalent relationship between Greece and Europe that continues to this day. Distraught over the lowly state to which Greece seemed to have fallen but ardent to see it rise from the ashes, the men and women who called themselves philhellenes used their tendentious classicism to rally support for the cause of liberating Greece from the "Turkish yoke."

In Chapter 5, we will see how, in the first decades of Greek independence, both Europeans and Greeks attempted to fashion the new nation according to an elaborate fantasy of what a country called "Greece" (and a city called "Athens") should look like. That fantasy would be reimagined in the twentieth century, when Western allies against the Soviet Union came, for political reasons of their own, to celebrate ancient Greece more for its invention of democracy than for its achievement of an aesthetic ideal. We finally return to the twenty-first century in Chapter 6, where we will witness a tenuous modern "Greek miracle" give way to a cruel new era of crisis. This most recent era has brought with it clamorous new invocations of the concept of classical debt alongside an onslaught of headlines and political cartoons that allude to ruined temples, hapless mythical heroes, Achilles's heels, and Trojan horses.

Finally, Chapter 7 will consider a number of ways in which the realities of the twenty-first century have served to expose just how untenable the Greek ideal is. But before we contemplate that ideal's overdue death, we need to consider its birth. Every time and place has its own great thinkers, artists, and leaders. What makes people think that classical Athens was so unique?

CHAPTER TWO

How Athens Built Its Brand

IN THE 1989 CULT-CLASSIC MOVIE *Bill and Ted's Excellent Adventure,* two dopey high school kids from San Dimas, California, travel through time in a magic phone booth. In every chapter of history that they visit, they collect a famous figure to bring back with them to California. Their first stop takes them to Athens, where the year is 410 BCE. Bill and Ted step out of the time machine and into a scene filled with tranquil white columns and chirping birds. Small groups of young men (in sandals, naturally) are gathered around Socrates, who is giving a lesson in philosophy: "Our lives are but specks of dust falling through the fingers of time." Dazzled by Ted's profound interjection "All we are is dust in the wind, dude," Socrates gladly accompanies the pair on the rest of their adventures through time. Back in California,

Bill and Ted take their new friends—Joan of Arc, Genghis Khan, Napoleon, and Abraham Lincoln, among others—to the San Dimas mall. On the mall escalator, Bill gives Socrates a friendly piece of advice: "Watch out for your robe, dude."

Bill and Ted's Excellent Adventure is a comedy, and its image of Athens is an obvious caricature of history. It is also a good indication of the way in which many Americans (and no doubt many people of other nationalities) are accustomed to imagining ancient Greece. This movie was one of my first introductions to Greek antiquity, and it taught me to picture Athens as a peaceful city of marble temples and civilized philosophical conversation. *Spartacus* and *Gladiator,* on the other hand, shaped my mental image of Rome as a cruel empire run on the backs of slaves. My seventh-grade Latin textbook (from the *Cambridge Latin Course,* still billed by Cambridge University Press as "the leading introductory Latin course") even featured a number of simple Latin sentences about a lazy and lustful slave named Grumio.[1] There are, by contrast, no obvious slaves in Bill and Ted's Athens, although one ancient census (from the late fourth century BCE) apparently put the city's slave population at twenty times that of its free citizens: 400,000 to 21,000.[2] In fact, the administration of democratic Athens rested largely in the hands not of "civil servants" but of public slaves.[3] Hollywood, though, is certainly not alone in portraying Rome as a practical, militaristic empire and Athens as a paradise of art, poetry, and contemplation. The dichotomy is false and facile, but it is also an ancient inheritance.

In the *Aeneid,* a first-century-BCE epic by the Roman poet Virgil, Aeneas, the ancestor of the Roman people, journeys to the underworld. There his dead father shows him a vision of Rome's future glory and tries to soothe any insecurity that future Romans might feel about their city's cultural inferiority to Greece. He prophesies that others (the Greeks) will sculpt more lifelike sculptures, develop finer rhetoric, and chart the heavens better than the Romans ever will. The Romans have a much greater charge: "You, Roman one," Aeneas's father tells him, "remember: you are to rule peoples with your power (these will be your skills), establish peace with rule of law, spare the conquered, and vanquish the proud."[4]

With these few lines, Virgil, writing a national epic for the emperor Augustus, managed to turn what seemed like a Roman shortcoming into a divinely mandated strength. Let the Greeks have their arts and keep their eyes on the stars and their heads in the clouds! Rome will do something better: it will build a great empire and subdue and bring peace to the world. This old idea about the fundamental difference between Greece and Rome has endured and has led to other equally lasting misunderstandings. In the first place, Rome's own artistic life was hardly lacking: Virgil's epic poem is just one proof of its rich literary culture. Just as importantly, the idea of a fundamental contrast between Athens and Rome has hindered generations of teachers and students (and moviemakers) from seeing classical Athens for what it really was: a well-oiled imperial machine. Athenians were just as invested in the accumulation and consolidation of political power as Romans ever were, and the Athens of 410 BCE—the Athens that Bill and Ted supposedly visit—was, in reality, a war-weary city still recovering from an oligarchic coup and fighting to hold on to a crumbling empire.

Classical Athens, the Athens of around 480–320 BCE, is of course not synonymous with ancient Greece: Greek antiquity spanned well over a millennium, and we know of about a thousand Greek city-states that existed between 600 and 300 BCE alone. Early Greek city-states and trading centers also spanned an enormous geographic range, from Cadiz to the Crimea. Of the other city-states, ancient Sparta has certainly enjoyed its fair share of fame; as one twentieth-century classicist put it, "Italian Humanists, Spanish Jesuits, French Calvinists, English Puritans, French Revolutionaries, German Romantics, English Aesthetes, French Nationalists, German Nazis have all looked to ancient Sparta."[5] To this list could easily be added, for example, today's American military, where Spartan honor is the gold standard (and Spartan-themed tattoos are common among soldiers).

Yet of all the Greek city-states, Athens has been the most influential in shaping both the narrative of Western identity and the course of modern Greek history. Today Athens's prestige and power remain strong in the global market of ideas. From academia to popular culture, ancient Athenians are cited to justify everything from military strategy and intervention (we will come to the Greek Civil War in Chapter 5) to new directions in literary theory: if Pericles did it, it must have been wise; if Socrates or Sophocles said it, it must (still) be true.

As paradoxical as it may seem, the idea of Athens as the peaceful meeting place of brilliant artists and intellectuals was constructed during the turbulent decades when the city's empire dominated the Aegean. Athens's continuing influence today is, moreover, owed more to the staying power of the city's ancient propaganda than to any objective reality. Corinthians wrote dramas and painted vases, Spartans philosophized, and great orators and engineers came from every corner of the ancient world, Greek and non-Greek. But the Athenians were so effective at celebrating, commemorating, and documenting themselves that the material evidence for their achievements—whether marble buildings or texts of plays, treatises, and speeches—survived antiquity better than most testaments to the life of other Greek places and populations.

It is the Athens suggested by sun-bleached ruins and glorified in so many ancient literary works that has become the West's secular Eden. That fantasy has had a number of practical and ideological consequences.

Even in the twenty-first century, those who attempt to define what it means to be a child of the West do so with reference to a truly "Athenian" ideal: the Athenians did not consciously "invent" Western civilization, but they did consciously create an idealized vision of themselves and their city. Constantly and convincingly they insisted that theirs was a city like none other, and that the rest of Greece therefore owed it both monetary tribute and a symbolic debt.

Imagine that we are taking a stroll on the grounds at a fifth-century-BCE version of a World Expo and come across the Athens pavilion. Before we even step inside, we know that certain key attributes of the city's "national brand" will be advertised within:

1. Athens saved Greece from "barbarians."
2. Athens is unique.
3. Athens is the home of the arts.

These three messages characterized Athens's brand throughout most of the classical period, in the years between the end of the Persian invasions of Greece and Greece's fall to the Macedonian successors of Alexander the Great. They are also the messages that have most influenced contemporary ideas about Athenian exceptionalism and have laid much of the conceptual groundwork for the idea of the West's abstract debt to Greece.

Yet in the last third of the fifth century, against the background of war with Sparta (the Peloponnesian War of 431 to 404 BCE), another powerful message was also built into the brand. As that war progressed and the Athenians' suffering intensified, many in the city developed a strong sense of nostalgia for what they saw as the better days of their ancestors. This nostalgia was focused largely on the generation that had led Greece to triumph over Persia more than half a century earlier—

in many ways the ancient Athenian counterpart to the United States' "Greatest Generation." It was in the context of that nostalgia that a new brand attribute began to crystallize. Phrased positively, its message ran something like this:

4. Athens is the product of exceptional ancestors.

Viewed from a different perspective, however, this could also be seen as a negative brand attribute that we can call 4′:

4′. Athens was much better in the past.

Elements 4 and 4′ are, of course, two sides of a single coin. The more the Athenians elevated the pedestal of their ancestors, the lower their own generation seemed to stand. This is a critical point: the idea that Athens (or, in vaguer and more modern terms, Greece) just isn't what it used to be is a trope as old as the Parthenon. This idea, too, would have enormous staying power, and today it remains at the heart of the West's uneasy relationship with modern Greece.

ATTRIBUTE 1: ATHENS SAVED GREECE FROM "BARBARIANS"

Despite its substantial population, Athens was of relative inconsequence for the broader geopolitics of the Mediterranean before about 500 BCE. At that time, the Persian Empire stretched from the Balkans to the Indus River valley and into northeastern Africa. The Persian king, Darius, undertook an enormous project of improving his empire's infrastructure and expanding its borders. Darius had hardly heard of Athens until the Greek cities on the west coast of Asia Minor rebelled against his rule in the Ionian Revolt of 499 BCE (Ionians were a kind of

Greek ethnic group: the Athenians identified as Ionians, while the Spartans saw themselves as Dorians). With substantial Athenian aid, the allied Ionian Greeks managed to burn and capture the city of Sardis, a Persian provincial capital and the western terminus of the Persian Empire's Royal Road.

In the *Histories,* an account of the Greco-Persian wars and their earliest roots, the Greek historian Herodotus (from Halicarnassus, Turkey's modern Bodrum) wrote that when news of the destruction of Sardis reached Darius, he had to ask an adviser who the Athenians were. As soon as he received the answer, he shot an arrow into the sky and made a prayer to have vengeance. He then "ordered one of his household slaves to utter to him three times, each time that his dinner was served, 'Master, remember the Athenians.' "[6] The slave's reminders did not go unheeded, and in time a series of wars between Persia and Greece began in earnest. The Athenians quickly came to believe that the part they played in those wars gave them license to build an empire and collect tribute from other Greeks for a defensive alliance against Persia.

In 492 BCE, Darius sent a campaign into Greece under the leadership of his son-in-law Mardonius. That expedition quickly collapsed, but the next year Darius dispatched emissaries to the Greeks demanding that they send earth and water as tokens of submission to his rule. Many of the Greek cities and states acquiesced, but Athens and Sparta remained defiant. At Athens, the Persian messenger was dragged off to the execution pit; at Sparta, the herald who delivered the message was hurled down a well. The attack that Darius launched on the heels of those insults marked the second campaign in what is known as the first Persian invasion of Greece. In the late summer of 490 BCE, the Battle of Marathon ended this first attempt by Persia to annex mainland Greece to its empire. The Greek forces in that battle consisted of Athenians, led by the general Miltiades, and men from the city-state of Plataea; the Spartans famously did not send troops because they were celebrating a solemn religious festival. The Athenians who died in the battle were, unusually, buried directly on the battlefield, and the city would long remember the *Marathonomachoi*—the "warriors of Marathon"—as icons of its Greatest Generation.

Darius's son Xerxes commanded the second invasion in person and managed much more destruction before he was forced to retreat from Greece in defeat. After his victory at the Battle of Thermopylae, in 480 BCE, the Athenians were seized with terror. Once Xerxes's troops managed to break through the mountain pass of Thermopylae, they headed toward Athens, where an ominous portent convinced the Athenians that their patron goddess, Athena, had already abandoned the city. According to Herodotus, Athenian legend had it that a great snake guarded the Acropolis. Every month the Athenians left honey-cake offerings for the snake, as if it were real. Now, for the first time, the offerings went untouched, and Athena's priestess interpreted this as a sign that the goddess had forsaken them. Most Athenians responded to the omen by packing up and evacuating their city. Thus when Xerxes and his troops reached Athens, they found the city all but deserted, and they seized that opportunity to sack and burn the citadel. One of the buildings destroyed in the fire was the Older Parthenon, which the Athenians had begun to build in Athena's honor shortly after the Greek triumph over Darius's forces at Marathon. Soon afterward, the Athenians commanded by Themistocles managed to lure the Persians to the strait between the Greek mainland and the island of Salamis. In the late summer of 480 BCE, those Athenians led the combined Greek forces to decisive victory in the naval Battle of Salamis.

After the Persians' defeat in the battle, the Athenians returned to their city. Confronted with massive heaps of rubble and scorched and broken statues, they set about clearing the debris from the sanctuary and leveling the entire site. Carefully, even ceremonially, they buried in mass graves the many damaged statues that had once stood on the Acropolis. The caches, which archeologists often refer to as the *Perserschutt* (German for "Persian rubble"), were discovered in the course of nineteenth-century excavations (more on those in Chapter 5). Many of the statues from the hordes are now celebrated as masterpieces of archaic (preclassical) Athenian sculpture, and today they are among the most highly prized works on display in the New Acropolis Museum. One, the Moschophoros (calf carrier), was found without his lower legs; today the museum has lovingly given him a new prosthetic set.

The Athenians began to prepare the Acropolis for rebuilding at about the same time at which they buried the damaged statues; the mass of the *Perserschutt* even helped bolster the terracing that was constructed to expand the buildable area. This was the first time in recorded history that such an extraordinary amount of debris was removed from the Acropolis, but it was hardly the last: some 2,300 years later, in the nineteenth century, the rulers of a Greece newly liberated from Ottoman rule embarked on their own program of clearing the Acropolis of centuries of postclassical interventions in an attempt to restore the site to its Periclean grandeur. I will return to the significance of that project, a profoundly important one for the story of Greece's relationship with its antiquity.

What is perhaps most remarkable about the undertaking in the early fifth century BCE is that the Athenians did not attempt to hide all the evidence of what their city had suffered. Some of the rubble was left exposed in a bold display of regeneration. One of the temples atop the Acropolis is the Erechtheion, supposedly built over the site where the gods Athena and Poseidon had competed to win the title of patron god of Athens. The Athenians who rebuilt the city constructed a section of

The Moschophoros statue and the torso of the Critios Boy among the "Persian rubble" excavated on the Athenian Acropolis in 1866.

View of a curtain wall on the Acropolis; column drums from the Older Parthenon are clearly visible.

a wall to the northeast of the Erechtheion by using remnants of the Older Parthenon, which they left exposed for everyone to see. Another wall to the northwest was built to incorporate fragments of the ruined temple of Athena Polias, or "Athena of the City"—burn-scarred statues from its pediments are also in the New Acropolis Museum. Both walls were testaments to temporary defeat and ultimate triumph over enemies who invaded from the east.

A few decades later, when the Athenians began to build a new Parthenon (the Parthenon whose ruins are visible today), they also left the foundation of the older building visible—yet another reminder of what the Persians had destroyed. Archeologists are still piecing together other ways in which narratives of Persia's defeat were incorporated into the city's very bones. In 2012, Samantha McAuliffe and John Papadopoulos published an article that revealed how the Propylaea, the massive gateway to the Acropolis, perfectly frames the view from the Acropolis over the gulf to the island of Salamis (the kind of inspired discovery that makes experts slap their foreheads and cry, "How could

I have missed that?").[7] Since its construction in the 430s BCE, the marble gateway, in framing the distant site of the battle, has served to turn the whole of the landscape into a monument of that Athenian triumph. And for centuries, the Athenians would regularly cite Salamis—a battle in which their city "saved" all other Greeks from enslavement by the Persians—as proof that the rest of Greece owed them admiration, loyalty, deference, and tribute. The architects of the Propylaea thus cleverly invited everyone who passed through it to gaze out at the water, imagine the battle being fought all over again, and acknowledge the debt to the valiant Athenians of old. The Persians waged war against many Greek states, but Athenians never missed a chance to promote themselves as the primary combatants and ultimate victors.

Athens's vision for its bigger, better Acropolis has even been likened to New York's 9/11 Memorial, which also integrated reminders of the attack against the United States into the memorial complex. There, the imprints of the fallen Twin Towers have been preserved and transformed into twin reflecting pools, each filled by massive waterfalls, beneath the One World Trade Center skyscraper. This new building, also known as the "Freedom Tower," is the tallest structure (at least for the moment) in the Western Hemisphere. In a 2014 article in the *New Yorker*, critic and classicist Daniel Mendelsohn underscored some of the points of comparison: like New York's Freedom Tower, the new Parthenon "rose as a replacement for a predecessor incinerated by enemies; it, too, towered over a plaza where the footprint of an earlier structure had been left deliberately visible."[8] In stitching ruins into the new fabric of their cityscape, both Athenians and New Yorkers proclaimed that their cities had risen again from ashes.

Like the 9/11 attacks, the conflict between Persia and the Greeks (and not just the Athenians) was viewed in antiquity as a clash of civilizations. Today, many historians even anachronistically place Herodotus's

The island and strait of Salamis (site of the 480 BCE Battle of Salamis) viewed through the Propylaea of the Athenian Acropolis.

narrative at the head of the tradition that separates the world into West and East. Herodotus saw the conflict between the Greeks and Persians as the latest in a long line of clashes between Greeks and "barbarians" generally, which he traced back to a series of abductions of women. Those abductions began, he claimed, when Phoenician traders kidnapped a Greek woman named Io (a rationalization of the ancient myth of Io, who had an affair with Zeus and was transformed into a cow). Eventually this unchecked tit-for-tat emboldened the Trojan prince Paris to abduct Helen, queen of Sparta, and the provocation gave rise to the Trojan War.

Herodotus did not, however, see the clash between Greeks and Persians in strict terms of points on the compass. The long-standing feud was more specific than that, for it pitted the Greeks—one of many peoples of Europe—against the barbarians of Asia, the mass of land separated from Europe by the strait of the Hellespont (the Dardanelles). Only over the course of the fifth century BCE would the Greek word *barbaros,* initially a generic word for non-Greek peoples, evolve into a pejorative term reserved largely for Persians and other peoples of Asia. Athenians defined themselves against the *barbaroi,* whom they portrayed as weak, dissolute, effeminate, and irrational. For Herodotus, one of the fundamental markers of difference between the Greeks and these barbarians revolved around the concept of freedom. The Greeks were, by their very nature, a people who loved their freedom and individuality, while the barbarians happily served as subjects of tyrants and kings.

In reality, cultural exchange between Greece and the Persian Empire was rich and productive. Athenian literature nevertheless tends to caricature the people of Asia. In the years after the Persian Wars, for a Greek to dress like a "Mede" (Media was part of the Persian Empire, but *Mede* was nearly synonymous with *Persian*) could signify a whole range of things, from (pretentious) sophistication to treacherous collaboration with barbarians. Ethnic humor that rings eerily modern already appears in Greek sources from this period. Take, for example, lines from a comedy by Aristophanes, *The Birds* (414 BCE). Here, two characters are asking another about the different species in a flock of varied and colorful birds:

> —Which prophecy-singing, mountain-soaring bird is this, who looks so out of place here?
> —This one is called *Mede.*
> —If he's a Mede, then how did he fly in here without a camel?[9]

The December 2, 2015, issue of *The Week* reported that at a town-hall meeting in Steenbergen, Holland, on the issue of Syrian refugees, one resident ordered, "Take your camels and f—— off." In addition to their many other gifts, the Athenians left a blueprint for seeing the world in terms of a contrast between "civilized" peoples, the cultural inheritors of the Greeks, and extravagant, idle desert barbarians (and their camels).

The rhetoric that Athens spun after the Persian Wars contrasted its people's religious reverence with iconoclastic Persian impiety. Yet according to Herodotus, Xerxes saw the destruction of Athens as the fulfillment of his father's prayer to avenge the burning of the sacred city of Sardis. The Persians justified their policy of sacking Greek temples by citing how the Greeks had burned their temple of Cybebe, an Anatolian mother goddess later worshipped as Cybele, or Magna Mater among the Romans.[10] In the course of the wars, both Greeks and Persians pillaged, burned, and laid waste each other's holy places. Nevertheless, as art historian Rachel Kousser has observed, "Following the

Acropolis sack such iconoclastic activity came to be seen as a paradigmatic example of 'Oriental' impiety and violence."[11] As they rebuilt their city from the rubble, stone by stone the Athenians also laid the foundations for ignorant assumptions that still color our views today. Another contemporary stereotype with an Athenian pedigree is that peoples of the "East"—first Persians, then Ottoman Turks and Arabs, and now Muslims more generally—do not value art and antiquities, do not grieve at the loss of humanity's heritage, and are all too happy to speed its destruction.

Athens used much more than its architecture to tell of its triumph over Persia. From the Assembly, that preeminent institution of Athenian democracy, to the Acropolis, from the theater to the marketplace, the tale was recounted time and again in a variety of forms: speeches, sculptures, plays, and paintings. The Athenians wasted no opportunity to instruct (or to "remind," as orators usually put it) the rest of the Greeks about how they had defeated Xerxes. They also continually celebrated their victories at Marathon and Salamis as high points of their history. Thanks in no small part to the success of Frank Miller's *300*, the Battle of Salamis stands in the shadow of Thermopylae in the popular imagination today. This was far from the case, though, in ancient Athens, where the fame of Salamis far eclipsed Leonidas's last stand. After all, the Spartans might have fought valiantly at Thermopylae, but in the end they suffered a crushing and total defeat. On the other hand, the Athenians who fought at Salamis won, and in doing so, they began the chain of events that eventually sent the Persians home.

In the decade after Xerxes retreated to Persia with what was left of his army, at least two Athenian playwrights ripped their own tragic plots from that headline. In the spring of 472 BCE, a play by Aeschylus titled *The Persians* debuted in Athens. *The Persians* was based on an even earlier play (now lost) by a poet named Phrynichus, one of the earliest known tragedians. Aeschylus's version is set at the royal palace in Persia, where Queen Atossa, Xerxes's mother and Darius's widow, anxiously awaits news of her son's campaigns in Greece. After a messenger arrives with a report of the defeat at Salamis, Atossa, together with the play's chorus of Persian elders, sings a lament that rouses the ghost of her late husband. Conjured at his graveside, Darius angrily rails against the hubris of his son Xerxes and prophesies more defeat for his son's armies. (*Hubris* is the ancient Greek vice of thinking that you are somehow better or greater than the gods.) At the end of the play, Xerxes finally returns home from Greece, a broken and humiliated man. As he mourns for the loss of his troops, the singing chorus concludes that the Ionians (really the Athenians) are, indeed, a brave people. "They are astonishingly warlike," Xerxes concedes. "I have beheld a catastrophe I never dreamed of."[12]

Classical Athens had no income tax; instead, rich men sponsored public projects, such as the building of warships or city walls. Each year, wealthy citizens were also called on to underwrite the high costs of the city's dramatic productions. Themistocles was the general who led the Athenians to victory at Salamis; he was also the producer of Phrynichus's play about the Persians. Pericles, the famous general and politician, provided the funds for Aeschylus's production. Aeschylus's *Persians* seems to have been one of Athens's earliest cultural exports: the play supposedly had a second performance among Greeks in Sicily, where it was an enormous success. The ruler of Sicily, a Greek named Hieron, reportedly arranged for the performance probably not long after his own victory over the Etruscans—another "barbarian" threat to Greek civilization—at the Battle of Cumae in 474 BCE.

In the past few decades, the scholar Edith Hall has done an enormous amount of work to unearth how the Greeks constructed their idea of the barbarian. In her 1989 book *Inventing the Barbarian,* she argued that Athenian tragedy was the crucible for many of the constructs of Easternness that are still in currency today, such as despotism, material extravagance, and cruelty and disregard for life.[13] More recently, she has reexamined responses to and reworkings of *The Persians* at various moments in modern history and has found that even contemporary productions "belong to a long tradition—over four centuries old—which has conflated the ancient victory of the Greeks over Persia at the battle of Salamis with more recent confrontations between the West and its subject peoples, in particular the Islamic world."[14]

It is not difficult to draw a line from the wails of Xerxes for Persia's downfall in Aeschylus's *Persians* to, say, the mentality on view in titles by contemporary military historians. Although Herodotus certainly did not frame the Persian Wars as a conflict between East and West in the way in which the conceit is now understood, this is exactly how popular historians tend to present those wars today. Barry Strauss's 2004 account of the Greek victory at Salamis gives the game away with its title: *The Battle of Salamis: The Naval Encounter That Saved Greece—and Western Civilization.*[15] The battle also receives a dedicated chapter in Victor Davis Hanson's book-length exploration of "why the West has won."[16] The Athenians themselves constantly insisted on the debt that the other Greeks had incurred to Athens on the day of the Battle of Salamis. "If it weren't for us," they may as well have been saying, "you'd all be speaking Persian right now." Today any configuration of Athens's victory at Salamis, or in the Persian Wars more generally, as the victory that saved the West from a fate of Eastern tyranny, dissolution, and terror is one that virtually buys ancient Athenian propaganda wholesale.

ATTRIBUTE 2: ATHENS IS UNIQUE

The Athenian Empire began life in 478 BCE as the Delian League, a Greek defensive alliance forged in the aftermath of the Greek wars against Persia. The league was formed ostensibly as a coalition to check Persian power and has often been cited as an ancient precedent for NATO, another league of states bound in alliance against a supposedly threatening Eastern power.[17] At first, the Delian League's common treasury was kept on the tiny Aegean island of Delos, but by the middle of the fifth century the Athenians had become powerful enough to co-opt the treasury and move it to the Acropolis for "safekeeping." The earliest Athenian tribute lists, records of the compulsory tax paid to Athens by its "allies" in return for military protection, date to 454 BCE. At the height of its empire, Athens received tribute from as many as four hundred other Greek communities. The city was able to invent itself as an imperial power so quickly largely because of its success in convincing other Greeks that it had saved them from "barbarians."

The Athenians often attributed their political and military success, including their victory over the Persians, to the depth of their collective commitment to Athens. One form of that commitment was the city's famed democracy. An aristocrat named Cleisthenes is typically credited with the radical reforms that transformed Athens into a democracy in 508 BCE. After those reforms, adult male citizens, regardless of wealth, had voting rights in the Assembly *(ekklesia)*. Five hundred were chosen by lot to serve for terms of one year on the Council *(boule),* which set the Assembly's agenda but could also circumvent the Assembly when moments of crisis demanded more urgent action. Participation, though, was far from universal: neither slaves nor women had voting rights, and in 451 BCE, a law was passed that further tightened qualifications for male participation by dictating that only children whose father and mother were both Athenians had rights to Athenian citizenship.

One of the most remarkable aspects of the city's democratic system was the set of rituals that reinforced it. One example involved a rope, freshly dipped in red paint, that was used to herd citizens out of the marketplace and into Assembly meetings. Anyone who turned up with streaks of red paint was exposed as a shirker of democratic duty. Another ritual that served to affirm the democracy was ostracism. Every year, the full body of male citizens voted on whether to hold an ostracism, and if they decided to do so, the entire marketplace was transformed into an enormous voting site. Each citizen wrote a name on a potsherd, called an *ostracon,* and the man with the most votes was exiled from Athens for a decade. This ritual was a way for the citizens to demonstrate how seriously they took their democracy. Men who were ostracized tended to be charismatic leaders with significant support—too much support, of the kind that potentially posed a threat to true democratic rule. In reality, ostracisms were rare events; there is solid evidence for just ten such occasions in the whole history of Athens's classical democracy. The potency of the ritual rested on the fact that the possibility of holding one was always annually there.

Athens thrived under its democracy only because the people believed that the state was worth dying for. They had many chances to die for it, since military service was compulsory and the citizens regularly voted—theirs was a direct democracy, after all—to send themselves to war. In the face of the constant flow of casualties, they developed ways of spinning death and defeat as patriotic virtues. Nathan Arrington, an art historian who has written extensively on the Athenian cult of the war dead, draws particular attention to the significance of the city's inscribed casualty lists. These stones were posted in the national cemetery, the *demosion sema,* as memorials to the men who had died in battle. As Arrington explains, the lists of names "showcased loss in order to create a rhetoric of struggle, thus becoming emblems of strength, power, and resilience."[18] In Athens, the casualty lists performed the additional task of effectively tracking the red column—the expenses of empire—in the city's ledger. These were balanced, in a manner, by tribute lists, which were posted on the Acropolis and tallied the annual intake of tribute collected from the allies: evidence that the empire stayed in the black. In one sense, then, everyone in Athens was freely invited to audit those metaphorical imperial books.

Casualty lists were permanent, stone memorials for the war dead, but the speeches given at their funerals were regarded as greater monuments still. These speeches, *epitaphioi logoi,* were pronounced during the public military funerals held after battles. They performed two important functions: first, they helped process and contain the city's collective grief; second, they worked to convince other citizen-soldiers that dying for Athens was the noblest of aspirations. They also gave orators an opportunity to paint a rhetorical image of Athens that inspired pride among those who belonged to the community and jealousy in those who did not. No one is quite sure when this practice first began, although its emergence is often associated with the Persian Wars. The only description of the public funeral is given by the Athenian historian Thucydides, who prefaces his famous account of a funeral oration by Pericles with a general account of the entire "ancestral custom." At public funerals, the bodies of the dead Athenians were laid out in cypress coffins, one of which was kept empty as a monument to the missing. Anyone who wanted to join the procession could do so, and women performed laments. Once "the bodies have been laid in the earth, a man chosen by the state, of approved wisdom and eminent reputation, pronounces over them an appropriate eulogy, after which all retire."[19]

Pericles was chosen by his fellow citizens to deliver the funeral oration in the winter of the first year of the Peloponnesian War, in 430 BCE. No one in Athens had a more eminent reputation: his mother belonged to one of the city's greatest noble families, the Alcmaeonids, and her uncle was none other than Cleisthenes, the man remembered as the father of Athenian democracy. Pericles's father had also been a politician and one of the most celebrated generals of the Persian Wars. In 479 BCE, he commanded the Athenian fleet at the naval Battle of Mycale, in the strait between the Aegean island of Samos and the west coast of modern Turkey. That Greek triumph, coupled with a simultaneous land victory at Plataea, effectively ended the Persians' second invasion of Greece. Pericles officially held the position of elected general in Athens, but Thucydides was clear on the extent of his influence: under his leadership, the city was "a democracy in name, but a rule by the first man in reality."[20]

Later generations remembered Pericles as the greatest orator the city had ever seen. He left no writings behind when he died, but Thucydides's rendition of this funeral oration is a masterpiece in its own right. Each phrase of the speech is a carefully crafted variation on a core of reliable themes: the greatness of Athens, the valor of its citizens, the nobility of its ancestors, and the honor and glory of dying for the city. The Athens evoked in the speech is a land where democracy rules and all citizens are equal before the laws, where poverty is no barrier to advancement, and where the only citizen worthy of the name is a politically engaged one. It also contains the sound bites still used today as slogans of the Athenian miracle: the Athenians are a people who "cultivate beauty with moderation, and wisdom without effeminacy"; "the entire city is an education for Greece."[21] In his speech, Pericles even supposedly asked his fellow Athenians to gaze on the power of their city every day and fall in love with it. He called on each citizen to become its *erastes*. In English the word is rendered as "lover," but in Greek it is more precisely the word for an active lover, the lover who pursues the beloved.[22] The idea of Athens on display in this speech has long been regarded as a historical reality. Shortly after World War I broke out, the sides of London buses were plastered with quotations from it. In 1938, the British classicist Gilbert Murray commented that those posters had been there "to remind us of the ideals which we had to defend."[23]

The funeral orations could be so over the top in their praise of Athens that even some Athenians were critical. Socrates, another great Athenian thinker who, like Pericles, left no writings behind when he died, apparently numbered among the critics. In *Menexenus,* a dialogue by his student Plato, Socrates gives a private recitation of a public funeral oration for a small group of close friends. He claims that he was taught the speech by Pericles's mistress, Aspasia. Little is known about her, but ancient sources preserve her reputation as a sparkling conversationalist and salon hostess: her house had the reputation of being a meeting place for the great and the good of Athens, and Socrates was supposedly a regular at her lively gatherings. The dramatic setting of *Menexenus* is draped with anticipation. Socrates's friend Menexenus has just returned from a meeting of the Council, which has been preparing to choose who will deliver the oration at the upcoming public funeral. Before he sets out to prove how formulaic these speeches are by delivering one of his own, Socrates praises, with more than a tinge of irony, the men who give them. "They deliver praise so well," he gushes, "that they enchant our souls." He continues in this vein of mock enthusiasm when he describes the effect the speeches have on him: "At once I feel as if I have become greater and nobler and more handsome," especially in the eyes of the crowds of foreigners who regularly came to hear the speeches. He even claims to get a "majestic high" on these occasions, a high that he comes down from only three or four days later: "Till then I had nearly thought I was living on the Islands of the Blessed—our rhetoricians are that good."[24]

Menexenus is often read as a satirical send-up of the funeral oration and, more generally, of the rhetoric of Athenian superiority, the very kind of rhetoric that many people seem willing to believe still today. Socrates's claims about how the orators make him feel—as a privileged Athenian, he is transformed in the glow of the praise—are certainly difficult to take at face value. Yet they are valuable as an indicator, however exaggerated, of the atmosphere that the state and its elected orator sought to create. Another of Socrates's students, Isocrates, was far more direct in his criticism of the institution of the public funeral. Isocrates was a renowned Athenian statesman and orator who was born in 436 BCE and lived for nearly a century, until 338. He was said to have died of grief over Philip of Macedon and Alexander the Great's defeat of Athens (and the whole of Greece) at the Battle of Chaeronea, the battle that heralded the beginning of the end of Athens's democracy and what today is considered its classical age. In the mid-fourth century BCE, Isocrates condemned the public funeral as part of the arrogant apparatus of the old imperial state. He also offered his own cutting interpretation of just why foreign visitors had been so eager to attend them. "They did not come to grieve with us over the dead," he explained, "but to revel in our misfortunes."[25] The Athenians' excessive efforts to prove that their city was worth dying for had resulted, at least in Isocrates's eyes, in far too many deaths.

ATTRIBUTE 3: ATHENS IS THE HOME OF THE ARTS

Pericles's claim in his funeral oration that Athenians "cultivate beauty with moderation" was a reference to the city's cultural achievements—

philosophy, poetry, drama, painting, sculpture, and architecture. As the Athenian scene from *Bill and Ted's Excellent Adventure* illustrates, Athens is today nearly synonymous with philosophy: Socrates, Plato, and Aristotle all taught, lectured, and made their philosophical careers there. Yet in antiquity, the cultural agenda of the state most emphasized the significance of Athenian art and drama. Today discussions of both of these hallmarks of Athenian culture all too easily gloss over the fact that most of the public art (including theatrical performances) created in fifth-century-BCE Athens was produced, at least officially, in the service of that state to complement and communicate the city's imperial program. Two of the most celebrated and enduring artistic legacies of ancient Athenian civilization, drama and architecture, offer special insight into how Athenians produced art in service of their city. Both were powerful tools used by Athens to shore up its political empire with the considerable soft power of cultural hegemony.

Theater festivals were organized and in large part financed by the city. The most costly and popular festival was the Great Dionysia, which was held every spring and featured tragedies, comedies, and choral performances. The festival was the highlight of the Athenian calendar, and over a span of about seventy years it hosted the debut of nearly every ancient Greek tragedy that survives today: Aeschylus's *Persians* (produced, as I have noted, by Pericles himself) and *Oresteia* trilogy, Sophocles's *Antigone* and *Oedipus the King,* and Euripides's *Medea* and *Women of Troy* all premiered at the Great Dionysia. The festival was also a manifestly political event. Like the state funerals, this was a regular opportunity for Athens to celebrate its power and advertise the ideology of its empire. The city did this by staging a whole host of civic, ideological performances alongside the plays and choruses. What happens on the red carpet on the night of the Academy Awards is just as important as the announcement of the awards, and the Super Bowl would hardly be the same without all the ceremonies around the football game: the singing of the national anthem, the coin toss, and the halftime show—even the much-anticipated (and staggeringly expensive) television commercials. The Great Dionysia likewise featured an entire suite of what classicist Simon Goldhill has called "preplay ceremonies."[26] These ceremonies did as much as the funeral orations to project Athens's powerful imperial persona, both to the city's residents and to the throngs of foreign dignitaries and tourists who traveled to the city for the occasion.

As long as Athens took in imperial tribute from other subject states, the Great Dionysia also coincided with the tribute's annual collection. Ambassadors came to Athens before the start of the festival to deliver their cities' payments and often stayed to take in the performances. One of the preplay ceremonies consisted of a brazen display of the tribute collected as silver from the fresh payments was paraded into the theater. In another kind of performance, Athenian boys who had come of age in the past year but whose fathers had died in war were presented with their own set of hoplite armor, a gift from the grateful city. Together, these two rituals served as further public tabulations of imperial profit and loss. Isocrates, who was so ashamed of the custom of the public military funeral, also bitterly resented both the parade of tribute and the presentation of war orphans at the theater festival. By the time he lodged his criticism, in the mid-fourth century BCE, neither ritual still took place: Athens no longer had an empire, and so there was no imperial tribute to display. Yet in Isocrates's mind, these practices had done a great deal of lasting damage. By enacting these civic rituals at the Great Dionysia, the Athenians had "sent a message to two groups." To the allies, they had displayed the tribute to highlight their material wealth, but "to the other Greeks they displayed the great number of orphans—and the consequences of their own arrogance."[27]

In regard to the war orphans, the Great Dionysia was highly coordinated with the public funerals for the war dead. At the end of each funeral oration, the speaker made a promise that the city would look after the war orphans as a surrogate parent. That promise was publicly fulfilled each year at the Great Dionysia, when the grown orphans were presented with their military armor and were urged to follow the example set by their fathers. The Great Dionysia also worked in concert with the public funerals in other ways, since both were an important site for the telling of patriotic stories drawn from Athenian mythology. In their speeches, the funeral orators typically surveyed major events in Athenian history. They began with exploits of the distant (or what we would call mythical) past, made their way to the triumphs over Persia, and finished with examples of Athenian heroism in more recent memory.

Year after year and over and over, the orators drew from a standard repertory of stories. These myths provided the city with a number of policy precedents. Tales of how the Athenian king Theseus had once intervened to ensure that even invaders of Thebes received proper burial after the battle, or of how the Athenians had once welcomed the persecuted children of Heracles into their city, justified their habit of intervening in other states' contemporary affairs. That habit was often called *polypragmosyne*—the ancient Greek word for sticking one's nose into other people's business. The city's claim to be the protector of Greece from barbarian threats was bolstered not just by the legacy of the Persian Wars but also by myths about how ancient Athenians had defeated invasions by Amazons and later by Eumolpus, king of Thrace (a Balkan region, now spread over parts of Greece, Bulgaria, and Turkey) and son of the god Poseidon.

Athenians used these kinds of myths to argue for everything from privileged positions in battle lines to their self-appointed status as the moral police of the Greek world. This repertory of legends also provided the material for a number of the tragedians' plots. During the years of the Peloponnesian War, these stories were a particular favorite of Euripides, one of Athens's most famous tragedians. The story of Eumolpus's invasion, which supposedly took place during the reign of the Athenian king Erechtheus, was the subject of a play titled *Erechtheus* by Euripides. Although it survives only in bits and pieces preserved on scraps of papyrus and in quotations by other ancient authors, we know that it begins as Eumolpus's forces are drawing nearer to Athens. King Erechtheus learns that in order to stop them, he must sacrifice his daughter. In one of the play's longest surviving scenes, his wife, Praxithea, makes a speech explaining why she is willing—even proud—to see her daughter offered up as a human sacrifice for Athens.

The first reason she states is that citizens must be willing to give their lives for the land that has given them life. Athenians held that their citizenry was autochthonous, literally born from the Attic earth. This was another characteristic—at its heart a claim for ethnic purity—on which Athenians especially prided themselves and that they believed made them exceptional. Praxithea explains that the Athenians' autochthony means that they are superior to other peoples, who have only settled their lands: "Other cities are founded as if by moves in a board game. . . . Anyone who moves from one city to live in another is like a round peg in a square hole."[28] In the course of her fifty-five lines (like Shakespeare, all ancient Greek playwrights composed in verse), she demonstrates an encyclopedic knowledge of Athenian patriotic values and conceits. She concludes with the thought that her daughter is hers only by descent; in truth, the girl belongs, like all Athenians, to the city.

Not all tragedies performed at the Great Dionysia took their plots from Athenian myths, but in classical Athens they were always packaged in celebrations of the Athenian state and its exceptionalism. Drama was nevertheless also the city's most successful cultural export. The reach of the city's dramatic tradition extended quickly, first across the Greek world, as early as the performance of Aeschylus's *Persians* in Sicily in the early fifth-century BCE. In the next century, Athenian tragedy—with all its plays and verses in praise of Athens—also traveled remarkably far into the East in the hands of Alexander the Great. In his *Life of Alexander,* the ancient biographer Plutarch reports that Alexander, an enormous fan of Athenian theater, demanded to be sent plays by the tragedians Euripides, Sophocles, and Aeschylus when he was on military campaign. In another work, Plutarch also notes that when Alexander "civilized" the world, children in the farthest reaches of Asia learned to recite lines by Sophocles and Euripides.[29]

Sophocles and Euripides also did their part to help foster a common sense of identity in the Greek-speaking world: Athenian tragedy was second only to the Persian Wars in the contribution that it made to fostering panhellenism, or solidarity around the notion of a common Greek (or Hellenic) identity. Tragedy also helped spread the Athenian dialect across Greece, just as the invention of the television helped spread a single standard form of Italian in Italy in the mid-twentieth century. We even have anecdotes from every corner of ancient Greece about cases of Euripidesmania, complete with screaming, fainting, and fits of insanity. Denis Feeney, a scholar of ancient Roman literary culture, has provided an account of the significance that Greek tragedy had, not just as an influence on Roman drama but as a very precondition for the birth of Latin literature some three centuries after the Greeks' wars with Persia. Feeney's investigation exposes the odd truth that in essence, Latin literature began with a translation project: the very first works written in Latin were the scripts of tragic plays, adapted by Italian poets from Greek scripts for Roman audiences.[30] Thanks in part to this help from the Romans, Athenian tragedy—that patriotic product of imperial ideology—entered the DNA of the Western literary tradition.

At home and abroad, Athenian drama served to showcase the city as one that valued and cultivated art and beauty. The same message was also built into the Athenian skyline. After Athens's destruction by Xerxes's Persians, elements of the Acropolis were rebuilt in such a way as to proclaim the city's triumph over barbarians: the city's foremost brand attribute. A generation later, in the second half of the fifth century, a whole host of new structures and statues rose up in the city under the auspices of an extravagant building program. Together they advanced an even grander program of advertising the city as the very wellspring of art and civilization. Athens thus invested heavily in a bid to consolidate its status as imperial capital largely by dressing the part.

The whole of the building program, especially as realized on the Acropolis, reflected what has been called an "integrated architectural concept."[31] In angles, proportions, and imagery, the structures and their sculptures presented a coherent vision of Athens as a city that revered and honored the gods and, with those gods' help, triumphed over its enemies. The myth of how Athenians once defeated a horde of invading Amazons—a myth traditionally recounted in the funeral orations—was also depicted on the Parthenon in a series of marble friezes known as the Western Metopes. If the theme of the city defeating an outside invader also rings familiar, it is because many art historians interpret those friezes as an allegory of Athens's definitive triumph over another set of barbarian invaders: the Persians.

The general and politician Pericles is remembered as the spiritual architect of the imperial building program. His transfer of the Delian League's treasury to Athens in the mid-fifth century BCE brought the city an unprecedented supply of wealth, and much of it was invested in construction and the general beautification of Athens. Each year that wealth grew larger as tribute poured in from the city's allies. In his *Life of Pericles,* Plutarch wrote that Pericles earned the epithet "Olympian" either because of his skill in political and military affairs or "because of the [buildings] with which he beautified the city."[32] His building program stretched across Athens and as far as Eleusis, the major religious site where the secret rites of the Eleusinian Mysteries were celebrated, in the northeast corner of Attica (the region controlled by the "capital" at Athens, comprising an area roughly the size of Luxembourg or about four-fifths of the state of Rhode Island). This program produced the Parthenon and the Erechtheion with its Porch of Caryatids, as well as a new monumental entryway to the Acropolis: the Propylaea, which frames the view out toward Salamis (if you have ever visited the Acropolis, you passed through it after a steep, often hot and slippery climb). It also included a number of other temples, statues, and even the city's Long Walls, referred to by Athenians as their city's "legs," a fortified corridor that stretched all the way to the port at Piraeus, Athens's lifeline to the sea.

Pericles's building program was an extraordinary undertaking in terms of material cost and human labor. Although some of its elements were completed with astonishing speed, others, such as the stone Theater of Dionysus, were not finished until late in the next century. Pericles came under heavy criticism, both from fellow citizens and other members of the Delian League, for his appropriation of the alliance's public funds. Plutarch reports that Pericles's enemies savaged him in the Assembly for such a frivolous use of their wealth: "Greece seems terribly insulted and subjected to haughty tyranny when she sees that, using her forced contributions to the war chest, *we* are gilding and tarting up our city, tricking her out—just like a conceited woman—with extravagant stones and statues and overpriced temples!"[33] Plutarch also stressed that in his own day some half a millennium later, the Periclean buildings still stood as "Greece's sole testaments that Athens' fabled power and its former wealth were no fiction." His much-quoted description of the enduring appeal of those buildings also foreshadows the kind of eighteenth-century German art criticism that we will encounter in Chapter 4: "In their beauty each building was, even then, instantly ancient, but in their perfection they are modern and new to this day: just so does a sort of freshness bloom perpetually over them, preserving an appearance untouched by time, as if the works were possessed of an ever-blossoming spirit mingled with an ageless soul."[34] Thanks to the building program more than anything else, Pericles's name is still synonymous with the artistic achievements of classical Athens: "Periclean Athens" is a kind of catchphrase often used for the city's supposed golden age in the fifth century. For the program's sculptural elements, including the great Parthenon frieze, Pericles retained the services of the artist Phidias, later the sculptor of the colossal cult statue in the temple of Zeus at Olympia, the only work on the Greek mainland later counted as one of the Seven Wonders of the World.

As they watched Pericles's buildings rise around Athens, some Athenians suspected—correctly, it turns out—that the structures' grandeur would shape posterity's view of their city. Sparta, Thucydides mused, was at least as great as Athens, yet if Sparta were to be abandoned, it would be difficult to persuade later generations of its former glory. This was only because it was never "decked out with temples and lavish buildings." For all its military fame, Sparta was never fortified in the classical period; it was not even a single city, but rather an association of rural villages spread over hills. Thucydides's reflection continued with what now seems like uncanny foresight: "But if this were to happen to Athens . . . the sheer sight of [the remains] would leave the impression that the city's power had been twice what it really is."[35] The Periclean building program certainly projected (and has left us with) an inflated sense of Athens's power in the Greek world. As cultural and political propaganda, this is exactly what all those beautiful buildings and sculptures were designed to do.

ATTRIBUTES 4 AND 4′: THE BURDEN OF THE PAST

Near the end of the second century BCE, the Greek league responsible for overseeing the religious site of Delphi issued a decree that granted special privileges to traveling actors from Athens. The decree claimed to award those privileges out of respect for Athens's status as the birthplace of drama: the city "herself manifestly pronounces the truth," the stone explains, "when she reminds the world that she is the *metropolis* [mother city] of all drama, because she invented and fostered both tragedy and comedy."[36] This move by the league thus marked one form of an attempt to help settle the symbolic debt that other Greeks allegedly owed to Athens.

Throughout antiquity, Athenians insisted that they had given other Greeks many gifts: the theater, certain religious rites (the Eleusinian Mysteries), philosophical academies, and, most important, the gift of safety from the threat of further Persian invasions. In the fifth century BCE, Athenians used that last point to justify their appropriation of the Delian League's entire treasury. With the help of those funds, their imperial ambitions were given visible expression under Pericles when, in the 430s BCE, he turned the whole of the city into a construction site. This kind of behavior, however, soon led the Peloponnesian League, with Sparta at the helm, to bring long-simmering tensions in Greece to a boil and precipitate the start of the Peloponnesian War. An unmistakable nostalgia for the past begins to emerge in the Athenian sources of this period. That nostalgia translated into Athenian brand attribute

4 (Athens is the product of exceptional ancestors), but also 4′ (Athens was much better in the past). Depending on how one looked at it, the Athenians were either lavishing well-deserved praise on their ancestors—the founders of the empire—or beginning to acknowledge that they did not measure up to them.

By far our best source for this later part of the fifth century is Thucydides's *History of the Peloponnesian War*. Thucydides served as a general in the war until he was exiled for a strategic failure in 423 BCE (his exile was precisely what afforded him the leisure and freedom to write his deeply insightful account). According to him, four separate infractions of a previous truce were formally cited as justifications for the war; these were its proximate causes. But the war's ultimate cause ("the truest reason, but the one that went completely unmentioned") was the fear that Athens's growing power inspired in the Spartans—not a people remembered for scaring easily.[37] Thucydides foreshadows Athens's defeat in the war in his rendering of a speech made by Pericles to the Athenian Assembly shortly before the violence broke out. In that speech, Pericles expresses high hopes for a good outcome, provided that the Athenians resist the temptation of combining their maneuvers against Sparta with schemes to add more territory to the empire.[38] The tragedy at the heart of Thucydides's account—and it is in fact often read as a kind of historical tragedy, with Athens in the role of the flawed and hubristic tragic hero—is that, in the absence of his leadership, Pericles's warning went unheeded. In the war's second year, Pericles died from a plague that burned through the already war-torn city.

As the Peloponnesian War progressed, one by one Athens's "allies" rose up against it. To put it gently, Athens always had an uneasy relationship with its imperial subjects. Flip casually to any page of fifth-century Greek history, and you may well find the Athenians treating, or at least regarding, allied cities and islands as subordinates; there are also good odds of catching Athens punishing allies for rebelling or other states for refusing to join the alliance. Aristotle, the Macedonian tutor of Alexander the Great, lived and worked for many years in Athens and was just one voice in the chorus of retrospective critics. In about 330 BCE, he observed that "once [the Athenians] secured the empire, they treated the allies rather despotically, except for Chios, Lesbos, and Samos—for they saw them as guardians of the empire."[39]

Athens could be incredibly harsh toward states that refused to obey it. When the city of Mytilene on the island of Lesbos tried to secede from Athenian rule, the Athenians first hastily ordered that all of Mytilene's men be executed and all its women and children enslaved. At a meeting of the Assembly, the Athenians reconsidered the issue in what is now known as the Mytilenean Debate of 427 BCE.[40] The question on the table was whether the death sentence should be carried out; after impassioned arguments on both sides, the Athenians decided to rescind it and were just barely able to get the message through before the executions could be carried out. About a decade later, in 416 BCE, the residents of the Cycladic island of Melos were not so fortunate (the debate over the Melians' fate is dramatized in Thucydides's renowned Melian Dialogue). When the Melians refused to bow to Athens's power and acquiesce to paying tribute, Athens handed down the same sentence that it had originally passed for the Mytileneans. This time there were no second thoughts.

Thucydides referred to the span of time between the defeat of Persia and the outbreak of the Peloponnesian War as the *pentecontaetia,* the "fifty-year period." This was the era in which Athens dominated the Greek world and its democracy flourished. During the last quarter of the fifth century, nostalgia for that age of unrivaled power and relative stability was enacted nowhere as vividly as on the Athenian stage.

The most famous comic playwright of the era, Aristophanes, wrote a number of plays premised on a protagonist's harebrained plan to restore the good old days. In *The Knights* of 424 BCE, a satire on Athenian life during the Peloponnesian War, Demos, the personified people of Athens (*demos* means "the people"; *demokratia* is "rule by the people"), is depicted as a withered old man. The utopian comic twist at the end of the play is that Demos emerges from backstage rejuvenated, restored to his former youthful glory, and accompanied by personified female peace treaties (a student of mine once called the play *Extreme Makeover: Demos Edition*). In *The Frogs* of 405 BCE, a play from two decades later, the concept is similar: Under its present leadership, Athens is in a bad way. To remedy the situation, the god of theater, Dionysus, decides to journey to the underworld to retrieve a dead tragedian in the hope that a great playwright of the past can save the city. Only a dead one will do, Dionysus explains, "because such poets no longer exist and the ones who are left are bad."[41] The great climax of the play is a contest between Aeschylus and Euripides, who vie for the chance to be brought back to life. In the end, it is Aeschylus—the great veteran of the Battle of Marathon—who wins the honor. This resolution was, of course, no more than a wishful flight of fancy. The year after *The Frogs* premiered, Athens fell to Sparta.

All this means that even before construction began on the Erechtheion in 421 BCE, calls were already ringing out to make Athens great again. In the first half of the fourth century, Athens even made an attempt to re-create the old empire. The short-lived Second Athenian Empire (378–355 BCE) was only a shadow of the first, and in the decades after its collapse, the mounting power of Macedon made clear that Athens would never regain its former command over the Aegean. Certain Athenians responded to that realization by embarking on an intensive project of curating the artifacts and legacy of their city's historic achievements. Those efforts made constant appeals to the old core messages of the brand. An inscription that allegedly preserves an oath sworn by Greek forces on the eve of the 479 BCE Battle of Plataea, the last Greek land battle against Persia during the second invasion of Greece, was put up in Attica. Statues of the great tragedians, whose careers collectively spanned, almost to the year, Athens's fifth-century imperial heyday, were set on display at the entrance to the theater. A new Monument of the Eponymous Heroes in the city's marketplace glorified the ten mythical heroes after whom the tribes, part of the organizational structure of Athenian democracy, were named.

These later Athenians, still "classical" from our perspective, were already suffering under the burden of the idealized past that they had constructed. The greatest tragedian of the fourth century, Astydamas (a name unfamiliar even to many classicists), is today best known for an epigram in which he lamented how hard it was to compete with the poets of the past. In one of his greatest speeches, the orator Demosthenes complained how unjust it was to compare living men with their illustrious predecessors. He told his courtroom opponent to "evaluate me against the orators of today," and not against the incomparable orators of the past, such as Pericles.[42]

By working so hard to construct a pedestal for their ancestors, the Athenians were catching themselves in a terrible and enduring bind. As they petitioned for Greece's respect—and independence from Alexander the Great's expanding empire—on the backs of their ancestors' achievements, they also ensured that later generations would always be viewed as a disappointment by comparison. This means that modern idealizations of the Athens of Sophocles and Socrates and of Plato and Demosthenes are idealizations of an Athens that on many counts was already anxious about its own decline. In seeking to rally support from other Greeks in the face of Macedon's mounting power, the city became particularly inclined to appeal to the abstract historical debt that Greece still owed it. This debt was owed because Athens had defeated the Persians, and also because the city had given Greece cultural gifts such as tragic and comic theater. These appeals were its best hope in the face of annihilation, but they also amounted to a ready acknowledgment that Athens was already failing to measure up to its past.

This idea that Athens "just isn't what it used to be" thus became packaged into the Athenian brand at a surprisingly early date. In 330 BCE, an aristocrat named Lycurgus, the greatest Athenian statesman of his generation, prosecuted a coppersmith named Leocrates for abandoning Athens in the critical moments that followed the city's defeat by Macedon in 338 at the Battle of Chaeronea. At one point in the speech, Lycurgus describes how severely the Athenian ancestors dealt with traitors and argues that the jurors must apply their precedent to Leocrates. "If you do not kill him," he asks, "how will you pass for descendants of those men?"[43] His question says it all: how could any living Athenians, or Greeks for that matter, ever be called the worthy descendants of such illustrious ancestors? Thus already in the period that we call "classical," this kind of question had begun to loom over the citizens of Athens. And still today a version of message 4', "Greece was much better in the past," continues to haunt Greeks and views of the Greeks. Unlike so many other supposed "gifts of the Greeks" (democracy, mathematics, philosophy, and others), it is rarely traced back to classical Athens. In this case, however, classical Athens really is where the idea started.

But just when and how did the modern era of disillusionment with Greece on these terms—for failing to live up to a more illustrious past—begin?

CHAPTER THREE

Colonizers of an Antique Land

TWENTY YEARS BEFORE SHE began her first term as Greece's minister of culture, Melina Mercouri served as a very different kind of representative for her country. In Jules Dassin's 1960 film *Never on Sunday,* she played a woman named Ilya, a hooker with a heart of gold and a passion for ancient Greek tragedy. Dassin, Mercouri's husband at the time, starred opposite her as Homer Thrace, an American tourist on pilgrimage to see the homeland of the ancient philosophers his father had raised him to love. At the beginning of the movie, as Homer's boat approaches the port of Piraeus, he cries out in glee, "There is the purity that was Greece!" After he steps off the boat, his illusions quickly disintegrate when he sees how far the Greeks have fallen. That night he meets Ilya when she intercedes to save him from a brawl. In the conversation that follows, he poses to her the questions eating away at him: "No society ever reached the heights that were attained by ancient Greece! It was the cradle of culture. It was a happy country. What happened? What made it fall?"

Homer Thrace's character in *Never on Sunday* is a stock type of Western tourist, disappointed to see how far modern Greece and Greeks fall short of the ideas in his mind. Disillusionment with Greece is a trope as ancient as it is common, but this particular form of it dates back to the later 1600s, when waves of travelers from northern Europe (especially Britain and France) set out on increasingly frequent expeditions to see Greece for themselves. During the second half of that century, in a kind of coda to Europe's Age of Discovery, a new kind of explorer emerged with sights set not on the geographic ends of the earth but on lands of remote antiquity. These travelers, too, saw themselves as discoverers, but they were seeking lost civilizations they had studied since they were young. In a manner of speaking, they would also prove to be just as much colonists as their South Seas and New World counterparts. Armed with grammars, dictionaries, and ancient texts, classically trained European gentlemen effectively planted their flags not in the soil of Ottoman Greece but amid its ancient ruins.

As the historian K. E. Fleming has argued, the impulse that guided their journeys "can be seen as representative of a different form of colonialism, in which the history and ideology, rather than territory, of another country have been claimed, invaded, and annexed."[1] In recent decades, especially since the beginning of the current financial crisis, historians, economists, and political scientists have pointed out various ways in which Greece, though never formally colonized by any European nation, does have a substantial legacy of subjection to European colonial power. That legacy began with the arrival of increasing numbers of European travelers in an era before the notion of the West's symbolic debt to Greece had yet been formulated. Those travelers were convinced that because of their classical education and personal passion for antiquity, they understood and appreciated Greece better than Greeks themselves could. This, in turn, led the travelers to develop an intensely proprietary attitude toward Greece, a land in which they felt a stake of ownership thanks to their putatively superior command of ancient Greek history, and even of Ancient Greek. It is no coincidence that at about the same time, European aristocrats also began to develop an insatiable appetite for antiquities from ancient Greek lands. Whether in person or through agents abroad, collectors embarked on a project of uprooting and relocating antiquity's tangible traces. They justified doing so by insisting that the artifacts would be more competently and lovingly safeguarded in other countries of Europe (such as Britain, France, or Germany), where they would keep company with truer heirs to the civilization that had created them.

Early modern Europeans were, however, hardly the first foreigners to view their Greek contemporaries as fallen from grace. Ancient Romans had been especially persuaded of the point. Cicero was a great admirer of Athenian drama, rhetoric, and philosophy, but when his younger brother took up a post in Asia Minor, he warned him to be wary of trusting local Greeks, except "for those extremely few who are worthy of ancient Greece."[2] Nearly a millennium later, in the 820s, the seventh Abbasid caliph, al-Ma'mun, engaged in a military campaign against the Byzantine Empire on the premise that his caliphate was ancient Greece's rightful successor. He painted the Byzantines "as villainous because they were not only Christians but also unworthy— and usurping—successors of the ancient Greeks."[3] For proof of his people's devotion to Greek antiquity, al-Ma'mun had only to point to his caliphate's capital in Baghdad, where all known ancient Greek scientific and philosophical texts were undergoing translation into Arabic.

That endeavor, the so-called Translation Movement, took place in the ninth and tenth centuries under the aegis of the House of Wisdom, an institution founded as part of an Islamic imperial ideology that proclaimed the renewal of scientific learning under Abbasid rule. Its translators focused almost exclusively on Greek works of science (mathematics, astronomy, medicine, geography) and philosophy.

Many centuries later, European travelers likewise saw Greece's modern inhabitants as unworthy successors of their ancient ancestors. But unlike the Abbasids, who sought to use ancient Greek wisdom as a practical tool for advancing their own philosophical and theological thought, the travelers belonged to an intellectual tradition dedicated to studying texts in Ancient Greek as examples of oratorical skill, moral advice, historical analysis, and poetic ingenuity. Abbasid translators, by contrast, had generally regarded Greek works of history and oratory as too culturally specific to ancient Greek civilization to be useful for Islamic intellectuals, many of whom had also opposed the translation of poetry on the principle that "poems do not lend themselves to translation and ought not to be translated."[4]

In Europe, the study of ancient Greek literary and historical works had started to flourish only during the Renaissance, when humanists ransacked monasteries looking for ancient manuscripts of all types. At first, very few of those scholars knew Ancient Greek, but that changed by the close of the fifteenth century when Aldus Manutius, Europe's first professional publisher, began to make Greek texts and grammars more widely and cheaply available by issuing printed editions from his press in Venice. Soon classical learning began to flourish in lands north of the Alps. In 1530, King Francis I of France established the Collège Royal, later the Collège de France, partially as an institution for the study of the classical languages: Greek, Latin, and Hebrew. A decade later, England's King Henry VIII appointed the first Regius (i.e., royal) Professor of Greek at Cambridge; another was inaugurated the next year at Oxford. By the 1600s, the study of Ancient Greek had become a pillar of education at prestigious universities across Europe. This meant that the literary and historical works that stood as testaments to the Athenian brand, with all their praise of Athenian exceptionalism, became a part of every gentleman's education.

In the mid-seventeenth century, some European students of antiquity also grew eager to supplement, and even to challenge, the ancient narratives with information gleaned from tangible, material artifacts: the hard evidence of coins, inscriptions, and monuments. No longer satisfied to study the written record alone, a new breed of antiquaries sought empirical experience of the past by apprehending it directly through their senses. And what better way to do so than by seeing the wonders of the "classical lands" (the Levant, Greece, and Italy) with their own eyes? In England, France, and elsewhere, antiquarian interests were bolstered by methodologies born of the Scientific Revolution. They also converged and intersected with enthusiasm for exploration and discovery—impulses that belonged to the broader context of the contemporary expansion of European empires, especially those of Britain and France. But despite their eagerness for adventure and first-hand encounters with the ancient past, many of the classically minded travelers who set foot in Greece could not help but experience some version of the same disillusionment that, some centuries later, threatened to ruin Homer Thrace's vacation.

By jumping from classical Athens to the era of Europe's "rediscovery" of Greece and the development of European proprietary attitudes toward its ancient past, we are leaping over two millennia of Greek history. Those intervening centuries naturally served to alter, conceal, and in many cases obliterate the ancient monuments that travelers so longed to see. Imagine a time-lapse sequence in a Hollywood version of the story of Greece: The camera is positioned on the Acropolis and focused on the Erechtheion's Porch of the Caryatids. In 322 BCE, Athens falls to successors of Alexander the Great. The Erechtheion disappears into a fog of smoke as the Roman general Sulla sacks and burns the Acropolis in March 86 BCE. In a swirl, the ancient temple is restored under the first Roman emperor, Augustus, who later incorporates rows of caryatids into his forum at Rome. In 267 CE, the Heruli, a Germanic people, lay waste the city. Soon, Rome begins its transition to Christianity under the emperor Constantine the Great, who in 324 CE founds a new capital, Constantinople. In a blink it is 395, and Alaric the Gaul is triumphantly marching his Visigoths into Athens. In 529, the Byzantine emperor Justinian closes Plato's famed Academy forever. In a flash, the Erechtheion becomes a church of Mary *Theometor* (Mother of God). Across the way, the Parthenon is rededicated to this other virgin, an upstart compared with Athena. When Constantinople is sacked during the Fourth Crusade, Athens comes under the control of European crusader states. For a quarter millennium of Frankish rule, the caryatids serve the Duchy of Athens in the shadow of the new tower that soars above the Acropolis. It is now a warm June day in 1458. Athens is captured again, this time by the Ottoman sultan Mehmed II, nicknamed "the Conqueror" for his conquest of Constantinople five years earlier. The harem of the garrison commander takes up residence inside the Erechtheion. We at last find ourselves in the later decades of the seventeenth century, watching as a trickle of passersby from England and France becomes a steady stream.

So many centuries of fires, invasions, demolitions, reuses, additions, and new constructions meant that these travelers encountered an Acropolis that Pericles would hardly have recognized. It was not for another two centuries or so that the site would be "purified" of those later interventions and restored to a vision of its fifth-century-BCE appearance (see Chapter 5). Thus, for the early European traveler who sought an unobstructed view of the city's classical grandeur, ancient texts were his handiest guides and imagination his most valuable spyglass.

Before I turn to some of their memoirs, though, I begin with a different and more local perspective. The most famous traveler to record his impressions of Athens in the seventeenth century was a Turk from the Ottoman capital at Istanbul. By the end of his lifetime, Ottoman territory would cover more than two million square miles, the greatest extent it would ever reach; in the mid-seventeenth century, empire on that kind of scale was still no more than a glimmer in the eyes of Britain and France. For this traveler, Athens was anything but a disappointment; it was one of the brightest jewels in the crown of his people's empire. Like the city that the Europeans also described, his Athens was undoubtedly an Athens of the imagination. But it was the product of a very different kind of imagination, and his account is a healthy reminder that the West's fantasy of the ancient city is only one among many.

THE BEASTLY PARTHENON

On August 10, 1630, a young man from Istanbul, still shy of his twentieth birthday, had a dream. In a bleary state between wake and sleep, he found himself in Istanbul's great Ahi Çelebi mosque and in the midst of Islam's prophets and saints. These souls had all gathered in the mosque to hear the Prophet Muhammed, in the company of his Companions, lead the morning prayer. When the prayer ended, the Prophet beckoned to the dreamer and told him to kiss his hand. At that moment the young man meant to beg for intercession but was surprised to hear a different request issue from his mouth: "Travel," he cried out, "O messenger of God!" At this, the Prophet smiled. He gave his blessing and told him, "You will be a world traveler and unique among men. The well-protected kingdoms through which you pass, the fortresses and towns, the strange and wonderful monuments, and each land's praiseworthy qualities and products, its food and its drink, its latitude and longitude—record all of these and compose a marvelous work."[5] So began the travels of Evliya Çelebi, the son of a jeweler at the Ottoman court of Sultan Murad IV (çelebi is an Ottoman title meaning "gentleman"). Spurred on, or so he claimed, by his dream—such dreams are a spiritual and literary trope in Islamic travel narratives—Evliya set out from his home in Istanbul on forty years' worth of journeys.

Decades into those travels, in the summer of 1668, Evliya arrived in a great ancient city. This city had first been founded, as "all the Christian and Coptic chroniclers agree," by the prophet Solomon and the Queen of Sheba; Evliya refers to her as Balqis, the name the Queen of Sheba usually goes by in the Islamic tradition.[6] He was dazzled by its sights: "Nowhere on the face of the earth in all the seven climes are there such noteworthy wonders and sight-worthy marvels." The highlight among the city's varied splendors was "a great, light-filled mosque" on the height of its citadel, "very famous among world travelers." "There is not such a resplendent mosque anywhere in the earth," he effused, "because no matter how many times you enter it, you will always discover some new example of artistry and workmanship." The whole city so impressed Evliya that, in his ten-volume *Book of Travels (Seyâhatnâme),* he pronounced that "anyone who has not seen this city should simply not call himself a world traveler."

The city was, of course, Athens; the mosque, with its sparkling dome and soaring minaret, was housed in the Parthenon. In the *Book of*

Travels, Evliya even provides one of the earliest detailed accounts of the Parthenon's Periclean-era sculptures. By his time, their bright colored paint had already worn away:

> Above the columns, which are sheltered by eaves, and above the walls are a remarkable and varied assembly of voluminous statues, made of white marble. If I were to describe these one by one, it would require an entire volume and would hinder the course of our travels. The human mind cannot indeed comprehend these images—they are white magic, beyond human capacity. One with the intellect of Aristotle would be dumbfounded at the sight of these statues and proclaim them a miracle, because to a discerning eye they seem to be alive.

In the second century CE, Plutarch had claimed that the buildings of the Acropolis seemed possessed of an ageless soul, but for Evliya it was these sculptures that appeared to have the breath of life in them. Today we confidently interpret these sculpted marbles from the Parthenon as depicting idealized scenes from the mythical history of Athens. But as Evliya craned his neck upward, he saw something very different: the carved marbles leaped out as a wild and writhing bestiary, brimming with animals, monsters, and scenes of the afterlife. There were elephants, giraffes, and rhinoceroses; the damned were there being tortured in hell while the elect luxuriated in paradise. All manner of creatures—animal, human, and divine—danced in the "white magic" of the sculpted stones: "Fearful and ugly demons, jinns [genies], Satan the Whisperer, the Sneak, the Farter, fairies, angels, dragons . . . the angels that bear up the throne of God."

And why not? If you have ever viewed these stones in Athens, London, or Paris, or even just in photographs, you have probably scratched your head trying to work out just how archeologists can come up with such detailed descriptions of what they depict. Many of the marbles are now so fragmentary or worn away that they seem nearly featureless, and a healthy imagination could see any number of fantastic images on their surfaces. It takes about as much faith to believe that certain slabs represent, say, Athens's war with the Amazons or centaurs battling Lapiths as it takes cynicism to brush off the suggestions of splashing sea sprites and wriggling centipedes.

As a chronicler, Evliya also provides an overview of Athens' pre-Islamic history. He notes that in more ancient times, this was the place where some seven thousand Greek philosophers and sages had gathered to collaborate on finding the cure for death. Among them were Pythagoras, Plato "the Divine," Aristotle, Galen, and Ptolemy; his catalog includes nearly every famous Greek scientific name and spans some eight hundred years of history as we reckon it today. In this vision of the city, all these men had lived and worked together, performing calculations and chemistry experiments in the rock hollows of the Acropolis. And although they never uncovered the secret of cheating death, their work led to discoveries of many cures for less serious conditions. Evliya marveled at how one could still sniff out the traces of their work: in the caves where they had labored, the air remained thick with the smell of arsenic, mercury, and sulfur, the olfactory footprints of alchemy. He also noted that these great scientists had all lived enormous lifetimes, of some three and four hundred years. When Hippocrates the physician and Plato the Divine finally died, the other sages and scientists renounced their ways and converted to Islam.

A CAUTIONARY TALE

Evliya spent his last years in Egypt, laboring to complete his *Book of Travels*. After 1682, we hear nothing more about him. This was also the year in which an account of travels in Greece was published in London: *A Journey into Greece* by a botanist named George Wheler. That work would come to stand at the head of the long English-language tradition of travel writing about Greece. Many from Europe had already passed through Greece, and some had written accounts of their journeys. Nevertheless, in the decades that followed its publication, Wheler's *Journey* became a model for subsequent travel writers to emulate for its structure, use of ancient sources, and even dismissive quips about the Greeks' fondness for "superstition." Wheler saw Greece—and his writing trained many others to see Greece—as a land whose Oriental decadence was only thrown into sharper relief by the visible ruins of better days. In the "Epistle Dedicatory" of his work, which was dedicated to England's restored Stuart king Charles II, Wheler flatly characterizes Greece as "a Country once Mistress of the Civil World . . . but now a Lamentable Example of the Instability of human things." All this stands in stark contrast to Evliya's vision of Athens as a city still humming with life and art.

George Wheler was born in 1651 in the Netherlands to an exiled English royalist family on the wrong side of Oliver Cromwell. The family returned to England not long after their son's birth, and Wheler was eventually sent to be educated at Oxford. In 1673, after he finished his studies, he set out on a tour that began in Europe and later took him to the Levant. His travels allowed him to cultivate his passion for botany, and he spent much of his time on tour collecting exotic plant samples (one of his greatest claims to fame is the introduction of Saint-John's-wort, the herbal antidepressant, to England from Turkey)

From 1675 to 1676, on the eastern legs of his journey, he traveled in the company of Jacob (Jacques) Spon, a Lyonnais physician who, in 1678, was the first to publish an account of their travels: *Voyage d'Italie, de Dalmatie, de Grèce et du Levant.* At first, Wheler had in mind simply to translate the Greek portion of Spon's *Voyage* for English speakers, but in the preface to his *Journey,* he explained that the scope of his ambitions had to change when "I found I had many useful Observations omitted" by Spon. Despite the many alleged defects in Spon's *Voyage,* Wheler lifted liberally from it as he composed his own travelogue.

Both Spon and Wheler approached Greece as Christian gentlemen who knew only the dead versions of the Greek language that they had studied in university tutorials at Oxford and Montpellier. Evliya, on the other hand, was an educated Ottoman Muslim raised amid the bustle of the sultan's court. He was also a polyglot and could speak the Greek of Istanbul's vibrant Greek community. He framed his travels not as a quest to uncover the remains of antiquity, but as a pilgrim's journey to visit the tombs of Islam's holy men, whose spirits he had encountered at the mosque in his dream. The *Book of Travels* is also a supremely important, if in many ways mysterious (just whom did Evliya write it for?), document of Ottoman imperialism. It is therefore the celebration of an illustrious present that provides a panorama of the empire, from its heart in Constantinople to the lands just beyond its borders. But for Wheler and Spon, whose works painted the first picture of modern Greece for many educated Europeans, the land's greatest allure lay in the fossils of past civilizations that it contained. If its present circumstances were of interest, it was because they served as an instructive illustration of just how far a great civilization can fall.

Ancient Greek literary texts were an especially powerful filter for European travelers who were given the chance to visit the ancient lands as "empirical" observers. Confronted with the melancholy of the

George Wheler and Jacob Spon marvel at the ruins of ancient Athens. From
Jacob Spon's *Voyagie door Italien, Dalmatien, Grieckenland, en de Levant. Gedaan in
de Jaren 1675 en 1676, door den Heer Jacob Spon, Doctor in de Medecijne tot Lion, en
Georgius Wheler* (Amsterdam: Jan ten Hoorn, 1689) (Dutch translation of Spon's
Voyage d'Italie, de Dalmatie, de Grèce et du Levant, fait aux années 1675 & 1676 [Lyon:
Antoin Cellier le Fils: 1679]).

ruins—Athens, in Wheler's words, was "now reduced to near the lowest
Ebb of Fortune"—again and again they returned to the fantasy that the
texts had allowed them to construct and indulge: of the city that "with
wonderful success, routed the numerous Armies of *Darius* and *Xerxes*'
and whose citizens became "Masters of the Ægean Seas."[7] Yet certain
ancient Greek texts also provided a blueprint for new formulations of
Greece's decline. Book 5 of Wheler's *Journey* is dedicated to Athens and
like Evliya's work, begins with a historical overview of the city from

its foundation. He makes no mention of "Christian and Coptic chroniclers," but only of "judicious historians" who attributed the city's foundation to King Cecrops, a half man, half snake born from the Attic earth and a symbol of the Athenians' pride in their genealogical connection to the land.[8] His potted history of early Athens is drawn entirely from ancient sources, such as Herodotus and Thucydides. He writes of Athena and Poseidon's contest for Athens, the city's transition from monarchy to democracy, its leading role in the Persian Wars, and its eventual defeat by Sparta and the Peloponnesian League. Wheler also pauses to observe how, in the aftermath of the Peloponnesian War, the city of Athens first set out on its path of precipitous decline:

> The *Athenians* soon began to slight the Vertue of their ancestors, and to give themselves over to Luxury and Idleness, loving their Ease so much, that they made it Treason for any to propose the Re-establishing of the Army, or the raising any money for the maintenance of it; preferring a lucky Satyrist, before the bravest Captain; and to hear a play, before the gaining of the greatest Conquest: which degenerous Disposition of theirs, in a short time, gave opportunity and leisure to the *Macedonians* to advance their monarchy, and extend it little by little over all *Greece*.[9]

Wheler's criticism would be repeated many times over by later travel writers. Yet it was hardly new; this paragraph, in fact, is lifted straight from the pages of antiquity.

In the mid-fourth century BCE, the Athenian orator Demosthenes delivered a set of political speeches urging his fellow Athenians to launch an expedition against Macedon (Macedon had recently attacked Olynthus, a city allied with Athens). In those speeches, the *Olynthiacs*,

Demosthenes rebuked his fellow citizens for their tendency to spend too much public money on theater and building projects—hallmarks of Athenian art and culture and touchstones of the city's brand—and not enough on military needs. Nearly half a millennium later, Plutarch turned those criticisms into the premise of an entire pamphlet titled *Whether the Athenians Were More Illustrious in War or in Wisdom*. He argued that the Athenians' love of theater had directly contributed to their downfall: "If we tabulate the cost of each tragedy," he complained, the Athenians spent more on "productions of Oedipuses and Antigones . . . than they spent in fighting for their supremacy and for their freedom from the barbarians."[10] In reality, then, George Wheler parroted an account of Athenian decline that had originated in an Athens that by today's chronologies was still in its classical prime. A theme of decline runs through the rest of his historical narrative, which culminates in a description of Greece's present "Turkish *Tyranny*." "The ancient greatness of Athens," Wheler finally sighs, "remains only a story in *Pausanias*."[11]

Pausanias, a Greek from Asia Minor, had embarked on an odyssey of his own in the second century CE, when Greece was still ruled by emperors in Rome. He traveled in Palestine, Egypt, Greece, and Rome, but his ten-book *Description of Greece* documents travels only in mainland Greece: Attica, the Peloponnese, and certain portions of the interior, including Thebes and Delphi. For Wheler, Spon, and the generations of European travelers who followed them, Pausanias's *Description* was a history handbook and travel guide rolled into one. It was also frustrating to use: Pausanias's journey followed circuitous routes, and his prose is dense with equally winding digressions. Classically educated travelers were nevertheless determined that Pausanias would direct their efforts to track down and describe the ancient monuments. As much as these travelers sought to apprehend antiquity with their own senses, they still relied heavily on the descriptions preserved in ancient literary sources. That kind of methodology inevitably left "the observer more impressed by an ancient past than what was actually present."[12]

Wheler, to be fair, did admit (like Jacob Spon) that Athens still had highlights. He called the Parthenon "the most beautiful piece of Antiquity remaining in the world" and (despite having relatively little basis for comparison) granted that the mosque within it was "the finest in the World." But in the few pages that he dedicated to the structure, he made only passing reference to its present occupants, making sure to note that "the *Turks*, according to their measure of Wit, have washed over the beautiful white Marble within, with lime."[13] His remarks linger briefly on the pediments and metopes, but in true Pausanian fashion he said nothing about the frieze: Pausanias was far more interested in the colossal chryselephantine statue of Athena inside the Parthenon than in the sculptural program that adorned the exterior—a longstanding source of frustration to art historians, who (like many scholars) often expect their sources to display interests and tastes in line with their own.

It is primarily due to the massive combined Anglo-French readership of Spon's *Voyage* and Wheler's *Journey* that this unlikely pair of antiquaries, a French physician and an English botanist, are today regarded as the fathers of Greek travel literature. If we limit this title to the Western European literary tradition, they have a fair claim to it: many subsequent French and British travelers first set foot in Greece with at least one of these works in mind (and sometimes in their luggage), primed to view the Greek landscape, ruins, and people through the lens of Spon's and Wheler's observations and prejudices. Their subsequent descriptions of Athens would also be overshadowed by wistfulness for the past coupled with sorrow at the condition of the city's present. In his dedication to Charles II, Wheler explicitly cast the downfall of Greece as a kind of cautionary tale. Any malcontent Englishman had only to contemplate Greece to "see the Miseries that other Nations are reduced to, and behold, as in a Picture, the Natural Fruits of Schism, Rebellion and Civil Discord." Given how much Wheler's and Spon's perspectives and impressions seem to differ from those of Evliya Çelebi, it can be easy to forget that the three men were contemporaries describing the same city. Wheler was even so moved by the plight of the Greeks that when he returned from his travels, he began to try to arrange for places for Greek students at Oxford. The Greek College at Gloucester Hall, Oxford, was inaugurated in 1699. It was short-lived, though, and dissolved in 1705 after enrolling only fifteen students.

VENETIANS AT THE GATES

One of the reasons that Spon's and Wheler's accounts are still so valuable today is deeply regrettable: they preserve descriptions of the Parthenon as it appeared before it was blown apart. In 1687, just five years after Wheler published his *Journey* (and Evliya disappeared from the historical record), the Parthenon and the "resplendent mosque" inside fell victim to the Ottomans' centuries-old feud with the Republic of Venice.

The Venetian siege of the Acropolis was ultimately the result of a failed Ottoman attempt to conquer Vienna, the white whale of the Turkish sultans' imperial ambitions. The Ottomans had first attempted to seize the city they saw as their gateway to Europe in 1529, during the reign of Suleiman the Magnificent. Despite defeat, the empire expanded enormously in that era, and Suleiman managed to annex both Egypt and a number of Venetian possessions to his lands. In 1683, Ottoman forces made another attempt on Vienna but were driven back again in the Battle of Vienna. Venice, backed by the Holy Roman Empire and a new Holy League, saw the Turks' weakened position after the battle as an opportunity to reclaim its own former Mediterranean possessions. A Venetian fleet was accordingly deployed to Greece under the command of Francesco Morosini; in late September 1687, its ships weighed anchor in the port of Piraeus. For nearly a week, Venetian forces laid siege to the Acropolis, where much of the Ottoman population had run to seek refuge. In the midst of the siege, late on the night of September 26, 1687, Venetian mortar shells struck the roof of the Parthenon. Sources from the era conflict on whether the artillery commanders had been aiming specifically at the Parthenon: against better counsel, the Ottomans had been using the building to store gunpowder supplies. Regardless of whether it was intended, the explosion was enormous. It shook the whole of the Acropolis and ignited a fire that took days to put out.

When the dust finally settled, the Parthenon was naturally in much worse shape than before. The explosion took hundreds of lives. It also brought down the building's roof (a late third-century-CE replacement for the original, which had been destroyed by fire in the middle of the century). Three of the structure's walls were blown out; countless ancient, Byzantine, and Ottoman-era artworks were broken; and the whole site was littered with debris. Well over half of the Parthenon's sculptures rained down in the explosion. All told, the Venetian siege caused the greatest physical damage to the Acropolis since it had been sacked by Xerxes in 480 BCE. On September 29, 1687, the Ottomans finally surrendered, and Morosini's Venetians raised their flag above the Propylaea, a new twist on the ancient triumphant view out toward Salamis.

The citadel nevertheless proved harder to keep than it had been to take. Morosini decided to resolve the problem once and for all by making a shocking proposal. Convinced that the Acropolis was simply

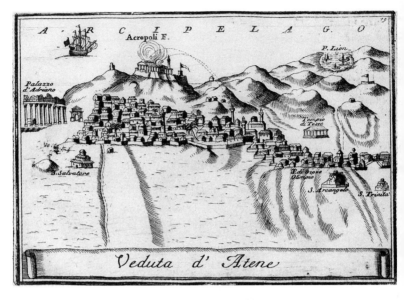

The Venetian bombardment of the Acropolis, led by Francesco Morosini in September 1687. From Vincenzo Maria Coronelli's *Morea, Negroponte & Adiacenze* (Venice, ca. 1708).

too difficult to defend, on the last day of 1687 he unveiled a plan to raze what was left of it. His council carefully weighed the suggestion but in the end decided that even this plan was too costly and laborious. In February, it voted simply to abandon the city altogether. Before leaving for good, Morosini took care to amass an impressive collection of souvenirs from his siege. He had hoped to load Venice's ships with even more loot, but in March he recorded his disappointment at having failed to extract the Parthenon's west pediment—the set of sculptures depicting Athena and Poseidon's contest for the city—from the building. His efforts left the sculptures in even worse condition, and his personal secretary managed to abscond with the head of one of the statues. As a proud Venetian—the year after his siege of Athens he would be proclaimed doge—Morosini had a particular taste for lions: Venice's symbol is a lion because the lion is the emblem of St. Mark, the city's patron saint. At the entrance to the Venetian Arsenal, you can still see two of the lions that Morosini shipped back to Venice from Greece. One is the celebrated *Lion of the Piraeus,* which he plundered from the port.

Morosini was far from the first to import antiquities to Venice in an effort to make it seem older. The Catholics' success in the Fourth Crusade—during which, despite Pope Innocent III's stern prohibition, crusaders ransacked and plundered Constantinople—went a long way toward lending Venice its ancient aura. This plunder helped enhance the city's splendor by magnifying its appearance of antiquity. As ancient a city as Venice might seem, it is also a city that for well over a millennium has tried to look much older than it is: the Venetian lagoon was settled only in the sixth century CE, and compared with many of its famous neighbors in Italy, Venice is a fairly young city. This "absence of a past" drove many Venetians to feel perfectly entitled to carry off art from the more ancient cities they invaded.[14] In Athens, Morosini's explosion dislodged a number of the Parthenon's sculpted marbles from the building's structure, which made some of them—though, to Morosini's great frustration, certainly not all—ripe for the picking. That explosion also happened to coincide with a new flurry of antiquities collecting spreading across Europe. Some of those collectors claimed to act in the artifacts' own interest. Many were ultimately motivated, as Morosini had been, more by the prospect of possessing antiquities than of preserving and studying them.

LOOT AMONG THE RUINS

A zeal for collecting coins, marbles (statues and reliefs), inscriptions, and even drawings of ancient ruins had first developed on the European continent (in Italy, France, Germany, and the Low Countries) at the tail end of the Renaissance, in the second half of the sixteenth century. The passion for collecting, like the boom in travel literature, soon became deeply entangled in the business of empire building. The spectacular fragmentation of the Parthenon at the hands of the Venetians occurred in the era when European monarchs were eagerly seeking to establish distant colonies, and it is little wonder that travelers developed a sense of entitlement to the antiquities harbored by classical lands. Those travelers effectively served as the men who led the charge on the ground for Europe's metaphorical colonization of classical antiquity.

Already by the seventeenth century, Europe's monarchs were scrambling to outdo one another's collections, and during the reign of King Charles I, the English joined in the competition. In 1624, the first successful British colony in the Caribbean was established in St. Kitts; in 1625, the first antiquities from Greece began to arrive in England thanks to the efforts of Thomas Howard, Earl of Arundel. Arundel was not fond of travel and made many acquisitions through agents abroad, including Thomas Roe, the British ambassador to the Ottoman court from 1621 to 1628. Arundel's greatest acquisition came through Roe via Smyrna: the Parian Marble, part of an ancient inscribed chronicle found in two pieces on the Cycladic island of Paros. At Arundel's urging, a polymath named John Selden produced an edition of the marbles in his collection. His *Marmora Arundeliana,* considered the first scientific work on ancient inscriptions to be issued in England, was published in London in 1628 and 1629.

After Arundel died, his son repurposed some of the antiquities from his father's beloved collection. The Parian Marble was permanently damaged when he had it converted into a hearthstone at Arundel House in London, where other marbles were built into the garden walls. The diarist John Evelyn was so appalled by this that he organized the removal of some of the stones to Oxford, where they were built right back into walls at the university's new Sheldonian Theatre, constructed between 1664 and 1669 from plans by Christopher Wren. In 1683, the year after George Wheler's *Journey* was published, Oxford's Ashmolean Museum was completed. The first such university museum, the Ashmolean was built to house manuscripts, antiquities, and other "curiosities" and specimens bequeathed by Elias Ashmole, a politician with further keen side interests in astrology and alchemy. Arundel's marbles were later relocated to that museum, but only after some two centuries of exposure to the English elements.

At about this time, the taste for collecting was also intensifying as the result of new intellectual movements in northern Europe. Toward the end of the 1680s, a quarrel over the matter of antiquity's greatness and inimitability ignited on both sides of the English Channel. On its first front in France, the debate went by the name of the *Querelle des Anciens et des Modernes,* the "Quarrel of the Ancients and the Moderns." In the British tradition, the row is often remembered as the "Battle of the Books" after the title of a satire later composed by Jonathan Swift (published as part of the prefatory material to his 1704 *Tale of a Tub*). In both countries, the question was whether ancient or modern learning was superior: had the world's greatest writers and thinkers already come and gone with classical antiquity, or could modern science improve on—and in some cases even disprove—ancient wisdom? In England, the most famous advocate in the Ancients' corner was the poet (and translator of the Homeric epics) Alexander Pope. The Moderns had their champion in the formidable Richard Bentley, polymathic Cambridge don, the father of textual criticism, the first titan of British classical scholarship, and (to put it politely) not a man known for suffering fools. Those in the Moderns' camp trusted more in the power of progress than in entrenched historical authority and held that scientific advances were capable of revealing the flaws of ancient thought. Influenced in part by the thinking of John Locke, whose 1690 *Essay Concerning Human Understanding* inaugurated the tradition of British Empiricism, such antiquaries developed a more robust framework for attempting to approach the past empirically. This, in turn, led them to value still more highly the material artifacts of ancient civilizations. Ancient historians, they believed, had inevitably produced subjective accounts, which meant that the best hope for a more objective understanding of antiquity lay in the study of its silent but observable remains.

Collecting was not always undertaken, of course, with such high-minded principles. One shocking case is that of a French Catholic priest named Michel Fourmont. Fourmont was a member of the Académie des Inscriptions et Belles-Lettres, one of the five academies of the Institut de France that had been established under King Louis XIV in 1663. In the late 1720s, when France's empire already extended from Nova Scotia to Louisiana and boasted of outposts in the Caribbean and on the Indian subcontinent, Louis XV dispatched Fourmont to Greece to collect antiquities—manuscripts, artworks, inscriptions, and coins. Today Fourmont is remembered for his ruthless approach to acquisition and his mendacious accounts of his archeological finds (a number of the inscriptions that he brought back to France were later outed as forgeries). In a notorious April 20, 1730, letter that Fourmont sent to Jean-Paul Bignon, librarian to King Louis, he even boasted of the trail of destruction that he was leaving behind him in Sparta. "For more than a month," he wrote, "I have been toiling with thirty workmen on the complete destruction of Sparta: every day I find something, and on some days I have found as many as twenty inscriptions. . . . I am becoming a barbarian here in Greece: it is no longer the seat of the Muses; ignorance has driven them out, and this makes me miss France, to where they've withdrawn."[15] Fourmont was no fool and was aware of the irony: he, an educated Frenchman, was carrying out acts of barbarism, all in nominal service of the Muses and in the name of the king and his royal collection. Fourmont's acknowledgment of his hypocrisy is an important reminder of the more insidious tactics of Europe's competitive scramble for ancient Greece.

A second case, equally important and illustrative, is that of the more mild-mannered Hans Sloane, a British physician who, like Wheler, had a taste for procuring both natural specimens and antiquities. In the late 1680s, Sloane first began furiously collecting flora and fauna in Jamaica during his service as physician to the British governor (Jamaica had come under British rule in 1655). By the time of his death in 1753, Britain's empire also contained considerable territories in North America and the Caribbean and was poised for expansion in India and the Pacific. Over his lifetime, Sloane amassed more than seventy-one thousand objects—animal, vegetable, and mineral—from around the world. His collection also included manuscripts, coins, and other things inventoried as "relating to the customs of ancient times," as well as "artificial objects" fashioned by native peoples. He bequeathed the entire collection to King George II, and on June 7, 1753, the British Parliament legislated its use as the basis for a new museum. The British Museum, like Paris's Louvre, St. Petersburg's Hermitage, and Munich's Glyptothek, was thus born of the necessity to house and display a vast collection that had already been accumulated. Like all these other museums, it is also an enduring monument to how deeply antiquarianism was intertwined with the ambitions and apparatus of empire—empire that even stretched into the ancient past.

DILETTANTES IN ATHENS

Nearly two decades before Parliament voted to create the British Museum, antiquarianism in Britain had already found another manner of institutional support in the form of a gentleman's society. On March 6, 1735, the first meeting of the Society of Dilettanti, formally a drinking club, was convened at the Bedford Head Tavern in London's Covent Garden. Its members were all aristocratic Englishmen who had already traveled to Italy and regarded themselves as connoisseurs of antiquity. In 1743, Horace Walpole, a Whig politician and dedicated antiquary, wrote a letter to his friend Horace Mann (a British diplomat, not the later American educational reformer) in which he made a wry and now-famous characterization of the qualifications, official and otherwise, for membership: the Society of Dilettanti, he explained to Mann, was "a club, for which the nominal qualification is having been in Italy, and the real one being drunk."[16]

At this time, the Grand Tour was already a rite of passage for wealthy northern Europeans, especially those freshly graduated from Oxford and Cambridge. The institution had first emerged in the 1670s on the heels of the publication of Richard Lassel's two-volume *The Voyage of Italy: or, A Compleat Journey through Italy* (published posthumously in Paris in 1670). By about 1720, it was firmly established as a fashionable pursuit for English noblemen, the capstone of their formal education and the last great hurrah of youth (and all its customary indiscretions). Most Grand Tourists departed from London, and for most of the seventeenth century the regular itinerary followed a loop through the middle of Europe. Typical stopping points included Paris, Geneva, Turin, Genoa, Florence, Rome, Naples, Venice, Munich, Vienna, Berlin, and Brussels. Rome and its ancient monuments were always advertised and remembered as the tour's great highlights. Itineraries to Greece and the Middle East began only later, near the turn of the nineteenth century, when the French Revolution and the Napoleonic Wars disrupted the usual paths of aristocratic tourism. Before then, northern Europeans who ventured to the Ottoman Empire usually did so with the excuse of mercantile, diplomatic, or—as would be the case for Dilettanti members—serious antiquarian business.

By the mid-eighteenth century, the Society of Dilettanti was thriving. Its meetings were opportunities for members to reminisce about their experiences on tour, compare notes, and build on travel-related knowledge and interests. In 1750, a man named James Stuart came to the society's attention when he published a work on recent archeological discoveries in Rome (*De obelisco Caesaris Augusti e Campo Martio nuperrime effosso* [On the obelisk of Caesar Augustus very recently excavated in the Campus Martius]). Along with his collaborator, Nicholas Revett, a painter and architectural enthusiast, Stuart was elected to the society's membership in absentia in 1751. From 1751 to 1754, the pair worked together in Athens. There they carefully documented the city's monuments, inscriptions, art, and artifacts. Thanks to a patchwork of funding, including a subvention from the society and about five hundred individual subscriptions, the first volume of their landmark *Antiquities of Athens* finally appeared in 1762. This volume was dedicated to some of Athens's less famous and impressive monuments and so was savaged in some corners on aesthetic grounds. The second volume, however, was a triumph. Issued in 1787, it included much-anticipated engravings of the Parthenon, frieze and all. A third volume followed in 1794 (the final volume, a supplement, was not published until 1830). *Antiquities of Athens* turned Stuart and Revett into celebrities, and Stuart came to be known as "the Athenian."

In 1758, while Stuart and Revett were still at work on the first installment of their magnum opus, the Frenchman Julien-David Le Roy published a similar work in France, *Les ruines des plus beaux monuments de la Grèce*. Stuart and Revett harshly criticized Le Roy for taking what they saw as an "impressionistic" approach to his drawings; their own, by contrast, would be roundly lauded for their precision and attention to detail. The images printed in *Antiquities of Athens* are now even largely credited with having sparked the neoclassical turn in architecture: the signature, "classical" look of so many banks, university campuses, and government buildings is owed largely to Stuart and Revett.

Stuart and Revett's drawings were celebrated for their accuracy and unprecedented eye for the details of ancient monuments. The images

The Philopappus monument in Athens; James Stuart and Nicholas Revett consult guides while a shepherd tends his flocks and a smoking janissary makes coffee. From James Stuart and Nicholas Revett's *The Antiquities of Athens Measured and Delineated by James Stuart F.R.S. and F.S.A. and Nicholas Revett Painters and Architects*, vol. 3, ed. Willey Reveley (London: John Nichols, 1794).

nevertheless also exemplify a style of British landscape illustration that was popular from the late seventeenth century into the early Victorian era. When they incorporated living people at all, such illustrations often depicted travelers admiring the view, as well as one or two exoticized natives drinking coffee or smoking (or both)—a touch of local color. The motif of relatively empty landscapes garnished with Orientalized natives was also persistent in contemporary representations of the "biblical lands." Architectural historian Mark Crinson has observed that illustrations of Palestine from the mid-nineteenth century "show barely populated 'present-day' scenes, where Arab culture was either little more than a distant minaret and a colorful costume, or, when it did intrude, it was implied that this 'religion of barbarism' . . . was to blame for current decay, idleness, and ruination."[17] This kind of illustration, which assumes and implies local disinterest in the monuments so valued by the European travelers, is a further symptom of the entitlement those travelers felt to the antiquities of Ottoman lands. After all, if the decadent locals were more interested in sipping their coffee than in attending to the monuments, why shouldn't well-informed passers-through remove whatever they could?

In 1764, two years after Stuart and Revett's first volume was published, Richard Chandler, a scholar of Ancient Greek at Magdalene College, Oxford, joined the Society of Dilettanti. Chandler would prove to be one of the earliest such travelers to show an interest in seeing the customs of contemporary Greeks as evidence of ancient Greek culture, and so to suggest the possibility of a clear continuity between ancient and modern Greek civilization. Together with Revett and a man named William Pars, Chandler set out on the society's first official, fully funded expedition. Their brief, which Chandler published in the preface to his 1775 memoir *Travels in Asia Minor,* was to spend a year exploring antiquities in the environs of Smyrna, modern Turkey's

Izmir. The society also instructed each of the members of the team to "keep a very minute Journal of every Day's occurrences and observations."[18] After they finished their work in and around Smyrna (*Ionian Antiquities* was published in 1769), the team departed for Athens. There, their mission from the society was "not to interfere with the labours of Messrs. Stuart and Revett, but solely to attend to those articles, which they had either omitted or not completed."[19] Another of their charges was to acquire marbles.

By the time Chandler arrived in Greece, Athens had already been thoroughly explored by other Europeans. His memoir of the time that he spent there, *Travels in Greece* (1776), owed much to the established tradition, and passages in it clearly paraphrase both Pausanias and Wheler. Chandler, however, was much more focused in his efforts to acquire antiquities than Spon and Wheler had been. His memoirs open a window into how some of these travelers rationalized their actions as attempts to salvage artworks and artifacts that, thanks to the apparent ignorance and indifference of the locals, were in danger of being lost forever. In describing the Parthenon, Chandler condemned the deeds of Morosini: the Venetian "was ambitious to enrich Venice with the spoils of Athens, and, by an attempt to take down the principal group [of statues], hastened their ruin." Nearly ninety years after the explosion, Chandler's assessment of the state of the Parthenon was gloomy: "It is to be regretted that so much admirable sculpture, as is still extant about this fabric, should be all likely to perish, as it were immaturely, from ignorant contempt and brutal violence. Numerous carved stones have disappeared; and many, lying in the ruinous heaps, moved our indignation at the barbarism daily exercised in defacing them."[20] Appalled to see antiquities casually recycled around the town (many ancient gravestones, for example, adorned the entries of private homes), the party leaped at an offer to purchase "two fine fragments of the frieze" from the Parthenon. They also gladly took a trunk (a "gift") containing the torso of a sculpture that had fallen from a metope and was lying abandoned in a garden.[21]

Despite his indignation at the locals' disregard for antiquities, Chandler showed greater interest in the life of Athens' contemporary inhabitants than Wheler or Stuart and Revett had. Although he followed Wheler in remarking on the Greeks' lack of learning and surplus of superstition, Chandler also recorded a number of detailed comments about the local peoples (Ottomans, Arabs, Greeks, and Albanians): their pastimes and ceremonies, habits (down to women's makeup routines), and various ethnic "characters." He even strained to identify strands of continuity between the ancient past and the Greek people's modern-day customs, pronouncing, for example, that "some of their dances are undoubtedly of remote antiquity."[22]

Chandler was thus beginning to add another kind of empirical evidence to the antiquaries' standard dossier. Like monuments, marbles, and medals, the ancient customs still practiced by local peoples could also provide valuable insight into the past. In his work, we catch a hint of an important development just beginning to take shape: the emergence of the notion that Greece's modern people really are descendants of the ancient Greeks, and that their culture and language have continued unbroken from ancient times. But despite the occasional glimpses of continuity that Chandler thought he discerned, he remained generally disappointed at the Greeks' ignorance about their own history. "The leisure of the Greeks," he grumbled, "is chiefly employed in reading legendary stories of their saints translated into the vulgar tongue. This and their nation they style *the Roman*."[23]

The word Chandler understood as "Romans" is more usually rendered as "Romiotes" (*Romioi* in Greek, *Romani* in Latin), while the Greek language was colloquially called Romaic *(Romaika)*. This was a holdover from the time when Greeks, as residents of the Roman Empire, had been a kind of Romans (in Romaic, ancient Romans strictly speaking were called *Romanoi*). Versions of these words were long used in Arabic and Persian to refer to Orthodox Christians, and *Rūm* was, in addition to a geographic designation for the region of Anatolia, a generic term for non-Muslim residents of the Ottoman Empire. In Greece, Chandler had rather hoped to find people who, like the ancient Greeks, styled themselves as "Hellenes" (in Greek mythology, the hero Hellen had engendered sons who went on to be the progenitors of the major Greek ethnic groups: Aeolians, Dorians, and Ionians).

When Richard Chandler made his expeditions for the Society of Dilettanti, the "colonization" of ancient Greece by northern and western European powers was pretty well complete. Some travelers, like Michel Fourmont, were unapologetic about speeding that effort along. Others, like Chandler himself, seem to have sincerely believed that they were acting to prevent antiquity's last traces from disappearing completely. In a revealing passage of his 1775 *Travels in Asia Minor,* Chandler lamented the fate of an ancient inscription he was forced to leave in place: "About half a century has elapsed since it was first discovered, and it still remains in the open air . . . destitute of a patron to rescue it from barbarism, and obtain its removal into the safer custody of some private museum, or, which is rather to be desired, some public repository."[24] It was nevertheless hardly the case that all the artifacts shipped out of Greece were destined, as Chandler would have liked, for museums and "public repositories."

European scholars, travelers, and collectors tended to assume that locals were all too happy to sell ancient treasures. The nature of the evidence, which consists mostly of the travelers' own memoirs, means that it is difficult to trace the other side of the story. Nevertheless, historians have begun to piece together evidence for local resistance to the collectors' efforts. Benjamin Anderson, a historian of eastern Mediterranean art, points out the importance of a story recorded by Thomas Roe, British ambassador to the Ottoman court in the 1620s and Thomas Arundel's man in Turkey. Roe facilitated many acquisitions but was prevented at least once by the local population from taking something he wanted. In his memoirs of his time as ambassador to the Ottomans, Roe recalled how he once learned that Istanbul's "Golden Gate," the ceremonial entryway to the city, contained ancient reliefs. With a bribe of "500 dollers" he persuaded the sultan's treasurer to come and have a look at the gate, but when he arrived, "the Castellano and the people began to mutine, and fell upon a strange conceit." The treasurer then asked Roe, via his interpreter, whether "I had any old booke of prophesy; inferring, that those statues were enchanted, and that wee knew, when they should be taken down, some great alteration should befall the city."[25] This anecdote is one illustration that local populations were well aware of the presence of antiquities and not always as indifferent to their fate as European collectors presumed.

And although travelers tended to dismiss local populations as ignorant, already in the seventeenth century native Greek antiquaries and informants were actively contributing to the European study of antiquity. Anastasia Stouraiti, a historian and specialist in Venetian visual and material culture, has emphasized how local Greeks in Venetian-held lands developed antiquarian expertise. "Indigenous archeological practices," she argues, greatly informed interactions between two different configurations of "locals" and "travelers": between European travelers and local Greeks in Greece, and between Greeks abroad and the antiquaries they met in Europe.[26]

Despite the richness and variety of interactions that must have characterized many travelers' experiences in Greece, the negative impressions that they recorded went a long way toward shaping assumptions that still color how inhabitants of the European West view Greeks today. Tenacious stereotypes about the Greeks' susceptibility to superstition, laziness, profligacy, corruption by Ottoman ways (or even fundamentally Oriental character), and failure to live up to the ancient inhabitants of their land were all planted in the modern Western mind by traveling scholars, collectors, and travel writers who journeyed to Greece and claimed its past for themselves centuries ago. In concert with their armchair colleagues back home in countries such as Britain and France, by the second half of the eighteenth century these travelers managed to convince both themselves and their countrymen that they had more valid claims to Greek antiquity and its material artifacts than anyone else, including the Greeks themselves. Like Caliph al-Ma'mun in Abbasid Baghdad, they found the modern Greeks unworthy successors of the ancients and so declared the Greek past their own possession. Unlike Evliya Çelebi, who reveled in the vitality of the Athenian present and all its sensory experiences, they saw the place as defined by its lack of resemblance to the shining city of Pericles, at least as they had imagined it.

In a study of Anglo-Greek relations in the early nineteenth century, C. M. Woodhouse, a politician and expert on Greek affairs who served at Britain's embassy in Greece during World War II, neatly summarized one popular position in eighteenth-century Britain: "The Greeks, if Greeks they could be called, were unworthy of their ancestors, whose true descendants were to be found in the colleges of Oxford and Cambridge."[27] This view continues to have surprising currency. A few years ago, a job in Greek literature was advertised at one of the universities mentioned by Woodhouse. When I asked a friend about the applicant pool, he told me that "only a few serious candidates"—that is, candidates with Oxbridge or London degrees—had applied. The rest of the applications, he scoffed, were from "just a load of Greeks."

Today that kind of dismissiveness, an inheritance from the early travelers, awkwardly coexists alongside the popular narrative of the West's enduring debt to Greece. In the seventeenth and eighteenth centuries, though, no such narrative colored the travelers views, because no such narrative did yet exist. When and how did it finally come into being?

CHAPTER FOUR

From State of Mind to Nation-State

THE PARTHENON IS THE STAR of a popular story about the Greek War of Independence. When Greek revolutionaries were besieging the Acropolis early in the war, the Ottoman forces atop it ran out of ammunition. Desperate to gather any metal they could, they set about pulling apart the Parthenon's columns to extract the lead fixtures inside. When the Greeks learned what the Ottomans were up to, they became distraught and reacted by sending ammunition up to the citadel with this message: "Here are bullets, don't touch the columns."[1]

One winter, when I was taking a series of lessons in Modern Greek, my teacher asked me what I thought about the story. Why, he prodded, would Greeks have so readily given such aid to their Turkish enemies? I answered that it was, I assumed, because they loved the Parthenon so much that they would rather lose the whole Acropolis than see it destroyed. My teacher, who knew I was a classicist (a career choice he thought very little of), laughed at my naïveté. "Wrong!" he replied with a smug grin. "They did it because foreigners love stuff like that, and they knew that if they played the part of good Hellenes, the Europeans would send them money." The Greeks may never have sent ammunition up with that message, and even if they did, we can only guess what their motivation was. Nevertheless, even if the incident never happened, the story, like my teacher's interpretation of it, is certainly illuminating.

In the late eighteenth and early nineteenth centuries, over the course of only a few decades, many foreigners went from dismissing Greeks as decadent, Orientalized shadows of their ancestors to championing their cause of independence. A dramatic evolution in ideas about Europe's stake in modern Greece began in the late eighteenth century, when new approaches to the study of Greek antiquity reshaped European estimations of Greece's continued significance for the modern world. This, in short, was the era in which "the idea that Hellas is the harmonious origin of civilization became popular in the West."[2] It is no coincidence, then, that at about the same time, a theory about the nature of the Greeks started to gain popularity in Europe and Greece alike. That idea held that contemporary Greeks were descended from ancient ones and that Hellenic culture had persisted without rupture since antiquity. Now, new generations of European thinkers and travelers to Greece thrilled at imagining that the habits and customs of flesh-and-blood Greeks could provide them with information about ancient practices. Soon the assumption of continuity became a driving ideological force of its own. As one historian has put it, "Greece's brief modern history has been shaped *entirely* by the socially-constructed belief that it enjoys an unbroken link with the classical past."[3]

By the nineteenth century, certain Greek humanists and revolutionaries, many of whom were themselves participants in the European Enlightenment, had come to internalize the notion that their people were descendants—by language, culture, and blood—of Pericles. For these thinkers, a classical lineage was much more attractive than traditional genealogies in medieval Byzantium, and even those revolutionaries who did not wholly believe in the idea recognized its usefulness for persuading Europeans to support the cause of Greek independence. At the same time, inspired by the resistance they saw building in Greece, many people in Europe also went from simply lamenting the loss of antiquity to committing themselves to its revival. With Greece's freedom secured, they hoped, a project of resurrecting the spirit of classical Athens for all of Europe could truly begin.

This immensely complex process, which unfolded over roughly half a century, can be distilled into three separate but complementary developments:

1. European scholars invented the impossible fantasy of the "Greek ideal," ostensibly the ancient Greek aesthetic but really an ideal of ancient Greece itself.
2. A Romantic notion took hold that contemporary Greeks were descendants of the ancients who had invented and lived that ideal.
3. Greek independence came to be seen as the first essential step toward widespread revival of the ancient spirit.

Combined, these shifts created the conditions for the invention of the European West's notional debt to the ancient Greeks. That idea would finally crystallize with the outbreak of the Greek War of Independence, when Greek revolutionaries and their European sympathizers began to insist on both the existence of such a debt and the obligation of its "debtors"—Britain, France, and even the United States—to begin to repay it by supporting the Greek cause. Requests for foreign aid to Greece became framed as an old favor being called in: "Mother Greece" had given Europe the gift of illumination and now stood in need of repayment. That conceit was formulated with help from the ancient Athenians, who had insisted that the rest of Greece owed them for the defeat of the Persians and the advancement of art and culture.

Here I will trace these radical developments through the contributions of six influential figures from this period: a pair of German classical scholars, Johann Joachim Winckelmann and Friedrich August Wolf; two very different Greek revolutionary thinkers, Adamantios Koraïs and Rigas Velestinlis; and a couple of British lords, Lord Elgin, whose name is synonymous in Greece with villainy, and Lord Byron, a poet remembered there as a national hero. Through their stories we will see Greece emerge as a nominally independent country, but one still beholden both politically and financially to the same nations whose travelers, scholars, and antiquaries had already colonized its antiquity. Many European intellectuals in this era would prove eager to accept the proposition that they were deeply indebted to ancient Greece. Yet many in Britain, France, and Germany also believed that because their countries had safeguarded antiquity for centuries and supported the War of Independence, they had also earned the right to intervene in Greek affairs.

THE ONLY WAY TO BECOME GREAT

In 1764, just two years after the first volume of Stuart and Revett's *Antiquities of Athens* appeared in England, Johann Winckelmann published a monumental work titled *Geschichte der Kunst des Alterthums*

(History of the art of antiquity). Winckelmann, the son of a cobbler and a weaver, had been born in 1717 in the Prussian town of Stendal. A voracious reader, he fought tenaciously to overcome childhood poverty and pursue his passion for art and antiquities. Years spent as personal librarian to aristocrats allowed him to develop an extraordinary, even encyclopedic, knowledge of the ancient past. By the time *History of the Art of Antiquity* was published, he was already one of the most esteemed members of Europe's Republic of Letters, an informal network of scholars that transcended national boundaries and whose lingua franca was Latin.

Winckelmann had first made his name in 1755 with his treatise *Gedanken über die Nachahmung der griechischen Werke in der Malerei und Bildhauerkunst* (Thoughts on the imitation of Greek works in painting and sculpture). There he introduced principles that would later come to be seen as representative of his life's work. He showered praise on classical Greece, arguing that its art had epitomized an aesthetic ideal of "noble simplicity and quiet grandeur." But he also insisted that Greece's sublime cultural achievements were of absolute importance to modernity: "The one way for us to become great, perhaps inimitable," he momentously declared in the essay, "is by imitating the ancients."[4] Although Winckelmann tempered that position in his subsequent writings, the pronouncement went on to develop a life of its own as a motto of Romantic Hellenism. That movement gained ground in the late eighteenth century, especially in Germany, when many authors and artists came to view ancient Greece as the remedy to a twin set of estrangements—from nature and the past—that they saw as lamentable side effects of the Enlightenment's emphasis on reason.[5]

Winckelmann himself was nevertheless careful to warn that only the finest expressions of the ancient artistic spirit should be emulated; throughout his life he dismissed the efforts of scholars who showed too little taste and discrimination in their interpretations of ancient art. In the same year in which he published his *History of the Art of Antiquity,* he wrote a letter to a friend decrying the rancorous lack of aesthetic judgment that marred the first volume of James Stuart and Nicholas Revett's *Antiquities of Athens* (see Chapter 3). To his mind, the pair had foolishly spilled great quantities of ink over Athens's minor monuments. Like the gruesome one-eyed Cyclops of Virgil's *Aeneid,* the British team's publication was a "massive, horrendous monster, dispossessed of sight."[6]

Only a few months after his famous 1755 essay was published, Winckelmann converted to Roman Catholicism and moved to Rome. There he worked at the Vatican, cataloging and describing the papal collections of ancient statues. During those years in Italy, he developed a peerless eye for Greek and Roman art and a preternatural instinct for spotting Roman copies of Greek original works. One of the most significant contributions of his *History of the Art of Antiquity,* the product of nearly a decade's work in the Vatican's extraordinary collections, was its abandonment of the old inventory-based approach to art and its turn toward the formulation of a grand narrative about their creation. Winckelmann divided his narrative into two parts. The first was a chronological "Investigation of Art with Regard to Its Essence," which spanned the period from prehistory to the Roman Empire by way of Egypt, Persia, Phoenicia, and Greece. The second was dedicated wholly to the ancient Greek achievement.

Winckelmann determined that Greek sculpture could be divided along chronological lines into four major styles, which he termed the Older, the High or Grand, the Beautiful, and the Style of Imitators. For him, that trajectory implied a parallel story of ascendancy, summit, and decline. The zenith mapped cleanly onto what we think of today as classical Athens, where the High Style was exemplified by the work of

Portrait of Johann Winckelmann (1768) by Anton von Maron (1731–1808).

Phidias, the master artist of Pericles's building program. Works of the Beautiful Style—brought to perfection by the Athenian sculptor Praxiteles—arose in the next phase, during the fourth century BCE. For Winckelmann, the finest expression of the Greek ideal in sculpture was the Apollo Belvedere, a marble copy of a bronze from the Beautiful epoch. With what he saw as its perfect proportions and simultaneous evocations of youthful grace and athletic, masculine strength, the Apollo Belvedere conjured for him an image of "eternal spring"—an echo of Plutarch's claim that Pericles's Athenian buildings seemed possessed of "an ever-blossoming spirit mingled with an ageless soul." As Winckelmann saw it, the rise of Alexander the Great and Macedonian hegemony had then ushered in the decline of art in the hands of Hellenistic "imitators." These chronological divisions largely underpin how Greek history and art history are still taught today, as falling into Archaic (Older), Classical (Grand and Beautiful) and Hellenistic (Imitative) periods.

As he worked among the sculptures at the Vatican, Winckelmann became convinced that whiteness, whether of a marble statue or human skin, contributed to aesthetic perfection. By the end of his life, however, he did come to acknowledge the polychromy (multicoloredness) of some ancient Greek sculptures. We know this because of evidence that he changed his opinion about a statue of Artemis discovered at Pompeii in 1760. Originally, visible traces of pigment had led him to identify the statue as Etruscan; later, after the first edition of *History of the Art of Antiquity* had already been published, he changed his mind and pronounced it Greek. The second edition of his magnum opus was published in 1776, but its text was inconsistent about incorporating his revised opinion, most likely because Winckelmann did not personally oversee the second edition through to publication. On June 6, 1768, he was murdered in his hotel bed by a man named Francesco Arcangeli during a stopover on a journey from the Tyrol to Trieste. (Arcangeli's objective was to steal the "medals" that Winckelmann had with him, which were ancient coins he had been given in Vienna by the Habsburg empress Maria Theresa. He had no idea that he was killing a luminary beloved throughout Europe, and he paid for his crime with a torturous death on a Catherine wheel.) Yet even if Winckelmann did eventually accept that some ancient Greek statues had, in fact, at first been brightly painted, over the next two centuries his pronouncements about the beauty of whiteness would become enormously influential and inform some of the sinister nineteenth- and twentieth-century theories about race (see Chapter 7).

Despite the controversy that Winckelmann's grand narrative of the history of ancient art initially provoked, in the nineteenth century he would come to be celebrated as the first to attempt to describe the panorama of antiquity's forest; earlier antiquaries had mostly obsessed over details of its trees (single coins, statues, and inscriptions). Yet Winckelmann also freely admitted that fantasy and imagination were major ingredients in the grand narrative that he pieced together. His imagination was stirred not only by encounters with ancient artifacts in the papal collections but also by extensive knowledge of ancient accounts of Athens's greatness. In *History of the Art of Antiquity,* he wrote of how, after the Athenian victory over the Persians at Salamis, "the Greeks now began to show an intensified love for their native land, for which so many courageous men had suffered injury and death, and which now could be regarded as secure against any human power." Athens's great flowering then came during the career of Pericles, "the most blissful times for art in Greece, and especially Athens." Later, during the ascendancy of the Macedonians, the Greeks "yielded to their natural inclination to idleness and revelry. . . . The poets and artists who busied themselves with providing entertainment sought out, in

The Apollo Belvedere. Roman copy (second century CE) in marble after a bronze by the Greek sculptor Leochares, ca. 350–320 BCE.

accordance with the taste of their time, the soft and pleasing, as the nation in its state of indolence sought to flatter its senses."[7] From the account of Athens as the bulwark against barbarians and cultivator of the arts down to its characterization as a city that met with early decline, these were the hallmarks of the Athenian brand—positive and negative alike—infused with fresh life.

Within little more than a generation after Winckelmann's death, by the end of the eighteenth century, the study of Greco-Roman antiquity had emerged in Germany as a separate university discipline. Today it might seem only natural that Classics departments are dedicated to the study of Greek and Roman antiquity, but that grouping is a peculiarity born largely of Winckelmann's work on Roman copies of Greek sculptures; by some other trick of history, the academic study of Ancient Greek might have been just as naturally paired with, say, Demotic Egyptian or Sanskrit or Classical Arabic. Yet in the early nineteenth century, German scholars of Greece and Rome grew anxious to keep their material free of contamination by "lesser" ancient civilizations. This was certainly the attitude of Friedrich August Wolf, who, from an early age, devoted himself to the literature of Greece and Rome as ardently as Winckelmann had pursued ancient art. At the age of eighteen, he enrolled at the University of Göttingen, where an oft-repeated legend in the history of classical scholarship has it that he enrolled in a subject—philology—that did not yet exist. For Wolf, "philology" was to be the empirical science of uncovering the human dimension of the past: a scholarly end in itself, and no longer a mere precursor to the study of law and theology. Before long, he was made professor at the University of Halle.

Although the traditional narrative has it that Wolf the philologist stood at odds with Winckelmann the Romantic idealist, intellectual historian Katherine Harloe has emphasized that the two shared a similar breadth and daring of approach in attempting to make comprehensive accounts of Greco-Roman antiquity.[8] In what has proved his most famous work, his 1795 *Prolegomena ad Homerum*, Wolf ventured a full analysis of the surviving Homeric poems, the *Iliad* and the *Odyssey*, which concluded that they had first been composed orally. The epics, he argued, were also not the product of a single genius but of multiple illiterate bards who had improvised as they performed. This piece of scholarship is still esteemed by classicists as one of the finest works of philology ever produced. Yet despite Wolf's groundbreaking and apparently "democratic" approach to the ancient epics, his insistence that philology break off from the study of theology and law was in reality rooted in chauvinism. The study of Greco-Roman antiquity was rich with potential in part because relatively good evidence for those ancient epochs had survived. But it was also simply not possible, he regretted, "to situate *Egyptians, Hebrews, Persians,* and other nations of the Orient in the same line with the *Greeks* and the *Romans,*" who had, to Wolf's mind, achieved a "true higher intellectual culture" (*Geisteskultur*).[9]

Once Greece achieved independence, the perspectives of Wolf and Winckelmann alike would profoundly shape its early years as a nation, when the new kingdom was ruled by a German-speaking king from Bavaria. Even today, Wolf's line of thought still has a hold. Although Wolf himself advocated the elite professionalization of philology (he wrote his major scholarly works in Latin), in a 2015 piece in the *Guardian*, one prominent classicist argued that everyone should have the chance to learn about ancient Greek civilization precisely because of its unmatched intellectual sophistication. Its author roundly acknowledged that ancient Greeks were greatly influenced by their "neighbors and predecessors" but ultimately maintained that the Greeks "asked a series of crucial questions that are difficult to identify in combination within any of the other cultures of the ancient Mediterranean or Near Eastern antiquity."[10] Boiled down to its essence, that last observation sounds much like Wolf's about the Greeks' and Romans' superior *Geisteskultur*.

RECOVER YOUR ANCIENT BRILLIANCE!

In 1762, just two years before Winckelmann's landmark *History of the Art of Antiquity* appeared, Tsar Peter III died, and his wife Catherine became Empress of Russia. She quickly began to pursue an aggressive program of expanding her kingdom's empire. In October 1768, four and a half months after Winckelmann's murder, the Ottoman Empire declared war on Russia. In 1770, Catherine dispatched one of her favorites, Alexei Grigoryevich Orlov (the man rumored to have murdered her husband, Tsar Peter), with a fleet to the eastern Mediterranean. Orlov's mission there was to provoke the Ottomans, and in mid-February he arrived in the Peloponnese, then known as the Morea, where Russian emissaries were already busy fomenting political unrest among the local nobles. This heralded the beginning of the Orlov Revolt. At first, the revolt proceeded successfully for the Greco-Russian side: broad swathes of the Peloponnese were temporarily liberated from Ottoman rule, while another front of rebellion opened up on the island of Crete. In July, Orlov scored another success when he led Russia in a decisive naval victory over the Ottomans at Chesme, a bay between the island of Chios and the west coast of Asia Minor. In 1774, the Ottomans finally conceded defeat to Russia and agreed to a treaty signed at Küçük Kaynarca in modern-day Bulgaria. Russia had roused the Greeks to rebellion with rhetoric that stirred their hopes of independence, but in the end the Greeks proved little more than pawns in a bigger game aimed at weakening the Ottoman Empire. The cause of Greek liberation was not mentioned in the treaty; Article 7 merely stipulated that the Ottomans would protect Christianity and the Christian churches in their territory. Without further Russian support, the last of the revolt was snuffed out.

In the aftermath of her war with the Ottomans, Catherine began to focus more intently on her ambitions to position Russia as the new heir to Byzantium. Her "Greek Plan" aimed at the revival of an Eastern Orthodox Empire with Constantinople as its capital. Under the plan's banner, she organized the resettlement of some quarter of a million Greeks in New Russia, an area north of the Black Sea (today a part of Ukraine). When her grandson—named Constantine, like the first and last of the Byzantine emperors—was born on April 27, 1779, the medallion that she issued to commemorate his birth featured Istanbul's Hagia Sophia Basilica, an early Christian cathedral that the Ottomans used as an imperial mosque. Russia seemed to offer the best hope for a liberation movement in Greece and actively campaigned for Greek support. The Russian platform emphasized three points: Greece and Russia's common Christian Orthodox heritage, Russia's success as a relative latecomer to the European Enlightenment, and the promises of the Greek Plan. Yet Catherine's ultimate failure to deliver on all these promises led the Greeks to see the importance of casting a wider net in a search for more reliable allies.

England and France, where the Orlov Revolt had captured the imagination of a number of prominent intellectuals, were the two most natural prospects. Already great admirers of Greek antiquity, Enlightenment thinkers there were inspired by the revolt to dream not just of Greek freedom but of seeing antiquity wholly reborn. Even while the revolt was still in progress, the French writer and philosopher Voltaire composed a poem titled "Pindaric Ode on the Current War in Greece." The poem declared that "now is the true time for crusades" and urged the French, British, and Italians to hearken to the Greek cause. Voltaire imagined that the goddess Athena herself was issuing this plea:

> I want to revive Athens. . . .
> Come out, be reborn, cherished Arts
> From these deplorable ruins
> That conceal you among their debris,
> Recover your ancient brilliance!

We can only wonder what Winckelmann would have made of the Orlov Revolt or of its contribution to the rise of the movement that, in the early nineteenth century, would come to be known as philhellenism, a highly politicized variety of "lovers of Greece" who supported its independence. Today the philhellenes are sometimes distinguished from Hellenists (adherents of Hellenism) who, like Winckelmann, studied, exalted, and nurtured a fantasy of Greek antiquity without any personal investment in the question of Greek independence. One scholar has finely articulated the difference between these two strains of Grecophile: the division "was, in a nutshell, the difference between those who could read their Sophocles with comfort when Greeks were fighting Turks and those who could not."[11] If Winckelmann's Hellenism was a state of mind, philhellenism would mark a call to action. Inspired by the courage the Greeks had shown in the Orlov Revolt, a first great wave of philhellenes was moved by the call of Voltaire's Athena. They dreamed of seeing Greeks liberate their land from Turkish tyranny, regain their ancestral greatness, and usher in a new enlightened age for Europe by rebuilding Athens in both spirit and stone. The great historical moment of the philhellenes would not come until the start of the nineteenth century; in the meantime, though, Greek revolutionaries began to recognize the selling power of a very seductive idea: that the long-suffering Greeks, whose ancestors had first brought Europe the light of civilization, were owed their liberation.

SEEDS OF REVOLUTION

Early European travelers often lamented that Greece was no longer a center of learning. Most of those travelers had studied Ancient Greek but had little or no knowledge of actual spoken Greek, so over and over they made this observation on the basis of ignorance. Within Greece, philosophy, theology, and literary study had persisted in schools and under the auspices of the Orthodox Church. A number of Greeks also vigorously participated in the conversations and debates of the European Enlightenment, which knew no national borders. Many of these intellectuals were members of the Greek diaspora that had spread under the Ottoman occupation; they lived, worked, and wrote in cities such as Paris, Vienna, and Bucharest. Radical political developments unfolding in other corners of the world only fanned their optimism. The Orlov Revolt may have inspired a first generation of Europeans to dream of a liberated Greece, but developments such as the successful American bid for independence, the French Revolution, and the Haitian Revolution also encouraged Greeks to see their own deliverance from tyranny as a real possibility.

Like their counterparts in western and northern Europe, Greek thinkers were also beginning to valorize secular accounts of history. Soon they began to use these fashionable new approaches to history as a basis for theorizing their people's independence. Paschalis Kitromilides, a scholar who has worked extensively on Greece and the Enlightenment, emphasizes the significance of the mid-eighteenth-century Greek translation of Charles Rollin's *Histoire ancienne* (Ancient history) for the Greek assimilation of the "continuity" theory of

Hellenic civilization. The full title of Rollin's thirteen-volume history, published in Paris between 1730 and 1738, was *The Ancient History of the Egyptians, Carthaginians, Assyrians, Babylonians, Medes and Persians, Macedonians, and Grecians* and so made bold claims for the scope of the work. In reality, though, the bulk of it was focused on the course of Greek civilization. Certain points of inaccuracy annoyed critics, many of whom regarded Rollin as little more than an uncritical compiler of other scholars' accounts, but his affable style and continuous narrative made *Ancient History* popular across Europe. Between 1749 and 1752, it was published in Greek translation by a press in Venice; soon it became the standard history book used in Greek schools. Kitromilides has called this development "the clearest indication that a sense of a connection between ancient and modern Greeks was in the making."[12]

The popularity of this new kind of history among Greeks signifies two important shifts, both of which would prove critical to the ideological underpinnings of independence. The first consisted in a move toward a secular vision of history and away from a model of thinking grounded in religious chronicles and the authority of the Orthodox Church. The second was a growing willingness among Greek intellectuals to accept, adopt, and internalize claims about the continuity of the Greek people and their culture from ancient to modern times. These claims were nothing radically new, and many modern scholars have stressed the persistence of classical learning among the Byzantine- and Ottoman-era elite. Yet with new Enlightenment theories of nationhood and with momentum building toward revolution, the ideas began to assume a more potent significance. Greek humanists worked to curate editions of ancient texts using European philological models. The notion that a single unbroken thread ran from Homer's time to the present day also led to new accounts and interpretations of literary history. Anthologies and handbooks came to include Greek literature and philosophy from antiquity to the end of the Byzantine Empire and even ventured to claim that contemporary Greek thinkers also belonged to the same long tradition. As travelers to Greece grew more eager to seek out traces of ancient habits and customs in the lives of everyday Greek people, more Greek intellectuals began to accept that this link with the splendors of ancient civilizations—especially Athens and Sparta—really existed. They too set out to identify and compile evidence for links to their ancient ancestors. This line of thought eventually led to a scholarly habit of seeing current (especially poor, rural) Greek customs as evidence for ancient culture; academic work founded on the premise of traceable continuity would remain popular into the 1970s, which saw the publication of titles such as *Greek Peasants, Ancient and Modern* and *The Ritual Lament in the Greek Tradition*.[13]

One of the most influential Greek thinkers of the European Enlightenment was Adamantios Koraïs, who was born in 1748 (just over thirty years after Winckelmann) into a silk-trading family of Smyrna in Asia Minor. Koraïs was the first major thinker to set the project of Greek liberty in the frame of the Enlightenment concept of a nation-state: a state that was home to a people who shared a common history and language, and where the people were the source of the state's sovereign power. As a diasporic Greek intellectual in Europe, Koraïs was shaped by both his own complex identity (as a thoroughly Europeanized Greek from Smyrna) and Enlightenment political ideals. He longed to see his people freed from the tyranny of the church and the Ottomans, but he also recognized that all of Europe had something at stake in Greek liberation.

After receiving a first-rate education in Smyrna, Koraïs moved to Amsterdam to manage his family's business interests. In 1782, he enrolled in the School of Medicine at the University of Montpellier; after six years of studies, he gave up medicine and settled in Paris in 1788, the year before the French Revolution broke out. In Paris, he devoted himself to his true passion, the study of Greek antiquity. Koraïs was the first Greek to be accepted among European classical circles and was even offered a post at the Collège de France despite having no formal university training in the field (he declined the position). Even when the Napoleonic Wars drove a wedge between France and Britain, Koraïs continued to correspond with scholars from both countries. On the back of his classical research, he also began carefully laying intellectual foundations for Greek independence. To his mind, though, independence still lay some half a century off; as an eyewitness of the revolutionaries' Reign of Terror in France (1793–1794), Koraïs had experienced firsthand the dangers of precipitous and bloody revolt. For him, any successful movement for Greece's liberation needed to rest on strong and principled groundwork. The slow but sure path lay through education, which would empower the Greek people to reawaken the spirit of ancient Athens first among themselves.

On this last point, Koraïs had sure allies in the philhellenes, but he also had to contend with prejudices that remained from a generation of Enlightenment thinkers who saw the Greeks as responsible for their own misfortunes. David Hume, polymath and leading figure of the Scottish Enlightenment, had offered a bleak estimation of the Greek people. In 1748, the year of Koraïs's birth, Hume published an essay, *Of National Characters,* in which he claimed that "the integrity, gravity, and bravery of the Turks, form an exact contrast to the deceit, levity, and cowardice of the modern Greeks." There Hume also observed how regime changes, waves of migration, and the general inconstancy of human affairs all have the power to degrade great peoples. Echoing a premise of the early European travelers to Greece, he argued that the Greeks were a first case in point: "The ingenuity, industry and activity of the ancient GREEKS," he scoffed, "have nothing in common with the stupidity and indolence of the present inhabitants of those regions."[14] Koraïs, by contrast, like many other Greek humanists, refused to place the fault in the innate character of the Greek people; for him, the blame lay with the Orthodox Church. He saw the church's corrupt and backward clergy as antiquated holdovers from medieval Byzantium and largely at fault for Greece's present condition, although centuries of Ottoman subjugation had certainly played their part. To his mind, Greece and the Greeks needed to be cleansed of an insidious double legacy of barbarism, Byzantine and Ottoman alike.

For all his lectures, letters, pamphlets, and unflagging advocacy of a carefully cleared path to independence, Koraïs never drew up anything like a clear blueprint for the practical architecture of a Greek nation-state. He did, however, write an essay "addressed to enlightened Europe," titled *Mémoire sur l'état actuel de la civilisation dans la Grèce* (Memorandum on the present state of civilization in Greece), which he penned under his Gallicized name Adamance Coray. The sixty-six-page treatise was published in Paris in 1803; in it, Koraïs formulated a number of intellectual arguments for Greek national sovereignty. The historian Thomas Gallant has distilled Koraïs's thought on Greek independence into these three principles:

1. The national boundaries of a Greek nation should correspond to the area of the Mediterranean dominated in antiquity by the Greek city-states.
2. The Greek language is the most essential indicator of Greek identity.
3. Greece's true cultural heritage lies in antiquity, and not in the Orthodox Christianity of medieval Byzantium.[15]

Despite the expansiveness of his thought, Koraïs remains best known today for his work to promote the revival of a more classical, "pure" version of the Greek language. The matter of linguistic continuity was fundamental because he found it much easier to cite the Greek language as proof of a continuous Hellenic tradition than to insist that the diverse and scattered Greek peoples were all descendants of Pericles. Yet Koraïs was troubled by the current state of spoken Greek, which had assimilated many words from Turkish, Italian, Albanian, and Slavic languages. Its grammar had also evolved and simplified since antiquity, and some points of difference (such as the disappearance of the infinitive verb form) particularly offended his sensibilities. For Koraïs, the foreign borrowings and structures that had sullied Greek speech were symptoms of the foreign, barbaric modes of thought that had also invaded the Greek land and infected the Greek people.

A broader debate over the so-called Greek Language Question had emerged at about the time of the Orlov Revolt. At its heart was the question of which version of the language, on a scale from the modern vernacular to formal Attic (ancient Athenian), was the most appropriate form of Greek. As revolutionary fervor in Greece approached its boiling point, the matter of language became an ideological focus of debates about the way forward. Archaists were proponents of a truly ancient form of the language, while vernacularists insisted on using the language that Greeks actually spoke. Yet vernacularists also believed that Greeks should cultivate their spoken language—as other Europeans did theirs—by outfitting it with the words, phrases, and structures needed to accommodate any level or subject of discussion. Koraïs was a devout linguist who "devoted himself, with a strict secular asceticism, to writing, translating, editing, and prefacing" Ancient Greek texts.[16]

Yet when it came to spoken Greek, he championed what he saw as a middle way; for all his commitment to antiquity, he knew that it would be just as impossible to resurrect true Ancient Greek as it would be to bring Pericles and Socrates back to life.

Instead, Koraïs became the leading advocate of a systematic cleansing, correcting, and light "ancientification" of the spoken language. This version of Greek was called *Katharevousa,* which means "purified; cleansed" (from the same Greek root that also gives us the word *catharsis*). Starting in the first century BCE, an Atticist movement in language and literature strove to resuscitate the Attic or Athenian version of Greek (that movement too had its detractors, who believed that literary Greek should reflect the spoken language). As a kind of modern-day Atticism—a "soft" imitation of Attic Greek—*Katharevousa* seemed to offer the best of both worlds: it retained the heart of the popular spoken language but expelled foreign "barbarisms" and so partially restored Greek to a purer state. Ever since travelers such as George Wheler and Jacob Spon had begun to visit Greece, European intellectuals—very few of whom understood spoken Greek—had dismissed the contemporary language as a debased corruption of the ancient one. Now Greeks had the chance to flip the hierarchy of language prestige on its head: *Katharevousa* would be proof that the Greeks were worthy not only of their ancient ancestors but also of Europe. In the end, *Katharevousa* was Koraïs's most concrete contribution to the new nation. Even before the War of Independence began, it was adopted by whole waves of prominent Greek thinkers; after the war ended, it became the de facto language of the Greek state. By the end of the twentieth century, *Katharevousa* would become all but obsolete in Greece, but that in no way diminishes Koraïs's contributions to the early ideological underpinnings of the Greek nation.

In the early years of the nineteenth century, Koraïs began actively to rally support for Greece in France by presenting public lectures in Paris on Greek affairs. He was a founding member of the Comité Philhellénique de Paris, one of the many European and North American philhellenic societies that formed once the War of Independence began and gathered money, supplies, and general support for the war's cause. Even when Greece gained independence, however, Koraïs continued to live as an expatriate in France. His biography is thus a vivid illustration of the reorientation of the Greek intellectual class toward western Europe and away from Russia. He and others like him found kindred spirits not among fellow Orthodox peoples but in European intellectuals who shared a combination of passionate Hellenism, Enlightenment values, and sympathy for the Greek people. In 1833, shortly after the Kingdom of Greece emerged as an independent state, Koraïs died in Paris at the age of eighty-five. Like Winckelmann, he had never visited the Greek mainland. Few thinkers have had more influence than this pair of men in determining Greece's fates as a nation; it is a testament to the power of the Greek ideal that both of them (like countless others who have lived under the spell of that idea) avoided setting foot in Athens but chose instead to behold the city of Pericles only ever with their minds' eye.

Certainly not every Greek—and not even every Greek intellectual living in France—shared the antiquity-oriented philhellenic vision of Adamantios Koraïs. For many revolutionaries, Byzantium offered a far more attractive model: the Byzantine Empire had covered much more territory than the ancient city-states and was united under a single, Christian emperor. One of the many who did not share Koraïs's wholesale distaste for the church and its heritage was Rigas Velestinlis (or Feraios), Koraïs's junior by about a decade. Like Koraïs, Velestinlis was inspired by the tradition of the Enlightenment and recognized the

Adamantios Koraïs depicted on a 100-drachma Greek banknote from 1973.

symbolic power in Europe of Greek antiquity. On most other points, the two differed in their views and approaches to independence. Koraïs was a man of thought, but Velestinlis had real credentials as a man of action: in his youth he even supposedly killed an Ottoman official. He was born in Thessaly, in northern Greece, and was educated and encouraged by Orthodox priests and monks (the patriarchate in Constantinople officially condemned revolutionary activity, but many members of the clergy supported independence movements). As opposed to Koraïs, a Parisian intellectual at heart, Velestinlis was active in the Balkans and the other diaspora capitals of Bucharest and Vienna. Unlike Koraïs, he was enthused by the violent revolution in France, and his grittier brand of patriotism favored the language spoken by the people.

Velestinlis's vision for the future of Greece was more internationalist than nationalist in spirit, and his most influential writing was a manifesto addressed to subjugated peoples in much of the Ottoman Empire. This pamphlet, titled *New Political Administration of the Inhabitants of Rumeli, Asia Minor, the Aegean Archipelago, Moldavia, and Walachia,* was published in Vienna in 1797. It consisted of the following:

1. A proclamation of revolution
2. A declaration of the "rights of man" in thirty-five articles (modeled after the Declaration of the Rights of Man and of the Citizen, the 1789 statement of the core principles and values of the French Revolution)
3. A constitution for a new Hellenic Republic, in 127 articles
4. A battle hymn

Its "proclamation of revolution" addressed "the people descended from the Hellenes . . . all those who groan under the unbearable tyranny of most loathsome Ottoman despotism," including diaspora Greeks who had been driven to seek refuge in other lands. Religion was immaterial: "I mean everyone," Rigas emphasized, "Christians and Turks, without religious distinction (for we are all children of God and children of Adam)." From the Balkans to the Cycladic islands to Asia Minor, all those who suffered under the Ottoman yoke were invited to join in his uprising.

That same year, Velestinlis also produced another radical document, a detailed map depicting an ambitious territorial expanse of a liberated Greece, which he printed "for the sake of Hellenes and Philhellenes."[17] The borders of his map contained a reclaimed Greek land that nearly corresponded to the territory of the Byzantine Empire at its height; this translated into a good portion of the Ottoman Empire of his time, including its capital at Istanbul, Byzantium's Constantinople. The printed map was as physically large as its proposed territory was ambitious: it consisted of twelve panels that, assembled, covered nearly fifty square feet. In time, the map would prove to be an early prototype of a dream that, in the early decades of Greek independence, later came to be called the "Great Idea": a national irredentist project aimed at reclaiming the entirety of the Greeks' ancestral homelands and reestabishing a Greek capital in Constantinople (Istanbul). Yet in the late eighteenth century, as Greek cultural historian Vangelis Calotychos has stressed, Velestinlis's map actually incorporated "a number of outcomes of a projected revolution." This was because "the exact terms of the entity to come out of any struggle for liberation differed greatly in the minds of many Greek patriots at the time."[18] With its sprawling dozen panels, the map could speak to all revolutionary aspirations: its outline was inspired by the borders of Byzantium, but it also took full advantage of European enthusiasm for ancient Greek place names.

Velestinlis might have been raised by Orthodox clergy, but he very well understood that his best hope of rallying support from abroad was to appeal to the European passion for Greek antiquity. Although he favored the vernacular Greek language, he also showed an incredible facility for molding Ancient Greek to his own ends. His radical vocabulary breathed new life into ancient words. One was the term *thnos*. In Ancient Greek, *ethnos* meant a nation of people (or even a "flock" or "swarm," say, of birds or bees), but his rhetoric reoriented the word's definition to mirror the sense of the French (and English) word *nation*, which had widened to encompass the new conceit of the nation-state. He also made a carefully calculated move to call the Greeks "descendants of the Hellenes"—not Romiotes, the term of Greek self-identification that had so disappointed eighteenth-century European travelers—and to call his hoped-for Greek state the Hellenic Republic. Velestinlis gave Europe everything that it could have hoped for in a standard bearer of revolution: he even incorporated a Greek mythical hero, Heracles, into the flag of the new republic. To Greeks he presented a different face and became enormously beloved for his battle hymns, composed in the people's vernacular. Yet with the help of Velestinlis's rhetorical and political skills, a radical shift in the coordinates of Greek identity was beginning to take place. Many

Greeks were now beginning to see themselves as members of a "Hellenic *ethnos*" rather than the "Romiote people."

Adamantios Koraïs had been horrified by the bloodshed of the French Revolution. Rigas Velestinlis took his inspiration for a secular and democratic Greek constitution directly from the Jacobins, the most radical and violent revolutionary faction in France. To rally support for his cause, he made overtures directly to Napoleon Bonaparte, supposedly by appealing to Napoleon's love of antiquity and its symbols: Velestinlis was said to have sent Napoleon a cigarette case made from laurel wood, taken from a tree that grew in a sanctuary of the god Apollo. Napoleon agreed to a meeting, but in 1798, as Velestinlis was traveling to see him in Italy, he was betrayed and arrested by Habsburg officials at Trieste (the Habsburgs were then allied with the Ottomans against Napoleon). He was transferred to Belgrade, where he was imprisoned and tortured before being extradited to Istanbul. He never arrived, though; on the way, he and his other "accomplices" were strangled to death by their captors. The popular tradition claims that his last words were something like "I sowed seed enough. Soon my people will harvest sweet fruit." Velestinlis's great map had ultimately helped cost him his life. In 1997, the two hundredth anniversary of its first printing, the Greek Ministry of Culture declared all surviving copies national monuments.

The martyrdom of Rigas Velestinlis further stirred the passion for revolution in Greece, and the story of his life and death also greatly moved many philhellenes. Some thirty years later, Henry Post, an agent of the New York Greek Committee for the Relief of the Greeks, included a dramatic narration of the tale as part of the memoir of his travels in Greece during the War of Independence. It ended with a vivid appraisal of the consequences of Velestinlis's assassination: "The Greeks, on learning the fate of their hero, gnashed their teeth in secret, and muttered vows of vengeance upon the heads of his murderers."[19]

LAST POOR PLUNDER FROM A BLEEDING LAND

The year of Velestinlis's death, 1798, was especially eventful throughout Europe and the Mediterranean. The Ottoman Empire suffered a major blow when Egypt, its semiautonomous protectorate, fell to Napoleon. Thomas Bruce, the 7th Earl of Elgin, was also appointed British ambassador to the Ottoman Porte. A Scottish aristocrat, Elgin had already spent several years in diplomatic service in Austria, Belgium, and Prussia. His eventual removal of nearly half the remaining sculptures from the Parthenon is one of the most notorious episodes of modern Greek history. Modern accounts of the controversy nevertheless tend to discuss it in isolation, as if it took place on a deserted Acropolis and in a historical vacuum, completely outside the growing momentum behind movements for Greek independence. By contrast, "serious" accounts of Greek history in this period often elide discussion of Elgin's actions, the implication being that their significance has been overstated as a result of the ongoing furor over the campaign to repatriate the Elgin Marbles. The deed is, nevertheless, of real historical significance because it ignited a chain of events in Britain that contributed immensely to the birth of a second wave of philhellenism.

Elgin set his eyes on the Parthenon even before he took up his post in Istanbul. From England, he began planning to conduct a survey of the Parthenon and to commission drawings and molds of its marbles. He envisioned that the images and reproductions, when put on display in Britain, would educate the public and guide it toward better taste. Years later he claimed that before leaving for Athens, he made inquiries of the British government as to whether it would be interested in sending artists from England to do the job, a matter he characterized as of national importance. Citing the obstacle of expense, the government allegedly gave a response that was "entirely negative."[20] Undeterred, Elgin employed an Italian landscape painter named Giovanni Battista Lusieri, who had previously worked as court painter in Naples to Ferdinand I, King of the Two Sicilies.

Once he arrived in Athens, Elgin's ambitions expanded well beyond casts and drawings. He hatched a plan to remove pieces of the Parthenon and put Lusieri in charge of the work. Just as they were ready to begin—the scaffolds were already up—they were stopped by the disdar, the military governor of the Acropolis. He informed them that if they wanted to detach the marbles, they had to obtain a *firman,* or a royal mandate, from the sultan. Elgin went to Constantinople to acquire one and, when he returned to Athens, was permitted to begin the work. The nature of this *firman* remains one of the biggest points of debate in the whole history of the controversy surrounding the marbles because no original copy exists. When the British House of Commons deliberated about purchasing the sculptures in 1816, the only version introduced into evidence was an English translation of an Italian translation of a letter supposedly sent by the grand vizier of Sultan Selim III to the chief judge and governor of Athens. The Italian version of the letter apparently contained these explicit orders of nonintervention in the work of Elgin's team:

> That no interruption may be given them, nor any obstacle thrown in their way by the Disdar . . . nor by any other person: that no one may meddle in the scaffolding or implements they may require in their works; and *that when they wish to take away any pieces of stone with old inscriptions or figures thereon, that no opposition be made thereto.*[21]

Even if this text faithfully reflected the original document, Elgin and Lusieri were incontrovertibly guilty of interpreting whatever permission was granted to them with enormous latitude. Like the Venetians who besieged the Acropolis in the seventeenth century, Elgin and his men also caused further damage to the sculptures and structure of the Parthenon with their crowbars and cranes. Another Englishman passing through Athens at the time, the clergyman and naturalist Edward Daniel Clarke, wrote in a travel memoir of how workmen in the process of removing a portion of a metope (a sculpted frieze) knocked off other pieces of marble near it, "scattering their white fragments with thundering noise amongst the ruins." The disdar, overseeing the works, "could no longer restrain his emotions; he actually took his pipe from his mouth and letting fall a tear, said in a most emphatic tone, 'Τέλος! [Telos!]'' positively declaring that nothing should induce him to consent to any further dilapidation of the building" (a *telos* is an "end" or "stopping point" in Greek and on this occasion meant something like Italian *basta,* "enough"). In a footnote, however, Clarke remarked that because the disdar was poor and had a family to support, "he was afterwards gradually prevailed upon to allow all the finest pieces of the Parthenon to be taken down."[22] As outraged as Clarke apparently was, the scene did not dissuade him from continuing to collect Greek antiquities of his own.

The notorious details of Elgin's decision, contrary to his original intention, to extract the marbles and ship them back to Britain remain controversial to this day. Lusieri's work spanned eleven years, from 1801 to 1811. By the time it was over, the team had packed up nearly half of the Parthenon's great frieze (247 feet from the original 524), fifteen of its ninety-two metopes, and a number of sculptures from the pediments—many of them badly broken by Morosini's explosion—along with a number of bits and pieces from other ancient buildings.

The first batch of sculpture was shipped from Athens on Elgin's own boat, which sank near Cythera, an island off the southern tip of the Peloponnese. The sculptures were salvaged, but Elgin's passage to England was temporarily thwarted: he was captured by troops of Napoleon when he departed from Constantinople at the end of his diplomatic service, in 1803. Elgin spent three years as a prisoner.

All the while, Lusieri continued acquiring antiquities from the Acropolis. One of his greatest prizes was a caryatid from the porch of the Erechtheion; in her place, Lusieri left a simple brick pillar to help bear the weight of the structure. The episode is now steeped in a legend that appeared almost immediately afterward. In his 1813 *Essay on Certain Points of Resemblance between the Ancient and Modern Greeks,* the English politician and Oxford graduate Frederick Sylvester North Douglas reported a moving version of the tale that he heard from "an illiterate servant of the Disdar of Athens" in Athens, a stop on his Grand Tour from 1810 to 1812:

> When the other χοριτζια [i.e., κορίτσια, "girls"] had lost their sister, they manifested their affliction by filling the air at the close of the evening with the most mournful sighs and lamentations, that he himself had often heard their complaints, and never without being so much affected as to be obliged to leave the citadel till they had ceased; and that the ravished sister was not deaf to their voice, but astonished the lower town, where she was placed, by answering in the same lamentable tones.[23]

The caryatid was packed up with the other loot from the Acropolis. The last shipment left Athens on a British naval ship that set sail in

April 1811 with Lusieri on board. Elgin, having apparently forgotten his more altruistic aim of cultivating public taste, now had in mind that all his acquisitions would go to Broomhall House, his ancestral country home in Scotland's Fife region.

The plans for beautifying Broomhall House were soon interrupted when Elgin underwent a highly public divorce from Mary Nisbet, his famously rich and beautiful wife, on grounds of her infidelity—a sensational scandal in upper-crust British society. Elgin quickly remarried, but his acquisitions in Athens had come at great personal cost, roughly £74,000, and his new wife did not bring the kind of resources to the marriage that would make up for his loss. Drowning in debt, he began to negotiate the sale of the marbles to the British government as early as 1811, the same year in which the last of them were shipped from Athens. He refused the government's first offer of £30,000 but managed to acquire enormous notoriety in the public eye. Eyewitness travelers had recorded their outrage at the marbles' removal; now members of the Society of Dilettanti publicly scoffed at the idea that the sculptures were of any real value. Soon, a rising literary figure stepped in to express his disgust over the whole affair.

This poet was also one of Elgin's most famous and bitter critics: George Gordon Byron, better known as Lord Byron. In June 1809, at the age of twenty-one, Byron set out on a two-year Grand Tour to the East (the Napoleonic Wars continued to make travel difficult on the old Continental routes). Three months before his departure, he published a satirical poem titled *English Bards and Scotch Reviewers,* a response to a panning that his poetry book *Hours of Idleness* had received the previous year in the *Edinburgh Review.* In that satire, he dismissed the efforts made by Elgin—and all other ridiculous antiquaries like him—to amass collections of antiquities. Let them, Byron declared,

"Waste useless thousands on their Phidian freaks, / Misshapen monuments and maim'd antiques."[24]

When Byron's Grand Tour finally brought him to Athens at the end of 1809, he was able to see firsthand the consequences of Elgin and Lusieri's handiwork. By the time he left Greece for Turkey in the spring of 1810, he had fallen in love with Greece and its people's cause for independence and radically altered his view of the significance of what Elgin had done. New, far harsher, verses against Elgin appeared in Byron's *Childe Harold's Pilgrimage*, a semiautobiographical poem about a young but world-weary man, Harold, and his travels from Spain to Greece. Byron composed the first two of the poem's four cantos while still on his tour; they were published in March 1812, the year after he returned to England. The second canto opens with an invocation to Athena (who had also starred in Voltaire's poem about the Orlov Revolt) and a question about what has happened to her ancient defenders: now they are "Gone—glimmering through the dream of things that were." Harold soon launches into open condemnation of Elgin's recent "dire" deed:

> What! shall it e'er be said by British tongue,
> Albion was happy in Athena's tears?
> Though in thy name the slaves her bosom wrung,
> Tell not the deed to blushing Europe's ears;
> The ocean queen, the free Britannia, bears
> The last poor plunder from a bleeding land.[25]

Toward the end of the canto, Harold ruminates on his hopes that Greece will secure independence from the Ottomans. In some of the most celebrated and quoted verses of the poem, he wonders who might take up the cause:

Fair Greece! sad relic of departed worth!

Immortal, though no more; though fallen, great!

Who now shall lead thy scatter'd children forth,

And long accustom'd bondage uncreate?[26]

These lines would often be excerpted as a rallying cry for the Greek cause. In particular, the verse that proclaims Greece a "sad relic of departed worth" has long been remembered as a kind of philhellenic motto, separated from its complex context within the difficult (and often ironic) poem. The 1812 cantos of *Childe Harold* were nonetheless such an instant hit (the poem's third canto appeared in 1816, the fourth and final one in 1818) that even Byron was stunned by how rapidly they increased his reputation: "I awoke one morning," he supposedly mused, "and found myself famous."[27] The combination of his newfound celebrity and the vitriol of his attacks on Lord Elgin created an enormous amount of publicity around the marbles and, ironically, only added to their value in the eyes of the British government. On February 15, 1816, Elgin reemerged from his life of quiet ignominy when he filed an official petition with the British government requesting that it purchase his collection. A special committee was formed to consider the matter. Its final report ran to twenty-seven pages, with well over one hundred more of appendices of documents submitted into evidence.

The committee's report exonerated Lord Elgin of any wrongdoing in acquiring the marbles—one of the major issues that it had been charged with considering. Its members heard testimony that locals in Athens had been glad to see the works get under way; they supposedly viewed Elgin's enterprise as a "means of bringing foreigners into their country, and of having money spent among them." Elgin, they found, did the sculptures a service, for the "Turks showed a total indifference and apathy as to the preservation of these remains, except when in a fit of wanton destruction, they sometimes carried their disregard so far as to do mischief by firing at them."[28] The committee deemed Elgin's collection eminently worthy of purchase and arrived at the "reasonable and sufficient" price of £35,000; satirical cartoonists in Britain meanwhile responded by pillorying Parliament for spending so much money on ancient marbles and so little on the poor. In the report's last paragraph, the committee expressed its sorrow at what had befallen Greece but ultimately concluded that, given the circumstances, "no country can be better adapted than our own to afford an honourable asylum to these monuments of the school of *Phidias,* and of the administration of *Pericles.*"[29] Britain, the committee determined, was the most suitable protector and most rightful heir of these masterpieces of Greek antiquity. The report was dated March 25, 1816; on July 11, Parliament passed the British Museum Act of 1816, "To Vest the Elgin Collection of Ancient Marbles and Sculptures to the Trustees of the British Museum for the Use of the Public." It also provided for the disbursement of Treasury funds to Elgin and made him a trustee of the British Museum. The same year, in April, Byron left England forever.

Elgin's Parthenon Marbles remain the pride of the British Museum, and their history is much more than a footnote in the story of European philhellenism and Greek independence. Elgin's actions helped turn Byron, one of the greatest luminaries of the era, into Europe's most celebrated and influential spokesman for the Greek cause. Byron's poetry in turn largely inspired the second stronger round of philhellenism born when the War of Independence broke out. This new surge grew out of a confluence of intellectual and political movements. Beneath its surface, rational Enlightenment ideals collided with the vibrant and restless spirit of Romanticism, which made for a messy internal logic. European philhellenes railed against Greece's subjection to a foreign oppressor even as their countries continued to expand their empires. Many philhellenes also subscribed to the paradox initially set by their interpretations of Winckelmann's work: precisely because the achievements of Greek antiquity were so inimitable, the only hope for the present age was to attempt to imitate them. For them, ancient Greece simultaneously represented the purity of mankind's childhood and humanity's cultural zenith. A return to the spirit of Athens would mark a return to a cultural Eden of sorts, but an Eden where knowledge would reign and free Europe from the bonds of Protestantism. This second-wave philhellenism blazed through Europe and even reached the shores of the newly independent United States. Thomas Jefferson, a friend and correspondent of Adamantios Koraïs, was one of the Greeks' most ardent supporters from a very safe distance at his plantation in Virginia.

MOTHER GREECE WANTS YOU

On April 11, 1814, Napoleon signed the Treaty of Fontainebleau in Paris, bringing an end to his reign as emperor in France. Once he conceded defeat to Russia, Prussia, and Austria, the Greek revolutionaries who had once placed such great hope in him had no choice but to take independence into their own hands. In September 1814, just months after Napoleon abdicated his throne, a new revolutionary group was born in Odessa, then part of the Russian Empire. The society, known enigmatically as the Filiki Etaireia (Friendly Society), was invitation only. Its organization was inspired by the Freemasons and other European secret societies that had also been formed to foster revolutions. By 1818, it had become the largest Greek revolutionary organization. Its members—rumor had it that Tsar Alexander I was among them—believed in the necessity of a violent uprising, but consensus was otherwise difficult to find. Some shared the principles of the late Rigas

Velestinlis; others dreamed that the overthrow of the Ottoman Empire would pave the way for a true return to the glories of Byzantium, with a Christian Orthodox emperor installed in a reclaimed Constantinople.

In April 1820, Alexander Ypsilantis, a Greek revolutionary born in Istanbul and educated at the court of the Russian tsars, was elected head of the organization. At the end of that same year, he seized an opportunity created by Ottoman infighting to advance his cause. Ali Pasha, the "Lion of Ioannina," who ruled for the sultan over much of northern Greece, declared a personal rebellion against the empire. When this window opened, Ypsilantis issued his revolutionary proclamation. In his 1821 "Address to the Greeks," he appealed to his countrymen: "Let us recollect, brave and generous Greeks, the liberty of the classic land of Greece, the battles of Marathon and Thermopylae; let us combat upon the tombs of our ancestors, who, to leave us free, fought and died." The document was widely circulated in English and was reprinted, for example, in Hezekiah Niles's *Weekly Register*, a magazine issued in Baltimore.[30] The rhetoric of antiquity that characterized these kinds of proclamations was clearly directed more at foreigners in Europe and the United States than at Greeks, for whom such historical allusions to Persian War battles would have resonated far less.[31] Ypsilantis was, however, nothing if not a compelling rhetorician; he even insinuated that he had secured the backing of Russia. Tsar Alexander I, however, quickly ordered an end to the revolt. The Orthodox Church also denounced it, and Gregory V, patriarch of Constantinople, excommunicated its architects. Gregory was nonetheless still put to death by order of the sultan in April 1821.

By that time, the revolt had already spread to the Peloponnese, which had long been a hotbed of local resistance to Ottoman rule. On March 17, Petros "Petrobey" Mavromichalis marched two thousand

Maniots (soldiers from Mani, a southern peninsula of the Peloponnese) to the city of Kalamata. They captured the city after two days of fighting, and on March 23, Mavromichalis dispatched a Greek declaration of independence authored by a fellow revolutionary, renowned intellectual, and committed "modernizer" of Greece, Alexandros Mavrocordatos, to the European powers. This declaration was later printed in English translation by Thomas Gordon, a British military officer and philhellene who participated in the War of Independence from 1821 until 1827. In 1828, Gordon again returned to Greece to pursue archeological work but ended up devoting most of his time to amassing documents and oral accounts of the revolution. In his two-volume history of the war, Gordon introduced Mavromichalis and Mavrocordatos's missive to Europe (part of an appendix to one of his chapters) as the "Manifesto addressed to Europe by Petros Mavromikhalis, Commander-in-Chief of the Spartan troops, and the Messenian senate, sitting at Calamata." This is the last paragraph of the manifesto as Gordon printed it; it is a loose translation of the original Greek version but an accurate representation of its content and spirit:

> We invoke the aid of all the civilized nations of Europe, that we may the more promptly attain to the goal of a just and sacred enterprise, reconquer our rights, and regenerate our unfortunate people. Greece, our mother, was the lamp that illuminated you; on this ground she reckons on your active philanthropy. Arms, money, and counsel, are what she expects from you. We promise you her lively gratitude, which she will prove by deeds in more prosperous times.[32]

Philhellenes now roundly came to accept the premise that Europe owed a great debt to Greece. One of the earliest expressions of this symbolic debt appears in a work by a British Romantic poet. In 1821, Percy Bysshe Shelley, an ardent philhellene, wrote a play titled *Hellas*. The play was an adaptation of Aeschylus's *Persians*, itself a dramatization of the Persian royal family's reaction to Xerxes's defeat by the Athenians in the Battle of Salamis (see Chapter 2). Shelley composed *Hellas* in Pisa, and it was the last work he published before his death. In it, he cast the Ottoman sultan in the tragic role of Aeschylus's King Xerxes; he also pledged proceeds from the sale of the play to the Greek cause. His view of the war—and of Europe's duty to support it—was made more than clear in the play's famous preface: "The apathy of the rulers of the civilized world to the astonishing circumstances of the descendants of that nation to which they owe their civilization—rising as it were from the ashes of their ruin, is something perfectly inexplicable to a mere spectator of the shews of this mortal scene. *We are all Greeks.* Our laws, our literature, our religion, our arts, have their root in Greece."[33]

The phrase "We are all Greeks" has, over the past two centuries, been quoted on countless occasions; in the context of the Greek economic crisis, it has gained a new lease of life as a slogan of solidarity (see Chapter 7). In the preface, Shelley nevertheless outlined a whole chain of indebtedness between Greece and other countries of Europe: in recent years, he explained, the "flower of [Greek] youth" had been returning to Greece from university study in France, Italy, and Germany and so bearing back to Greece the light of ancient learning "of which their ancestors were the original source." The relationship that Shelley constructed, then, was one of absolute mutual dependence across time between Greeks and the rest of Europe.[34]

Shelley dedicated *Hellas* to Alexandros Mavrocordatos, whom he and his wife, Mary, had met, and with whom they had developed a close personal, intellectual, and political relationship in Pisa. This was the same Mavrocordatos who authored Mavromichalis's proclamation of

Greek independence and plea to Europe to come to the aid of the Greek cause. Shelley inscribed his play to him as "an imperfect token of the admiration, sympathy, and friendship of the author." He thus laid bare his agreement with the terms of the debt as formulated by Mavrocordatos: now was the time for Europe to meet its ancient obligations.

The Greek revolutionaries sought "arms, money, and counsel" from Europe. The British began to answer that call when, on the last day of February 1823, the first meeting of the London Greek (or Philhellenic) Committee was convened. The committee was formed to aid the Greek cause primarily by raising funds, and its existence reflected the wide general support in Britain for Greek independence. Despite Britain's official position of neutrality, George Canning, British foreign secretary from 1822, allowed the committee to raise money privately by selling subscriptions. One of its first goals was to attract Lord Byron to its ranks. *Childe Harold's Pilgrimage* had succeeded in rallying public support for Greece, but in an explanatory note published with the poem, Byron had expressed doubts about Greece's prospects for freedom: "The Greeks will never be independent; they will never be sovereigns as heretofore, and God forbid they ever should!" Instead, he ventured that Greece could become an Ottoman equivalent of a British colony, "not independent . . . but free and industrious."[35] As with his estimation of Lord Elgin, Byron eventually revised this opinion.

Byron joined the committee in its second wave of membership, as did a handful of classical scholars, although "most of its members knew nothing about the revolution they had pledged to support."[36] The provisional government, remembered as the First Hellenic Republic, meanwhile began to send emissaries around Europe in the hopes of securing loans for the new state. The London Greek Committee eventually sent a military unit to aid Greece on the ground, but its "grand object," in the words of one of its founding members, Lieutenant-Colonel

Leicester Stanhope, "was to impress on the public mind the stability and security of the Greek government, and to procure her an efficient loan."[37] Members of the committee were instrumental in brokering and financing what are now remembered as Greece's "independence loans." In 1823, Edward Blaquiere, a veteran of the Napoleonic Wars and another of the committee's founders, published a pamphlet trumpeting the investment potential presented by the Greek revolution. Philhellenism had paved the way for a surge of sympathy for Greece, and potential investors salivated when they read Blaquiere's claim that a liberated Greece "may calculate upon becoming one of the most opulent nations of Europe."[38] In short, this admirable, prestigious, and fashionable cause seemed to be coupled with a great opportunity for profit.

In November 1823, the committee sent its own military expedition to Greece, with the terribly unqualified Byron as its leader. There he cut something of an embarrassing figure and was often spotted lounging about the camp sporting an ancient Greek–style helmet. Back in England, however, his hearts-and-minds campaign was hugely successful at rallying support. With substantial help from the London Greek Committee, in 1824 Ioannis Orlandos and Andreas Louriotis, two Greek deputies, managed to procure a first British loan of £800,000. The loan, backed by members of the committee and by the London bank of Loughman, O'Brien, Ellice & Co., was a risky one for investors. Repayment depended on the revolution's success, and this high risk translated into high costs for the Greek borrowers. After interest and other loan-issuance fees and commissions were deducted, the Greeks saw only £348,000, or 44 percent, of the nominal principal. As collateral, the temporary government pledged all its "national property." Another loan followed the next year, this time negotiated directly with the London bank of Jacob & Samson and Ricardo. Representatives from both the London Greek Committee, many of whose members had per sonally invested in the Greek debt, and Jacob & Samson and Ricardo were appointed to a board of control formed to oversee both loans. The second loan, issued in the hopes of stabilizing the first, was still by all accounts squandered: it went mostly toward purchasing steamboats built with British parts and overpriced frigates from the United States.

Today the names of Romantic poets such as Byron and Shelley are usually not thought of in conjunction with such high-level financial intrigue. Yet thus it was that a committee founded on principles of philhellenism became deeply embroiled in the first Greek debt crisis, which began within months of the birth of the Greek state. Philhellenes who idealized ancient Greece and idolized Lord Byron, himself a member of the committee, midwifed Greece's rebirth with their financial speculation. Within just a few years, the committee became mired in scandal because of its mismanagement of the loans. Greece seemed to be failing to establish a constitution rooted in liberal Enlightenment principles, and the committee's initial enthusiasm soon gave way to doubt, disinterest, and worry over lost investments. In 1826, the short-lived London Greek Committee disbanded, and in 1828 the First Hellenic Republic defaulted on the independence loans, which philhellenes had brokered at great expense to Greece.

Efforts by artists, writers, and statesmen throughout Europe also immensely helped raise public awareness about the war and inspire sympathy for the Greeks. In the United States, Edward Everett, a German-educated classicist and major politician, was just one of many philhellenes to give speeches in support of the revolutionaries; in France, the Romantic painter Eugène Delacroix cultivated sympathy for the Greek people with canvases that included his enormous (over thirteen feet tall) 1824 *Scène des massacres de Scio,* a bleak and heartrending depiction of an 1822 Ottoman massacre on the island of Chios. On January 19, 1824, American congressman Daniel Webster delivered a speech in the

U.S. House of Representatives urging the passage of a motion he had made at the end of the previous year to dispatch money and an envoy to Greece in support of the struggle for independence. Together with Mavrocordatos's plea for British aid and Shelley's preface to *Hellas,* that speech is one of the earliest clear articulations of a country's perceived debt to Greece. In it, Webster listed a number of American inheritances from the ancient Greeks: "This free form of government, this popular assembly, the common council held for the common good. . . . This practice of free debate and public discussion." "Even the edifice in which we assemble," he pleaded, "these proportioned columns, this ornamented architecture, all remind us that Greece has existed, and that we, like the rest of mankind, are greatly her debtors."[39] The concept of the West's classical debt had finally found its feet.

The previous year, in 1823, the United States had, however, adopted a principle of nonintervention in internal European affairs as part of the Monroe Doctrine. In light of that policy, Webster's motion was ultimately defeated. As in the case of Britain, though, American national politics did not prevent individuals from making private interventions. Roughly a thousand men from Europe and North America—many of them self-proclaimed philhellenes, but many others mercenary soldiers out of work since the end of the Napoleonic Wars—journeyed to join the Greeks. A third of them never returned home; some died in battle, but far more died, like Byron, after succumbing to disease. On April 19, 1824, Byron passed away after an excruciating fever. He is still remembered as a freedom fighter in Greece, where many streets and living men bear his name.

On July 6, 1827, all the Great Powers finally agreed to the prospect of military intervention in Greece's war. Together they signed the Treaty of London for the "pacification of Greece." The treaty's terms dictated that the Ottoman Empire recognize Greece's independence, but also that the Greeks accept the Ottoman sultan as "Lord paramount" of their land. Confident in the strength of their forces, the Ottomans refused to sign. On October 20, 1827, the navies of the Great Powers clashed with the Ottoman and Egyptian armadas in the Bay of Navarino, off the western coast of the Peloponnese. The result was a spectacular Ottoman defeat, and by the end of 1828 Britain, France, and Russia began to agree among themselves to a series of protocols that called for the creation of an autonomous Greek state confirmed by a *firman* of the sultan.

When the Great Powers finally resolved to back the creation of a fully independent state in 1829, they also determined that it would be ruled by an absolute, hereditary monarch of their choosing. Their choice fell on an unlikely figure: with the backing of Britain, France, and Russia and a ratifying vote by the newly formed Greek National Assembly, on February 6, 1833, a seventeen-year old named Otto, the second son of King Ludwig I of Bavaria, arrived in Greece, escorted by the British navy, to assume his crown. Greece was nominally free but under Europe's control. No longer beholden to the Ottoman sultan, Greece found a new ruler in Europe's appointed prince, a teenager whose vision for his new Athens would depend in equal parts on Johann Winckelmann's fantasies, the neoclassical movement sparked by James Stuart and Nicholas Revett, and the ancient pillars of the Athenian brand.

CHAPTER FIVE

Greek Miracle 2.0

THE FLOWERING OF PHILOSOPHY, literature, art, architecture, and democracy in classical Greece is often called the "Greek miracle," a phrase that began to gain currency in the second half of the nineteenth century. One of the first to use it was the scholar Joseph Ernest Renan, the first professor of Hebrew at the Collège de France and an influential theorist of nationhood, race, and the virtues of French imperialism's "civilizing mission." In an 1883 autobiography, *Souvenirs d'enfance et de jeunesse* (Memories of childhood and youth), Renan wrote of an epiphany that he experienced on the Acropolis in 1865. It was then, in the course of a sojourn in Athens, that he had a revelation of *le miracle grec,* "a thing which has existed only once, which had never been seen before, which will never be seen again, but the effect of which will last for ever, an eternal type of beauty, without a single blemish."[1] His account is a testament to the peculiar power that classical Athens has enjoyed to make itself felt for generations of modern admirers, however accidental or unsuspecting; as one scholar has put it, "Standing on the Acropolis, Renan adopts the same stance as his ancient Athenian counterparts—he comes to regard all other civilizations as equally crude and barbarian."[2] Since the late 1800s, Renan's notion of an ancient Greek miracle has been elaborated, challenged, rejected, and reinvented many times over, but the phrase has also managed to find a permanent home in our vocabulary.

Another, very different kind of Greek miracle—hailed as a modern economic miracle—began in the middle of the twentieth century. From 1950 to the early 1970s, Greece experienced a generation of thrilling prosperity and earned the title of fastest-growing economy in Europe. A second, truly miraculous, wave of affluence rolled in again in the early years of the new millennium. Between 2001, when Greece adopted the euro, and the peak of the country's most recent economic boom— just before the wave broke, with disastrous consequences, at the end of 2009—the country's gross domestic product (GDP) increased by more than 250 percent. The idea of an ancient Greek miracle has had its critics, but by all accounts this latest one really was too good to be true. With the help of some creative accountants, the Greek government had concealed massive amounts of debt to meet the European Union's conditions for entering the Eurozone.

By the end of the decade, the jig was up, but in the meantime Greece had lived a new dream, however illusory, as a European success story. In that dream's vivid last hours, antiquity—or really a Western fantasy of antiquity—played a starring role in two spectacular moments of international theater. The first was the 2004 Summer Olympics in Athens; the second was the opening of the New Acropolis Museum in

June 2009. On both of those occasions, each coordinated with a global audience in mind, the brand image that Greece presented was a whitewashed fantasy of the classical past. At its heart, this was a version of the fiction that we watched develop in Chapters 3 and 4: the idea that Periclean Athens really had been everything the ancient Athenians claimed it was; that ancient Greece was the most enlightened civilization the world had ever known; and that the best way forward for modern Greece—and for the European West—was to revive something of its spirit.

The path that led Greece from independence to the Eurozone was long and difficult: through regional wars, world wars, and civil war and through democracy and dictatorship. Yet in the tumultuous decades and centuries that followed independence, Greece shaped its modern identity to the mold of the ancient fantasy cast by European scholars, travelers, and philhellenes. In this chapter, we will see how that fantasy continued to evolve once the state was formed. We will take a rapid tour through modern Greek history, pausing at a handful of moments that each served to thrust the country and its classical past into the international spotlight. At each of those moments, certain of the country's leaders strove to embrace and enact aspects of the classicism that Europe had come to project onto Greece. We will see Athens rebuilt, literally, at the hands of European kings, German architects, and Greek archeologists in attempts to revive its Periclean grandeur. We will also witness the city reinvented in the twentieth century as the mythical birthplace of Western values, when liberal democracy in the Anglo-American mode became articulated as the greatest source of the West's debt to Greece.

The course of nearly two centuries of Greek independence finally culminated in the exuberant celebrations of the first decade of the twenty-first century. Together, the Olympics and the unveiling of the New Acropolis Museum appeared to mark the brilliant but logical endpoint of a long and difficult journey. Toward the end of the third millennium's first decade, it seemed that Greece was wholly commanding, fully in control, of the great ancient past to which its people were heirs and to which the country owed statehood. In retrospect, it is difficult not to look back on the two events as the miracle's unintended farewell celebrations. Just six months after the New Acropolis Museum opened, Greece's credit rating was downgraded by all three major rating agencies, the first clear sign that a wondrous age would soon be succeeded by a new era of crisis.

ATHENS GETS A FACELIFT

In the first years of Greek independence, the administration of the young Bavarian king Otto undertook a program to modernize Athens and erase the many architectural layers that had shaped and altered its appearance in the centuries that had passed since antiquity. The first seeds of this transformation were sown even before the War of Independence broke out in 1821 by the Filomousos Etaireia (Society of Friends of the Muses). The society was founded in 1813 for its own manner of revolutionary purpose: to educate Greeks along European models and promote philhellenism more generally. About half of its first members were Greek, most of them Athenian intellectual elites. The majority of the other members were British, with a handful from elsewhere in Europe. Some had pasts as exporters of antiquities, which they justified on the grounds that spiriting antiquities out of Greece was the best hope for their preservation. The position of the society, however, was that artifacts had to be kept in Greece, where they would be used to educate future generations of the budding state. Language in its constitution explicitly tied the recovery and collection of antiquities to broader purposes of education. Article 4 stipulated that funds would be raised to "serve the purpose of enlightening the Greek spirit of the young through the study of sciences, publications of useful books, help for poor students, discovery of antiquities, collection of stone inscriptions, statues and utensils and of anything else worthy of attention."[3] Article 9 held that members of the society would assist visiting travelers by accompanying them to ancient monuments and offering them any help that they required—short, of course, of shipping artifacts out of Greece. Before long, the society was effectively operating as Greece's first archeological superintendency.

The charter mission of the Filomousos Etaireia reflected the new significance of material artifacts in the context of Greek independence, when they were reimagined as a vital, physical link between the people and their ancient ancestors. Previously, homes and other buildings had been constructed in and around ruins. Inscriptions, even funerary headstones, were regularly transformed into paving stones, while ancient sarcophagi proved handy vessels for water storage. Early European travelers had expressed shock at this casual repurposing of artifacts, even though antiquities removed from Greece also had a habit of turning up at British manors as mantelpieces and garden decorations. Now, they were pressed into the service of nation building as they came to be viewed as proof of the continuity of Hellenic civilization from antiquity to the present day. The existence of ancient Greek relics and ruins on any given piece of land further testified that the land had historically been inhabited by Greeks and so rightly belonged to the country of Greece. Archeologist Yannis Hamilakis has formulated just why the location, collection, and preservation of antiquities became one of the most urgent endeavors of the newborn state. Although ancient stories and texts certainly played a part in nation building, "it was the materiality of ancient sites, buildings, remnants, and artefacts, their physicality, visibility, tangible nature, and embodied presence, that provided the objective (in both senses of the word) reality of the nation."[4] Even while the War of Independence was still ongoing, the provisional government of the First Hellenic Republic passed a resolution that officially nationalized all antiquities. The same order, issued on February 8, 1826, also charged the Filomousos Etaireia with acquiring ancient artifacts and keeping them safe.

When Europe installed Prince Otto of Bavaria on the throne, the country, though ostensibly independent, embarked on what in practical terms was another period of foreign rule. Because King Otto was so young when he was made king, three regents were chosen from the court of his father, King Ludwig I of Bavaria, and appointed to govern on Otto's behalf. In Greece today, the term *Bavarokratia* (Bavarian rule) is often used to refer to this regency period (1832–1835); sometimes it is applied to the entirety of Otto's reign. Like the parallel terms *Frankokratia* (the period when European crusaders ruled Greece) and *Turkokratia* (the era of Turkish, Ottoman rule), the word conjures up memories of another period of Greek captivity by foreigners and still has bitter associations.

Plans for a redesigned Athens began to take shape even before the city was officially inaugurated as the country's new capital. In 1828, during the War of Independence, Greek revolutionary forces captured Nauplio, a port town in the northeast of the Peloponnese, and declared it their capital. Nauplio was thus Otto's capital, too, when he assumed the throne in 1832. By 1834, he and his regents had transferred the government seat to Athens. At that time, Athens was, both politically and practically, an insignificant town; its population in 1821 is estimated to have been around 12,000. European travelers often remarked that it resembled an African village: it was dotted with palm

An 1819 aquatint by Edward Dodwell (1767–1832) of a view of the Parthenon before Greek independence.

trees, and camels and donkeys were the chief means of transport over the steep and narrow streets. Yet the city's historical importance and symbolic significance were too much for the Bavarians to resist, and there is little doubt that the young king dreamed of positioning himself, from his seat in Athens, as a new Pericles for a new and glorious Greek age.

In May 1832, Stamatios Cleanthes and Eduard Schaubert were commissioned by the provisional government to prepare a design for the city. Cleanthes was a Greek veteran of the War of Independence; Schaubert was a Prussian architect. Both were trained at Berlin's Bauakedemie (Academy of Architecture) by Karl Friedrich Schinkel, the neoclassical architect largely responsible for transforming Berlin, in the aftermath of the Napoleonic Wars, from a hodgepodge of chaotic medieval quarters into a modern capital city. Cleanthes and Schaubert's proposal was approved by the same decree of the provisional government that announced the capital's transfer. The extent of Schinkel's direct contribution to Cleanthes and Schaubert's plans is unclear, but those plans bore the unmistakable influence of his neoclassical reenvisioning of Berlin.

Cleanthes and Schaubert's design ultimately turned out to be too ambitious and costly, in large part because it called for enormous and expensive government expropriation of private property. Otto's father sent one of his favorite court architects, Leo von Klenze, to revise the plans. Klenze's work in Munich had already made him one of Europe's most influential proponents of neoclassicism. In Greece, his first order of business was to see to the protection of actual ancient monuments, and he immediately set about devising a program for conservation and restoration of the Acropolis. Meanwhile, Schinkel drafted plans to construct a new royal palace for Otto atop the Acropolis. The plan was fueled by the site's obvious symbolic appeal but was rejected on both practical and ideological grounds: the rocky citadel had no water source, and King Ludwig was insistent that nothing new be built among the ancient monuments. (Schinkel, in the tradition of many German Hellenic idealists, never set foot in Athens.) In the end, the honor of designing Otto's new palace went to yet another Bavarian court architect, Friedrich von Gärtner. In 1835, Ludwig turned up in Athens with Gärtner in tow; in January 1836, the king of Bavaria ceremonially laid the foundation stone for a new neoclassical palace, now the Hellenic Parliament.

In 1839, after Otto had dismissed his regents, work on his Othonian University, today's National and Kapodistrian University of Athens, began. The main university building was designed by Otto's court architect, Hans Christian Hansen of Denmark. Together with the Academy of Athens and the National Library of Greece, both by Hansen's brother, Theophil, these structures are known as the city's "trilogy." Theophil is

Idealized view of classical Athens as imagined by architect Leo von Klenze (1784–1864) (oil on canvas, 1846).

most famous today for Vienna's Austrian Parliament building, another grand neoclassical structure built to evoke both the grandeur of ancient temples and classical Athenian democracy.

Under the rule of King Otto, this whole host of new buildings served to project a European fantasy of classicism onto the city. A two-pronged program called for the demolition of postclassical structures and the building of a number of new civic buildings. Greece's rulers aimed both to revive the city's splendorous classical appearance and to transform it into a respectable European royal capital. The new structures were designed according to the principles of the Greek Revival, the architectural movement sparked in the second half of the eighteenth century largely by the detailed illustrations of James Stuart and Nicholas Revett's *Antiquities of Athens*. In a sense, then, the Hellenic Parliament

The Academy of Athens (built 1859–1885), part of the neoclassical trilogy by the Hansen brothers of Denmark.

building and the city's trilogy are copies of copies of imaginary models originally inspired by Athens's own ruins. This European neoclassical vision for Athens led to some very impractical urban planning. In the early twentieth century, the British journalist William Miller wryly noted that "wide, shadeless streets and the glare of the marble houses may not be so well suited as narrow lanes and Turkish buildings to the heat of the summer." "It might have been better," he observed, "if the plan of modern Athens had been made in Byzantium rather than in Germany."[5]

As new, classically inspired buildings went up around the city, older ones were cleared away in a program of architectural and archeological "purification." *Katharevousa,* the "purified" version of Greek advanced by Adamantios Koraïs, was designed to purge the foreign "barbarisms" that had, over millennia, invaded the Greek language. A similar ideology motivated new plans to tear down and scrub away several centuries' worth of material traces that foreign, "barbaric" peoples had left in Greece's physical landscape. Otto's circle of advisers and architects eagerly adopted the view that Athens would have to be rid of those more undesirable layers of history. One of Klenze's first proposals was to remove all postclassical structures from the Acropolis and to dismantle and demolish even the Byzantine monuments— churches among them—in the neighboring quarters below it. Klenze himself played master of ceremonies when Otto inaugurated the Parthenon restoration program on August 28, 1834. The details of that occasion have been masterfully laid out by architectural historian Eleni Bastéa. In a highly choreographed pageant, local girls, dressed in a German fantasy of ancient Athenian attire (all white, of course), surrounded Otto and Klenze as Otto enthroned himself at the Parthenon. Amid the Bavarian pomp and circumstance—the crowd was greeted by a military band—Klenze delivered a speech in German in which he made an ambitious promise to the king: "Your Majesty . . . all the remains of barbarity will be removed, here as in all Greece, and the remains of the glorious past will be brought in new light, as the solid foundation of a glorious present and future."[6] This speech was tantamount to a declaration that from that time onward, Greece's antiquities would rest in the hands of the state.

In 1835, the same year in which King Otto ousted his unpopular Bavarian council of regents and became absolute monarch, demolition of the Acropolis began under the direction of Ludwig Ross, Otto's head conservator. Soon, new institutions were founded with the purpose of uncovering and preserving the old relics of the new nation. The Archeological Society at Athens and its journal, *Arkhaiologiki Efimeris* (Archeological journal), were established in 1837; for nearly a quarter of a century, the periodical would remain an official state publication.

The purification program that began in earnest under Ross, today remembered as Greece's first official superintendent of antiquities, was later continued by the Archeological Society. The task was massive: the Acropolis was thick with rubble and ruins, mortar shells, garbage, debris, and even the occasional human bone. Progress on the site's ritual cleansing was slow but steady. In 1837, a medieval castle nestled in and around the gateway to the Acropolis was dismantled and carted away. In 1842, one of the most offensive structures, the mosque in the Parthenon, at which Evliya Çelebi had marveled when he visited Athens (see Chapter 3), was entirely removed except for the lower part of its minaret. A few decades later, the rest of the minaret would also disappear, along with the "Frankish Tower" that had dominated the Acropolis's skyline for centuries. Between 1834 and 1854, the first phase of *anastilosis,* or reconstruction of ancient monuments, also began for the Acropolis's most famous Periclean buildings: the Parthenon, the Erechtheion, the Propylaea, and the Temple of Athena Nike.

The efforts made in these decades to unearth, rebuild, and showcase the golden age of Periclean Athens were carried out by Europeans and by Greek intellectuals who had, until just recently, been living abroad in Europe. The program was not met with universal support, and many of Athens's longtime residents reasonably feared that they stood to lose their property and livelihoods in the name of historical preservation. In recent decades, archeologists and historians have been able to uncover and piece together the story of how officials in Otto's Greece executed their purification of the Acropolis and of other ancient sites despite this resistance. That story has been documented in detail by Yannis Hamilakis, whose *The Nation and Its Ruins* underscores the ceremonial nature and purpose behind the destruction and removal of the postclassical buildings. There he calls the process a "ritual purification of the site from what were seen as the remnants of 'barbarism' and the material manifestations of the occupation of Greece by foreign invaders."[7] The irony, of course, was that all this work was carried out under the direction of Greece's latest wave of foreign invaders, Otto's Bavarian court.

One vivid account of the Acropolis's purification is recounted in an illustrated children's book on sale in the bookstore of the New Acropolis Museum. Eleni Hadjoudi-Tounta's *Adventures of the Acropolis Marbled Girls* ("a true story that took place on the rock of the Acropolis") makes, like many other children's books for sale in that gift shop, an emotional plea to children and their parents for the return of the Elgin Marbles from the British Museum. The richly illustrated book is set during the reign of King Otto; its main character is Zissis Sotiriou, a Serbian who fought for Greece in the War of Independence and later became a guardian of antiquities on the Acropolis. In the story, Sotiriou approaches Kyriakos Pittakis, Greece's first superintendent of antiquities, and asks to be allowed to serve as a guard of the Acropolis's ruins. Sotiriou promises Pittakis, "I will help to turn [i.e., tear] down all the Turkish houses and mosques that have been erected on the rock."[8] Soon after Pittakis grants Sotiriou's request, the Erechtheion's caryatids, Sotiriou's "daughters," confide in him that they have received word of their sister's whereabouts in the British Museum. "She feels loneliness. . . . She thinks of you day and night. She is trapped, however, like a partridge in the trap. She wants to be near you again. She does not like to get old in a terrible wet place. I have also seen the spots she has from parasites, since she lives without any sun and light in this foreign country. She is crying each time she remembers you."[9] Like most historical books meant for children, *Adventures of the Acropolis Marbled Girls* is simple and direct. Its casual references to Lord Elgin's "theft" and the Greeks' condition of slavery under the Ottomans, coupled with its celebration of Zissis Sotiriou and his offer to aid in the Acropolis's purification, make for a powerful reflection of how deeply archeology is still entwined with nationalism and national memory today. The early chapters in the archeological history of the modern Greek state, so marked by concern for restoring Greece's classical "purity," did much to program Greece's identity as an independent country: they shaped abiding memories of Greece's centuries under the "Turkish yoke," of the barbarism that had to be exorcised from the landscape, and of the damage, both literal and symbolic, that Elgin and other foreigners like him had wrought.

UNEARTHING THE NATION

As enthusiastic as he was about restoring Athens and ruling Greece, King Otto had a rocky time during his reign. He loved Greece and the Greek people but knew very well that the feeling was far from mutual. In 1843, fairly early in his reign, unrest over his absolute monarchy nearly set off another revolution. A crowd led by Yannis Makriyannis, a hero of the War of Independence, gathered in the square in front of the palace and demanded to be granted a constitution; the site is now Athens's iconic Syntagma (Constitution) Square. The next year, in 1844, the "Great Idea" that dominated Greek foreign policy (and spending) into the twentieth century was at last fully formulated. In Chapter 4 we saw the first stirrings toward that plan in the form of Rigas Velestinilis's radical and enormous (in all senses) map of a liberated Greece. The Great Idea made its formal debut in a speech by Ioannis Kolettis, an influential member of Parliament. Kolettis claimed that "the Kingdom of Greece is not Greece" but only "one part, the smallest and the poorest." He argued that Greece in its truest, most whole sense boasted "two main centers of Hellenism: Athens, the capital of the Greek kingdom, [and] 'The City' [Constantinople], the dream and hope of all Greeks." As one Greek cultural historian points out, Kolettis's speech is a mismatch with Western visions of Greece, "which place Athens at their center": Athens might stand as a metonym in the West for Greek classical antiquity, but in this formative era of nationhood, "Constantinople became the symbol of an imaginary Panhellenic union organized on the common ground of the Greek language and the Orthodox faith."[10] This expansive vision of Greece's rightful borders was one that King Otto was eager to pursue.

Over the next two decades, Otto's relationship with his subjects nevertheless deteriorated. Meanwhile, Britain and France, two of the European Great Powers to which he owed his throne, were rankled by his conspiring to side with Russia in the Crimean War as part of maneuvers to realize the dream of the Great Idea. The unrest finally came to a head in October 1862, when the king departed from Athens with his wife, Queen Amalia—the target of an assassination attempt two years earlier—on a tour of the Peloponnese. One of the aims of the trip was for the royal couple to connect with their people, but the situation was already beyond repair. In their absence from Athens, a coup was launched; Otto and Amalia tried to return to their palace but were blocked by their own royal navy at the port of Piraeus. The *Bavarokratia* had come to an end, and Otto returned, brokenhearted, to Bavaria. Soon the Great Powers installed another European prince on the throne: George of Denmark, who would rule from 1863 until his death in 1913. Otto died in 1867; legend has it that with his last breath he called out, "Griechenland, mein Griechenland, mein liebes Griechenland" (Greece, my Greece, my beloved Greece). He was buried, on his instructions, in Greek national costume.

During both Otto's and George's reigns, Greece witnessed enormous efforts to restore, curate, and preserve the nation's antiquities and newly designated archeological sites. Yet it also saw waves of resistance to the government's aspirations to a new "Europeanness." Some Greek intellectuals called on their compatriots to reject European notions of classicism and instead to study and interpret the ancient texts for themselves—after all, those texts had been written in Greek. Provoked, in part, by a new theory that the Greeks were not "Greek" after all (discussed later in this chapter), many thinkers in Greece turned to the crafting of national historical narratives. Those narratives attempted to rectify views of Greek history that owed much to the ideology of philhellenism and saw the two millennia between classical antiquity and the modern nation-state as a long dark age in Greek history, marked only by continued decline and the spread of Eastern, Oriental lethargy.

Kyriakos Pittakis, the superintendent of antiquities in the children's story about the caryatids, is remembered as the man who founded the institution of Greek national archeology in the formative years of the state. He was a veteran of the War of Independence and the figure who, during the war, allegedly arranged to send more ammunition to the Ottoman forces atop the Acropolis rather than see the Parthenon's columns destroyed for the metal inside them. That story may well be apocryphal and seems to have originated with the funeral oration that the poet and statesman Alexandros Rangavis delivered at Pittakis's funeral on October 24, 1863. By all accounts, however, Pittakis really was tireless in his devotion to protecting antiquities. Leo von Klenze remembered that whenever Pittakis "saw anyone approach [antiquities], he leapt in the greatest anxiety over stick and stone to the place where the greatest danger threatened."[11] In 1863, the last year of his service as superintendent, Pittakis revived Klenze's dream of building an Acropolis museum. He also greatly expanded the activity of the Archeological Society of Athens (which he had helped found) outside Athens and Attica. He personally oversaw the first excavations at the Peloponnesian site of Mycenae, the fabled home of King Agamemnon, the Homeric hero killed by his wife, Clytemnestra, when he returned home from the Trojan War.

In the mid-nineteenth century, foreign archeological schools also began to crop up in Athens. The first, the École française d'Athènes, was founded in 1846 by decree of King Louis Philippe I "for the study of language, history, and Greek antiquities." The school was largely an outgrowth of European Hellenism; Théophile Homolle, the director of the school from 1891 to 1903, attributed its existence "to two revolutions: political and literary; the Greek revolution and the revolution of Romanticism."[12] Not to be outdone, by the end of the nineteenth century, the Germans (1874), Americans (1881), British (1886), and Austrians (1898) had all established their own institutions. Today, seventeen countries have national archeological schools headquartered in Athens, and many of those schools have satellite branches at major excavation sites elsewhere in Greece. They are officially recognized by the Greek government, and one of their most important roles is to facilitate the granting of (limited and therefore much-coveted) state-issued archeological permits. Over their histories, the schools have also served as political and intelligence bases for their home countries' maneuvering in the region. By the second half of the nineteenth century, the French school was grooming future diplomats; in the twentieth century, especially during World War II, members of the schools were called on to aid their governments in gathering intelligence. The director of the German Archeological Institute in Athens, Walter Wrede, was even head of the Nazi Party in Greece. Who, after all, knew the local terrain better than an archeologist?

In 1882, a year after the American school was founded in Athens, Pittakis's successor, Panayiotis Evstratiadis, renewed the efforts to clear debris and remove postclassical structures from the Acropolis. Evstratiadis had been trained as a classical philologist in Germany and served as Greece's superintendent of antiquities for two decades, from 1864 until 1884. Under his watch, an architectural competition was announced to secure plans for a national archeological museum. In 1829, Ioannis Kapodistrias, Greece's first prime minister, had established a temporary museum for the nation's antiquities on Aegina, an island about seventeen miles to the southwest of Athens. The collections were nevertheless still in need of a permanent home. Construction of a museum in the capital finally began in 1866, early in the reign of Greece's King George I. At about the same time, work also started on a museum of the Acropolis. This first museum was completed in 1874 and was (unlike the new one) actually situated atop the Acropolis, built discreetly into the rock bed. The first Greek National Archeological Museum finally opened its doors fifteen years later. Its plan was based on a German architect's neoclassical design, which was then modified by Panagis Kalkos, the chief architect in charge of construction. Kalkos was Athenian but had also been trained in Munich in the principles of neoclassicism.

Meanwhile, the excavation efforts of Evstratiadis and his successor, Panayiotis Kavvadias, had vastly increased the need for new storage and exhibition space. Archeological finds on the Acropolis accumulated along with towering piles of rubble as teams under the superintendents' direction hewed down to the bedrock at the base of the Periclean-era monuments. In the process, archeologists discovered thousands of pieces of sculptures and monuments. In 1886, Kavvadias's team hit on

View of the Acropolis ca. 1880, with considerable mounds of earth piled up by archeological work carried out under Kyriakos Pittakis, Greece's first superintendent of antiquities.

a second cache of Persian rubble (the *Perserschutt* mentioned in Chapter 2). The most exciting find was a collection of fourteen statues of young girls, *korai,* which had been broken during the Persian sack of the city in 480 BCE and then ritually buried by the Athenians. Many in Europe reacted with excitement, but some were dismayed that these *korai* did not match their fantasy of the ancient Athenians' superb aesthetic—a fantasy inherited largely, of course, from interpretations of Winckelmann's writing on the Greek ideal. In a 1901 essay titled "Athènes antique," French political theorist, poet, and critic Charles Maurras expressed dismay at the girls' gaudy and "Oriental" appearance. "But what!" he wrote, "so the Athens of the Pisistratids, that Athens which saw the first critical edition of Homer, was a city without taste after all? The women went around loaded up with ridiculous ornaments? . . . Alas! I said: won't someone rid me of these Chinese girls!"[13]

Maurras's exclamation reflected his indignation over the *korai* and their fracturing of his fantasy of classical Athens and Athenians. A few generations before, early in the history of the Greek state, a much larger scandal had erupted in Greece when Jakob Philipp Fallmerayer, a historian from the Tyrol (in today's northeastern Italy), introduced a new theory about the "true" ethnicity of contemporary Greeks. Like Winckelmann, Fallmerayer was a brilliant scholar of humble origins. His parents were farmers, and as a young man Fallmerayer supported himself by working as a shepherd. After serving Bavaria in the Napoleonic Wars, he became a professor and scholar of history. In 1830, the first volume of his *Geschichte der Halbinsel Morea während des Mittelalters* (History of the Morea Peninsula in the Middle Ages) appeared. The work caused an uproar; it opened with the pronouncement that "the race of the Hellenes has been eradicated in Europe" and argued that during the "barbarian invasions" of late antiquity, the native Greeks had been completely wiped out of the Peloponnese. Fallmerayer maintained that the area was later repopulated not by Greeks but by Slavic peoples from the north. The consequence? No drop of pure "Hellenic" blood flowed in Greece's contemporary Christian population.

The book hit a nerve in Greece, where the entire identity of the brand-new nation seemed to depend on the premise of continuity with antiquity. Fallmerayer's ghost is often said to haunt the Greek people to this day. A century and a half after the hypothesis was introduced, it found a new lease on life in the lead-up to the June 1986 Oxford Union debate about the Elgin Marbles. At the debate, Melina Mercouri expressed her outrage over this "new theory" about the Greek people's racial makeup: "Of late, a new theory has been proposed, this one is a

beauty. Mr. Gavin Stamp, I shall have the honor of meeting him tonight, proposes the notion that modern Greeks are not descendants of
Pericles. Wow! Our marbles have been taken. Who will lay claim to
the bones of our ancestors?"[14] In a piece titled "Keeping Our Marbles,"
which ran in the December 10, 1983, issue of the conservative British
magazine *Spectator,* Gavin Stamp, an architectural historian and Mercouri's debate opponent, had essentially reformulated Fallmerayer's
premise when he argued that modern Greece "has very little connection with the nation and people who carved the marbles and who
designed that refined and sophisticated building to which they were
once fixed." Stamp went right for the national jugular in declaring that
"racially . . . the present inhabitants of Greece are not descended from
the race of Pericles. As with the rest of Europe, the southern tip of
the Balkan peninsula has seen many migrations and population movements over the last two thousand years."[15] Despite what Mercouri
claimed, then, Stamp's theory was far from new.

Fallmerayer is not a household name among historians today, but
his thesis is still cited (as we will see in Chapter 6) to dismiss the notion that modern Greeks have any legitimate ties to ancient ones. In
Fallmerayer's day, his ideas provoked enormous reaction and a great
deal of reflection. Various Greek strains of rebuttal quickly appeared:
some denounced his claims as mean spirited and historically inaccurate; others were prompted to work to build a new understanding of
the *longue durée* of Greek history that was more nuanced than the state's
antiquity-driven narrative. Fallmerayer maintained that Byzantium
was, by definition, an inferior civilization because its people's blood
and character were Slavic. He personally harbored suspicions about
continued Russian ambitions to resurrect Byzantium: Russia, to his
mind, was the dangerous last outpost of Byzantine imperial autoc-
racy. Greece's medieval history had, it is true, been a source of embar-

rassment for certain Greek thinkers of the European Enlightenment, especially those who, like Adamantios Koraïs, saw the church and its clergy as representing barbarism on a par with that shown by the Ottomans. Nevertheless, scholars in recent decades have stressed how the Orthodox religion and the church so associated with the Byzantine legacy played a foundational role in the orientation of the new national consciousness. Despite the patriarchate's official prohibition of the revolution, many of the clergy had supported it. Even King Otto embraced this aspect of his people's history: after all, the rallying cry of the War of Independence had been "For Christ's holy faith and the freedom of the fatherland!"

The early decades of independence generally saw lively and often vitriolic debates about the nature of Greek identity. One 1842 article in the short-lived periodical *Evropaïkos Eranistis* (European compiler) explicitly posed a new, seemingly crucial, question: "What is Greece? East or West?" The author began with the reflection that "perhaps this question seems, at first glance, uninteresting," but "any politically engaged man who does not concern himself with studying and answering this question is like a sailor who sails the ocean with neither map nor compass." The real issue, he argued, was whether European civilization was foreign and antithetical to Greece or already and innately Greek, given that the origins of European values and aesthetics lay in Greek antiquity. The "East" in his conception was, of course, not the "Oriental," Ottoman East, but Orthodox Russia—Samuel P. Huntington's Orthodox Civilization, a direct descendant of Byzantium. "West," by contrast, was a byword for Britain and France. The author compared his question to the riddle of the Sphinx—"Whoever does not solve it is destroyed"—but coyly spent twenty-five pages arguing that Greek identity lay somewhere between the two poles. This unsigned article was written by a budding philosopher and historian named Markos Renieres.

When he wrote the essay, he was twenty-seven years old; twenty-five years later, in 1867, he became governor of the National Bank of Greece.

Fallmerayer's shocking theory provided Greek thinkers with a new impetus for finding ways of incorporating Byzantium—Greece's "Eastern" legacy—into an overarching historical narrative that still emphasized the endurance and continuity of the Hellenic people. The historian (and novelist and poet) Spiridion Zampelios provided an influential framework for rethinking the character and role of Byzantium. In his 1857 *Byzantine Studies,* he proposed a tripartite division of Greek history into ancient, medieval, and modern periods. Within his schema, Byzantium no longer represented a decline from or rupture with the glories of antiquity. Instead, Greece's medieval ages marked an era of fruitful cultural production, during which Christianity creatively refashioned and gave fresh expression to ancient civilization. Zampelios coined the adjective *hellenochristianikos* (Helleno-Christian) to describe the single Greek identity that had been born of antiquity and Christianity alike. His division of historical periods was soon adopted by Constantine Paparrigopoulos, a professor at the University of Athens and the historian remembered today as the father of Greek national historiography. Paparrigopoulos's five-volume *History of the Greek Nation from Antiquity to Modern Times,* published over the course of 1860–1874, accounted for the whole of Greek history in a single, continuous narrative that fully incorporated and valued the rise of Christianity and the age of the Byzantine Empire.

WHERE ARE YOUR BEAUTIFUL OLYMPIC GAMES?

Even as Greek intellectuals strove to broaden the public's appreciation of a greater expanse of Greek history, works to "purify" the Acropolis of its postclassical, foreign "barbarisms" continued apace. By 1890, the project was more or less complete, but against the background of that national success the government's finances were starting to crumble. In 1878, after more than a decade of negotiations, the Great Powers had finally arranged a settlement between Greece and the bondholders who remained from the era of the Independence Loans, brokered between the provisional Greek government and foreign lenders early in the War of Independence (see Chapter 4). Soon the country began to borrow from Europe again, and throughout the 1880s it did so at a frenetic pace. Much of the money from these loans went toward infrastructure improvements, but Greece also used the injection of funds to expand its military power in anticipation of war with Ottoman Turkey, since it continued to aspire to realize the dream of the Great Idea. The state's heavy borrowing, coupled with an unforeseen export crisis, soon spelled financial disaster.

In the late nineteenth century, Greece's largest industry was based on the export of currants, most of which were sold in European and American markets for use in the production of sweetening syrups (along the lines of today's corn syrup) and cheap alcoholic beverages. In 1893, vast overproduction of Greek currants, coupled with new restrictions introduced in major import markets abroad, resulted in the great "currant crisis." As the effects of the crisis spread to every level of Greek society, half of the government's budget had to go just toward servicing outstanding loans. On December 10, 1893, Greek prime minister Charilaos Trikoupis made a difficult admission in a speech before the Hellenic Parliament. In recent years, the media have delighted in dusting off his sound bite: "Unfortunately," Trikoupis pronounced, "we are bankrupt."

Just a few short years after this total economic collapse, Greece nevertheless managed to stage a major, enormously expensive international event. In 1896, Athens hosted the first Olympic Games held under the auspices of the newly formed International Olympic Committee. Decades earlier, in 1846, the Greek businessman and War of Independence veteran Evangelis Zappas had presented King Otto with an offer to fund a revival of the ancient games. Zappas's vision was largely inspired by Alexandros Soutsos, a Greek poet of Romanticism, who in 1833 had published a poem titled *Dialogue of the Dead* in the Greek newspaper *Helios*. In the poem, the ghost of the ancient Athenian philosopher Plato calls on Greece's modern people to revive their ancestors' ancient traditions: "Have you wretches pondered what your Hellas once was? Tell me, where are your ancient centuries? Where are your beautiful Olympic games?"[16]

Plato's pleadings aside, many Greeks were opposed to the idea: an ancient festival had no place in a modern and still-modernizing country. Antiathleticists proposed that Greece instead hold agricultural and industrial expositions to showcase more appropriately its modern identity as an industrialized European nation. Zappas was persistent and in 1856 published an article in *Helios* declaring his resolve to sponsor a revival out of his own pocket. King Otto eventually agreed to a compromise: Zappas could fund the games, but only in conjunction with the expositions. Zappas acted quickly to endow the Olympic Trust Fund, and in 1859 the first attempt at revived games saw contests in wrestling and track and field events. For well over a millennium in antiquity, the Olympic festival had always been held in honor of Zeus at his sanctuary of Olympia. Even today, Olympia, located in the northwest Peloponnese, is a long journey, nearly two hundred miles from Athens. Zappas's insistence on holding the "Olympian" revival in Athens reflected the Greek capital's role as the modern site and symbol of the entire ancient miracle.

In 1856, the games were nevertheless overshadowed by the national exposition that took place alongside them, a point often forgotten in modern accounts of the Olympics' history and revival. The expositions contributed enormously to the consolidation of a sense of unified Greek identity; they were the first such event to bring together Greeks from throughout the Mediterranean, including areas still under Ottoman control. When Zappas died in 1865, his cousin Konstantinos carried on his legacy of commitment to the athletic side of the event. By the second celebration of the games, in 1870, Athens's newly refurbished ancient stadium was ready to seat thirty thousand spectators. The complex had been reconstructed from the ruins of the stadium used for the athletic competitions at the ancient Panathenaea, a festival held in honor of the goddess Athena's birthday. The first modern restoration and rebuilding of the ancient Panathenaic stadium, a monument to the glory of classical Athens, was complemented by the construction of a neoclassical structure, the Zappeion. Named after the famous advocates of the games and located in Athens's National Garden, the Zappeion was inaugurated in time for the fourth games, in 1888. Its purpose was to host both indoor events and the expositions on which the antiathleticists, including Prime Minister Trikoupis, continued to insist. The building served as the press base at the 2004 games; today it is mostly used as a conference and exhibition center.

Early Greek movements to revive the Olympics reflected the growing interest in large-scale athletic games that was also stirring elsewhere in Europe: Greece's first international Olympics arose from a confluence of athletic movements of both nationalist and internationalist spirit. Beginning in 1850, for example, athletic contests meant to encourage physical activity among the working class had been organized around the small market town of Much Wenlock in northern England. In 1890, those games made a particular impression on one noteworthy spectator, Pierre de Coubertin, a French historian and longtime advocate of a large-scale Olympic revival. In 1894, Coubertin hosted a conference at the Sorbonne in Paris to present a proposal for a truly international set of contests. The conferees agreed to stage them in 1896 and after some debate decided unanimously that Athens would be the site. In Greece, the royal family welcomed the news. King George's son, Crown Prince Constantine, happily stepped in as president of the organizing committee. Despite financial difficulties—in what would prove to be the start of a great Olympic tradition, the cost of the games was much greater than budgeted—the opening ceremony was held on April 6, 1896. The day was symbolic: it fell on Easter Monday, the same day on which the country celebrated the seventy-fifth anniversary of its declaration of independence from the Ottoman Empire.

Amid the financial crisis caused in large part by the collapse of the currant market, Greece even managed to reconstruct the Panathenaic Stadium again, this time entirely in marble. Today the stadium is often simply referred to as Kallimarmaro, the "Beautiful Marble." Athletes from some fourteen nations came to compete; Prince Constantine gave a speech, and his father King George blessed the event. A large choir sang what is now known as the Olympic Hymn, with lyrics by the poet Kostis Palamas and music by the renowned opera composer Spyridon Samaras. One of the greatest causes of excitement was the debut of the marathon. The race was proposed by Michel Bréal, a renowned French linguist, philologist (he wrote major works on Iranian, Greek, and Latin grammar and mythology), and educational official. Bréal was inspired by the ancient story of the messenger Pheidippides; the story has a number of different versions, but the most famous one tells of how, after the Battle of Marathon in 490 BCE, he raced back to Athens, a distance of about twenty-five miles, to report news of the Greek victory to his fellow Athenians. In one ancient source, a work by the postclassical ancient Greek author Lucian, he delivered the news ("Joy to you, we've won!"), then died on the spot from fatigue. Still today, Bréal's race honors an Athenian messenger who brought news of the Persian defeat, a Greek triumph over "barbarism," in the Battle of Marathon.

In 1896, the outcome of the first modern marathon seemed a triumph of poetic justice. Its winner was Spyridon Louis, a twenty-three-year-old Greek water carrier who crossed the finish line ahead of twelve other contestants representing five different countries. Crowds were delighted; it was the first track and field win for Greece at the games, and it had happened in the most symbolically charged event. During the last part of the race, King George's sons, Constantine and George, joined Louis for his last lap. Louis later claimed that he paced his steps at the end of the race by chanting the Greek national anthem. His victory in the marathon—at the time referred to as the "Hellenic event"—was the highlight of the games, and as a trophy he was awarded a pure silver cup designed by Bréal himself.

The closing ceremony, held on the morning of April 12, was again presided over by the royal family. It featured the singing of an Olympic ode, composed and performed in Ancient Greek by the Oxford classical scholar and multievent competitor George Stuart Robertson (Robertson's discus throw of 25.19 meters at the games is the worst in Olympic history). In the end, the whole affair was hailed as a triumph and an enormous credit to its hosts. On the heels of humiliating bankruptcy, Greece had achieved a major public relations coup. Spectators and the media all agreed that the ancient athletic spirit—the spirit that had sculpted, both in flesh and in marble, the beautiful bodies of Winckelmann's Greek ideal—had been magnificently revived in Athens. A major tourist attraction, in a way these games also marked the major international debut of the newly purified Acropolis. One curious scholar who managed to catch part of the event was Basil

Lanneau Gildersleeve, the most renowned American classicist of his day. In a February 1897 article in the *Atlantic Monthly,* he delighted in his memory of how "the cry 'Zíto I Ellás!' (Long live Greece!) hallowed the new Olympic games." The exuberant slogan was one that the many foreign athletes and crowd members were apparently "quick to catch."[17] In 1896, the first Athenian Olympics celebrated the triumph of the country's tenacious ancient spirit over the recent financial collapse. In the summer of 2004, by contrast, Greece's Olympic organizers could never have guessed that a new debt crisis lay just around the corner.

COLD WAR CLASSICS

The twentieth century was marked in Greece, as it was in Britain, France, Germany, the United States, and elsewhere, by countless new engagements with Greek antiquity and controversies over its significance in the modern era. It was, however, the advent of the Cold War and the Greek Civil War that saw the most radical recasting since the Greek War of Independence of the West's self-avowed symbolic debt to Greece. In an 1824 speech before the House of Representatives, American congressman Daniel Webster had pleaded for U.S. intervention in the War of Independence by reciting a list of American inheritances from the ancient Greeks, "which all remind us that Greece has existed, and that we, like the rest of mankind, are greatly her debtors" (see Chapter 4). Strikingly absent from his list was the single word *democracy.* Webster named other aspects of the political process—"This free form of government, this popular assembly, the common council held for the common good"—but it was not until well over a century later that the single term *democracy* became a by-

word for the greatest legacy of classical Athens and the strongest jus-
ification for the West's classical debt.

World War II had arrived in Greece on October 28, 1940, when Ioannis Metaxas, general, prime minister, and dictator during Greece's
era of fascism from 1936 to 1941, refused to accede to Italy's demand of
unconditional surrender. Metaxas styled his regime as the "Third Hel-
enic Civilization," a synthesis of the aggressive militaristic ancient
societies of Greece and Alexander's Macedonia (the First Hellenic Civilization) and Byzantine Orthodox Christianity (the Second). Yet, despite
Metaxas's fascist ideology—his concept of the Third Hellenic Civilization largely mirrored the ideological underpinnings of Hitler's Third
Reich—by April 1941, German troops had conquered Athens and raised
the Nazi flag over the Acropolis. The Greek government, led by King
George II, went into exile.

The brutality of the occupation that followed has been attributed
in part to German disappointment at the reality of modern Greece and
Greeks. In 1935, a professor at the University of Cambridge named Eliza
Butler published an influential book titled *The Tyranny of Greece over Germany*.[18] In it, she claimed that ever since Winckelmann, the German
people had suffered from a consuming hyperobsession with the Greek
ideal—a classicizing idealization of art, architecture, the human body,
and civilization as a whole. Her argument was so provocative that the
book was outright banned in Germany. Since that book's publication,
other scholars have revised and nuanced many of its arguments. Yet
Butler might have found quick confirmation of her work in an innova-
tion introduced at the 1936 Summer Olympics in Berlin. In advance of
those games, the Olympic torch was lighted in Greece and conveyed
by relay to the site of the games. Its July arrival in Berlin was laden with
symbolism: the flame underscored the connection between the ancient

and modern Olympics, but it also served to stress the Third Reich's origins in an Aryan classical Greece.

When Germany invaded Greece in 1941, propaganda encouraged soldiers to view the Greeks' race as related to their own. On a number of occasions, Adolf Hitler held forth about the biological link between the peoples. Over dinner on February 4, 1942, he boasted to his guests that "the Greek profile and that of the Caesars is that of the men of the North of ours, and I wager that I could find amongst our peasants two hundred heads of that type."[19] The phrase "Greek profile" had been made famous by Winckelmann, who had called it "the chief characteristic of a high beauty" (see Chapter 7).[20] Historian Mark Mazower has nevertheless emphasized how, even as occupying German soldiers "visited the classical sites as dutiful 'war tourists'" in Greece, they came to harbor "considerable ambivalence towards Pericles' modern descendants."[21] The Greeks' stock, they now suspected, had been fundamentally corrupted—not by Slavic blood, as Jacob Fallmerayer had proposed a century earlier, but by miscegenation with ancient Semitic peoples. In the course of the extraordinarily violent and destructive Axis occupation of Greece, some 400,000 civilians (60,000 of them Jewish) were murdered or died from starvation. Thousands of antiquities were unearthed (and damaged in the process) and some were stolen; museums were raided and ancient monuments vandalized. Axis troops murdered and dehumanized the people of Greece, but they also plundered the land's past—a past they believed was most rightfully theirs.

German forces withdrew from Athens in the autumn of 1944, but the country's liberation brought only brief respite. In 1946 Greece descended into a brutal civil war fought between the national government and members of the Soviet-backed Greek Communist Party. Britain and the United States aggressively backed the nationalists. In a speech before Congress on March 12, 1947, President Harry S. Truman

announced the Truman Doctrine, a pledge to dispatch "American ci-
vilian military personnel" to Greece and Turkey, along with four hundred million dollars in aid, in an effort to stop the incursion of Soviet
communism. Truman likened the gravity of the situation to the eve
of World War II and assured Congress that "this is an investment in
world freedom and world peace." His policy would have immense consequences for the reshaping of Western identity in uncompromising
terms of democracy.

The Greek Civil War ended in 1949 with a victory for the government's army. With enormous foreign financial support, particularly
through the United States' Marshall Plan, Greece set out on the path
of modernization that gave rise to the "Greek economic miracle" of the
later twentieth century. At the same time, the concept of "Hellenism"
found still new definition in the hands of Western powers. As historian and sociologist Despina Lalaki has argued, the notion of Hellenism
became a tool used to shape and create new "distinctions between the
Democratic West and the Communist East."[22] Her work emphasizes
the role that American archeologists played in mediating that transformation. Some of those archeologists, most notably Carl Blegen (after
whom the library of the American School of Classical Studies in Athens
is named) insisted that their work in the country had confirmed for
them the fundamentally good (non-Communist) character of the
Greeks. When American forces arrived to combat communism in 1947,
the United States presented its mission as one of "safeguarding democracy for the country that has been charged as its first progenitor." "To
save Greece," Lalaki writes, was cast as a vital mission "to save the
American soul."[23]

In the aftermath of the Greek Civil War, the ruling party in Greece
made constant efforts to affirm "Western" identity and values. In 1961,
amid the country's new economic miracle, Greece gained its first

admittance to the European Economic Community (the EEC, or European Common Market). The prime minister at the time was Constantine (Konstantinos) Karamanlis, a towering figure in the modern history of Greece whose life and political career spanned much of the twentieth century. During his first term as prime minister, he was also the leader of the country's new anti-Communist Right. His campaign to join the Common Market began in 1958. When the Treaty of Association gained Greece entry three years later, Karamanlis's chief negotiator is said to have pronounced that Greece had finally "rejoined the mainstream of Western history."[24] In Greece, he nevertheless "came under fire from the opposition for betraying the cause of Hellenism in the interests of NATO and the Americans."[25]

The new Anglo-American "democratic" ideal of classical antiquity was paraded in Greece by leaders intent on proving to Britain and the United States that it was on the right side of history. The aim of their campaign was nowhere else so clear as in the *Acropolis Sound and Light Show,* which debuted in 1959, the year after Karamanlis began his campaign for Greece's entry into the European Common Market. That show, a dazzling homage to Periclean Athens, was a spectacular production that ran night after night for more than four decades, enough to put the most successful Broadway producer to shame. When King Otto and Leo von Klenze inaugurated the Acropolis's restoration program in 1834, the site was grandly illuminated for the occasion. More than a hundred years later, a more extravagant and far more prolonged display of lights on the Acropolis served as a massive advertisement of the Greek state's commitment not only to its own antiquities but also to the values of Western democracy.

The forty-five-minute show was sponsored, three times a night in high tourist season, by the Greek National Tourist Organization. At the beginning of each show, a voice recording proudly proclaimed through loudspeakers: "Tonight on this hill we shall revive once more the Golden Age of Athens!" That pronouncement was followed by a pastiche of passages from Herodotus's and Thucydides's ancient accounts of Athenian greatness. Art historian Elizabeth Marlowe has analyzed the show as an expression of Cold War sentiment and politics. She underscores how, throughout the script of the show, "the Persians are presented as cardboard-cut-out bad guys, 'reckless,' 'bloodthirsty' and 'barbaric,' while the Athenians are ever 'courageous,' 'noble' and 'heroic.'"[26] The show even featured the "voice" of Pericles himself, delivering excerpts from Thucydides's account of his funeral oration, that ancient manifesto of the Athenian brand (see Chapter 2).

In *The Invention of Athens: The Funeral Oration in the Classical City*, classicist Nicole Loraux noted how the twentieth century produced "innumerable conflicting interpretations of Pericles' epitaphios." In France, the value of *fraternité* was read between its lines; in Germany, the speech stood as a testament to the depth of the Athenian patriotic character; in England, the speech became a "hymn to individual, positive, action-oriented liberty and to classical Athens—an expanding imperialist Athens, busy like the British Commonwealth, comfortable like liberal societies."[27] The most influential piece of propaganda from classical Athens has been repeatedly transformed into new strains of national propaganda. It is no coincidence, as Marlowe points out, that the portions of the funeral oration blasted at the light show were "those that bear the closest resemblance to European and American ideas of democracy." The show's Pericles declared: "The constitution which governs us has been given the name of Democracy. Her purpose is the service of the greatest number. We are all equal before the Law. Only personal merit opens the way to honor."[28] In 1937, the regime of the Greek fascist dictator Ioannis Metaxas had issued an order banning the study of Pericles's funeral oration in schools "because the undue praise of democratic ideals in the *epitaphios* may be misunderstood by students as an indirect critique of the strong government policy and of the tendencies of the present state more generally."[29] Now, in the context of the Cold War, the speech was recast as the founding document of Western liberal democracy, to which some Greek leaders were now eager to pledge their allegiance.

The *Acropolis Sound and Light Show* is also the best example of the convergence of Karamanlis's emphasis on national tourism and his political objectives. It is largely to his vision that we owe today's travel-agent plugs for Greece as a land of island paradises, incomparable light, and ruins that still bear witness to Western civilization's early days. During his premiership, Melina Mercouri and Jules Dassin's internationally successful 1960 film *Never on Sunday,* about an American tourist's experience in Greece, was released (see Chapter 3). The same year, the country's official ambassador to the United Kingdom also garnered wide foreign recognition, both for himself and for Greece, when the first major English translation of his poems appeared in print. The poet was George (Giorgos) Seferis, a career diplomat whose international group of friends included many literary luminaries. His poems had already been translated into English by Henry Miller and Lawrence Durrell, among others, but Rex Warner's 1960 volume *Poems* made a large sample of his work readily available to an English-speaking audience. In December 1963, just six months after Karamanlis handed over the reins of government, Seferis became the first Greek to be awarded the Nobel Prize in Literature. That prize was, in part, a testament to the appeal that Greece's apparent embrace of its classical heritage continued to have in Europe.

Seferis was one of the most successful poets in an intellectual circle that touted a concept its members called Hellenicity *(hellenikotita);* these artists and thinkers "endeavoured to promote Greek culture in the West, as a reminder to the European Occident of its cultural debt to the Greek Orient."[30] By the time Seferis's Nobel Prize was awarded, Greece certainly seemed to have found its feet as an "occidental," European nation. The country was politically stable and experiencing its greatest growth period yet (between 1961 and 1973, the GDP grew annually by an average of 9 percent). Europe's hopes for the country were finally being realized: it was achieving success as a functional and prosperous European state, all while the poetry of Seferis—one of the first Greek poets to achieve widespread success in translation—served as elegant, poignant proof that the people's modern soul remained one with their ancestors' spirit.

Seferis's work is rich in allusions to ancient Greece: to Odysseus, who, like the Smyrnean-born Seferis himself, traveled as an exile far from his home; to gleaming marbles; to the mythical plots of Athenian tragedies; and to the evocative landscape of Delphi. Non-Greek readers were drawn to the way in which his verses and essays resurrected antiquity, if often with guarded ambivalence, in a modernist idiom. The theme of antiquity's persistence and weight in the present day is especially palpable in Seferis's celebrated *Mythistorema* (Mythical narrative), first published in Greek in 1935. Like the Homeric epics, the poem is structured in twenty-four parts; it is also the first poem in Rex Warner's influential 1960 English translation and became immensely well known to Greeks and non-Greeks alike. A passage from its third part ("Remember the baths where you were slain," an allusion to Aeschylus's *Oresteia*) was even chosen for recitation at the opening ceremony of the 2004 Summer Olympics in Athens. In a part of the ceremony titled "Allegory," a woman dressed in black stood at the edge of a body of water, clutching the head of a white marble sculpture in her arms. She, or rather a voice-over, performed these lines from Seferis's poem:

> I awoke with this marble head between my hands
> Which tires my elbow out. Where can I put it down?
> It was falling into the dream as I rose from the dream
> And so our lives grew one, hard now to be separated.[31]

On the American network NBC, one commentator pronounced, even as the recitation was still ongoing, "This is a poem about the fate of all Greeks, who from the day they are born are linked to their ancient heritage."

That explanation reduces Seferis's lines to a straightforward declaration of the Greek people's steady continuity from antiquity to the present day. In reality, these lines, like the entire Mythistorema, suggest a far more complex uncertainty about the ancient past and the weight of its legacy. Yet the commentator's gloss on the poem (surely suggested by some official promotional materials) is a fair reflection of the reputation that Seferis and his poetry earned with international audiences. At the 1963 Nobel Prize presentation ceremony, Anders Österling, permanent secretary of the Swedish Academy, stressed Seferis's role as continuer of the ancient tradition: "Seferis is today the representative Hellenic poet, carrying on the classical heritage."[32] In his Nobel lecture, Seferis celebrated the wealth and tradition of modern Greek poetry but also invoked the unities of language and landscape that connect the Greek people to antiquity: "This language shows the imprints of deeds and attitudes repeated throughout the ages down to our own. These imprints sometimes have a surprising way of simplifying problems of interpretation that seem very difficult to others. I will not say that we are of the same blood, for I abhor racial theories but we have always lived in the same country and have seen the same mountains slope into the sea."[33] In the 1960s, Seferis thus seemed to give international audiences everything they could hope for in a modern Greek poet: he was elegant, witty, and diplomatic by profession, while his poems evoked both the gleam of antiquity and the thread of continuity connecting Greece's present and past. Not long after that momentous Nobel Prize, however, the seemingly clear path to full integration in Europe hit a barrier. On April 21, 1967, a group of colonels staged a coup, known as the Junta, and imposed a military dictatorship. The Junta lasted until 1974, when the Turkish invasion of Cyprus set off a chain of events that led to the restoration of democracy.

Three years later, in November 1977, the Greek archeologist Manolis Andronikos announced that he had uncovered the former Macedonian capital of Aegae and the royal tomb of King Philip II (father of Alexander the Great) in the small northern Greek town of Vergina. Years later, as the Cold War drew to a close, that monumental discovery would show that Greece's insistence on the respect that its antiquity is owed—and on the entire international community's classical debt—can complicate the course of Western democratic progress as much as it can justify it. Today, many archeologists remain uncertain about the tomb's true occupants, but that doubt has not prevented the site from playing a role in a still-ongoing geopolitical controversy. When the Republic of Macedonia was born of the fractured Yugoslav Federation on September 8, 1991, a decade and a half after the tomb's discovery, Greek communities across the world rancorously protested its use of the name "Macedonia." Macedonia is the name of the northern region of Greece that encompasses both Vergina and the country's second city of Thessaloniki.

In classical antiquity, the Macedonians' credentials as Greeks were a matter of heated debate: in the fifth century BCE, the Macedonian king had to beg to be allowed to participate in the Greek Olympics, and when Philip and Alexander invaded Greece in the mid-fourth century BCE, their campaign was painted as the latest in a long series of barbarian invasions. For centuries, historical narratives had tied Greece's decline in antiquity to the coming of the Macedonians. Andronikos's discovery was nevertheless quickly marshaled as incontrovertible proof of the protesters' rallying cry, "Macedonia is Greek!" Alexander the Great's empire was now enfolded forever into the catalog of Greek achievements, and the former Yugoslav republic seemed to be positioning itself as the latest foreign state with aims to co-opt Greece's past for itself. In 1992, the Greek government even responded by issuing a stamp featuring Andronikos amid a collage of finds from the alleged royal tombs at Vergina. Greece's protestations, rooted largely in the archeological "evidence," constitute the main reason that its northeastern neighbor is still generally known—and recognized by the United Nations—not as the Republic of Macedonia, but as the Former Yugoslav Republic of Macedonia, or more commonly FYROM.

THE GOD ABANDONS THE MIRACLE

We have already encountered Melina Mercouri a few times in this book in two different roles as a kind of representative of Greece: at the 1986 Oxford Union debate (Chapter 1) and in the 1960 film *Never on Sunday* (Chapter 3). When she participated in the debate, she was in her first term as Greek minister of culture. That term lasted from 1981 to 1989; she was sixty years old when she took the position and had some twenty film credits to her name. As minister, Mercouri was a passionate advocate for the return of the Parthenon Marbles to Greece ("And Parthenon marbles they are," she insisted at the Oxford debate: "There are no such things as the Elgin Marbles"),[34] and in 1982 Greece filed a formal peti tion for the restitution of the marbles through UNESCO. Under her direction, the popular tourist area at the foot of the Acropolis also became fully pedestrianized and closed off to traffic; she was likewise responsible for the vision behind the "European Capital of Culture" program. Since 1985, that initiative has designated a European city to host, for one calendar year, a whole suite of activities designed to celebrate and showcase "European" culture. In 1985, four years after Greece was allowed to rejoin the European Economic Community (EEC), precursor of the 1993 European Union (after its temporary expulsion because of the Junta), Athens became the first city to win the designation of Europe's cultural capital. The supposed wellspring of Western civilization thus became Europe's first official poster child.

Shortly after Mercouri's first term as minister ended, Greece suffered a highly publicized embarrassment when it lost a bid to host the 1996 Summer Olympics, the hundredth-anniversary games. Mercouri led the campaign, stylized as one to bring the games "home." She, like many others both in Greece and abroad, was shocked and outraged when the honor was awarded by vote of the International Olympic Committee (IOC) to Atlanta, Georgia. At a meeting in Tokyo on September 18, 1990, Atlanta received fifty-one votes, Athens thirty-five. "Coca-Cola," Mercouri declared, "has won over the Parthenon temple."[35] In 1992, the Italian branch of Coca-Cola added insult to injury when it ran an advertisement in the newspaper *Corriere della Sera* that reconfigured the Parthenon columns as Coke bottles. The image provoked enormous outrage in the Greek media, which was further fueled by rumors that Coca-Cola had rigged the IOC vote in 1990.

Throughout the campaign to host the 1996 games, Greece was perceived as relying far too much on the premise of a symbolic debt to Greece: the international community owed the country respect because of its antiquity. A similar sentiment colored the controversy over the

Republic of Macedonia's choice of name in 1991, at the apparent conclusion of the Cold War. Both issues foregrounded what one scholar has called a perceived "Greek propensity for wielding a symbolic narrative over more pragmatic strategies," or, in other words, for overreliance on the conceit of classical debt.[36] When the IOC's disappointing decision was handed down in 1990, Greek officials spun the outcome as an offensive refusal by the international community to acknowledge Greece's unparalleled contributions to world culture. A widely quoted statement by Andreas Papandreou, a former Panhellenic Socialist Movement (PASOK) prime minister, captured the general feeling of outrage over this unacknowledged and therefore unpaid debt: "I express my deep regret that the international community did not respect history and the spirit of the Olympic Games and, yet again, committed an injustice against Greece."[37] Athens nominally lost the vote because committee members worried that the city's notorious pollution and traffic congestion would hinder the games, as well as because of Greece's apparent inability to host such a large-scale event; the country would have needed three billion dollars' worth of infrastructure improvements to do so. Speculation was strong, however, that the choice of Atlanta had been largely affected by widespread resentment over the presumptuous tone of the Greek campaign. That tone was especially clear in the rhetoric of Spyros Metaxas, the committee's president, who had emphatically underscored Greece's "historical right" to host the games. When the decision was announced, he swore that his country would never make another bid.[38]

Greece nevertheless did just that, in terms that both addressed the IOCs earlier concerns about Athens's fitness as a venue and were less insistent on the country's historically determined "right" to host the games. At an IOC meeting in Lausanne, Switzerland, on September 5, 1997, Athens was declared host city for the 2004 Summer Olympics

Between the 1997 IOC vote and the 2004 Summer Olympics, Greece succeeded in its bid to enter the European Monetary Union. The triumph was largely the result of the government's aggressive macroeconomic stabilizing policies. Those policies served to reduce the country's debt and to curtail inflation, but they also involved the privatization, from the early 1990s onward, of banks, telecommunications, and utility companies. Greece thus rebounded robustly from the stagflation, or lack of economic growth combined with inflation, that it had suffered along with the rest of Europe in the 1980s. By the close of the millennium, it was reaping the benefits of another economic boom. When euro notes and coins debuted on January 1, 2002, Greece counted itself one of twelve members of Europe's pioneering new common currency area, the Eurozone. The economy was thriving, and over the course of the decade Greece enjoyed high growth rates—the second highest in the Eurozone—and relatively low inflation, given the country's record.

The Athens 2004 Organizing Committee spent nearly two billion dollars in preparation for the games, and the Greek government invested billions more in the country's infrastructure. Airports, rail lines, hospitals, museums, and archeological sites all benefited from major upgrades and improvements. For the second time since the birth of the modern state, the government was pouring an enormous amount of money into giving Athens a makeover meant both to modernize the city and to emphasize its ancient, classical past. In 2000, as preparations for the games got under way in earnest, an invitation-only competition was announced to solicit plans for a new Acropolis museum. Three previous contests had ended in failure, but feverish anticipation of the Olympics renewed the country's commitment to a workable plan. Ideally the museum would be completed in time for the games, when Greece could take advantage of the international media presence and position the museum as a plea for the return of the Parthenon Marbles. The winning design was by Franco-Swiss radical architect Bernard Tschumi and his Greek collaborator, Michael Photiades, who proposed a steel, glass, concrete, and marble structure that promised to take full advantage of the building site's view of the Acropolis and the "Attic light" so touted by the tourism industry. The "glass house" for the Parthenon opened in 2009, half a decade after Athens had hosted the Summer Olympics.

To the world's surprise, when August 2004 arrived, the country was otherwise ready—or at least ready enough—for the games to begin. Now, as Greece basked in its European economic prosperity, it had the chance to put its illustrious history—the ancient font of the much-glorified and idealized "Olympic spirit"—on display once more before a world audience. The games' mascots, Athena and "Phevos" (*Phoibos,* pronounced *Fivos* in Modern Greek, was an ancient epithet of the god Apollo) were inspired by ancient *daidala,* roughly anthropomorphic statues from one of the earliest phases of ancient Greek art. They symbolized exactly the image that Greece as a country was hoping to portray. The organizing committee explained that "their creation was inspired by an ancient Greek doll and their names are linked to ancient Greece, yet the two siblings are children of modern times. . . . In this way Phevos and Athena represent the link between Greek history and the modern Olympic Games."[39]

Dimitris Papaioannou, already a well-known avant-garde visual and performance artist, director, and choreographer, was named artistic director of both the opening and the closing ceremonies. The first part of the opening ceremony, "Allegory," included the extract from Seferis's *Mythistorema* quoted earlier in this chapter and showcased Greece as the wellspring of culture and civilization, home of the inventors of life like marble statuary, the discoverers of geometry, and so on. It was also a celebration of humanity's natural inquisitiveness, spirituality, and yearning for love. The second part was, by contrast, a celebration entirely dedicated to Greece's own history, recounted through a parade of its art and culture. For about ten minutes of that spectacular pageant, called *Klepsydra* (Hourglass), hundreds of lavishly costumed participants enacted poses that transformed the best-known icons of Greek art into stunning *tableaux vivants*. Nearly seven of those minutes were devoted to living reperformances of ancient artworks, which ran a vast gamut from Minoan frescoes to figurines of the Hellenistic era. For forty seconds, a living diorama of the Parthenon frieze turned the ceremony into yet another platform for Greece's plea for the return of the Elgin Marbles. Papaioannou also worked in other sly statements: in a nod to the old Great Idea, his pageant included evocations of mosaics from Istanbul's Hagia Sophia.

As critics noted, one of the most striking aspects of *Klepsydra* was the way in which it projected a Europeanized, whitewashed version of the Greek ideal to audiences around the globe. Nearly all the classical sculptures—the small army of archaic statues of young men *(kouroi)*, the living tableaux of the Parthenon frieze, the caryatids, and the discus throwers and other ancient athletes—were noticeably lacking in color. As archaeologist Dimitris Plantzos has noted, this was "a representation that the *ancient* Greeks themselves would have found difficult to come to terms with: they, for one, would have been mystified by the pristine whiteness of their paraded statuary."[40] If Winckelmann knew about the brightness of ancient statues in the late eighteenth century, Papaioannou certainly did at the beginning of the twenty-first.

Some critics also grumbled over the Olympic ceremonies' sentimental kitschiness and overreliance on a jumble of ancient imagery. In other quarters, though, Papaioannou was hailed as a new Yannis Makriyannis, the great general of the Greek War of Independence (in

Still from Dimitris Papaioannou's *Klepsydra* procession at the opening ceremony of the 2004 Summer Olympics in Athens. Such *kouroi* were usually brightly painted in antiquity, but Papaioannou chose to present them as white.

2005, Greece's president awarded Papaioannou the Golden Cross of the Order of Honor for his contribution to the Olympics). Proud national sentiment ran strong over the next half decade and culminated in another grand public presentation of Greece's classical heritage. On June 20, 2009, 135 years after the first Acropolis Museum was completed, the New Acropolis Museum finally opened its doors to the public. The museum had been built amid a host of controversies over its finance and location, in an area rich with archeological remains. In 2007, another public relations storm surrounded the proposed demolition of two neighborhood buildings, not because they stood on the construction site, but because they supposedly obstructed views of the Acropolis archeological park. Both buildings, one neoclassical, the other art deco (decorated, allegedly, by a friend of Picasso's), were listed as national monuments.

The owner of the neoclassical house, the composer Vangelis Papathanassiou (the "Vangelis" best known for the *Chariots of Fire* theme song), declared that the Greek government was waging "architectural terrorism" in the name of antiquity.[41] His response echoed the resistance that local Athenians had voiced, for example, to the early archeological purification program. Campaigns to save the buildings were successful, but controversy continued to surround the museum. Some critics and visitors were irked at the prominence given to the classical history of the Acropolis. In a sense, the museum more permanently enshrines the vision of antiquity that had been ephemerally paraded at the opening ceremony of the 2004 Athens Olympics: it is a celebration, above all, of the glory of ancient Athens.

It is no secret that the museum was designed to pull on international heartstrings: the urgency behind its construction was intimately tied to the campaign for the Parthenon Marbles' reunification in Athens. The top level of the building is devoted to the Parthenon and its ancient frieze, or really to the loss of about half of it to early antiquities scavengers. Enormous windows allow visitors to look up to the Parthenon on the Acropolis and encourage lamentation over the injustice of the marbles' absence. At the display of the caryatids (copies have been installed at the Erechtheion on the Acropolis), a lonely base awaits the return of the sixth, abducted sister, the marbled girl held "like a partridge in a trap" in the British Museum. Despite the criticism of the museum's politics of display, the structure was showered with architectural prizes and hailed across the world as a monumental artistic achievement. Like Phevos and Athena, the mascots of the Athens Olympics, it styles itself as both a testament to Greece's link to the ancient past and as a "child of modern times." In Greece's great decade of economic prosperity, its years as the standard bearer of European modernity, the face that the country chose to present to the world was much like a *kouros* in Papaioannou's pageant or even a stanza of Seferis's poetry: strong, controlled, and imbued with an exuberant ancient spirit, yet proudly and strikingly modern.

Six months after the glass house of the New Acropolis Museum welcomed its first visitors, the more fragile and illusory edifice of Greek economic prosperity collapsed. After revelations were made of the country's deep debt to masses of international creditors, Greece quickly began to pay an embarrassing price for the long insistence by Greeks and foreigners alike that the world owed so much to it.

CHAPTER SIX

Classical Debt in Crisis

THE GLOBAL FINANCIAL CRISIS BEGAN when a housing bubble burst in the United States in 2007. Many in Greece remained optimistic that they would survive the foreign crashes unscathed. The numbers soon told a different story: between 2008 and 2010, Greek GDP fell by about 20 percent. Slowly but surely, a backlog of irregularities in national accounting started to come to light. In the late 1990s and the early years of the twenty-first century, the country had taken out loans at a rapid pace, which only intensified as its leaders sought to cover up a growing deficit. New loans went, in part, toward improving the national infrastructure: the Summer Olympics of 2004 were a public relations triumph but an enormously costly affair. Much of the freshly borrowed money nevertheless had to be earmarked to financing preexisting debt. In October 2009, the social-democratic party PASOK came to power again after national elections. Shortly after taking office, Prime Minister George Papandreou pronounced the national economy in "intensive care." His government warned that the deficit would run high the next year; it also revealed that deficits of previous years, during the former New Democracy administration, had been greater than reported. Largely as a result of these admissions, over fifteen days in December 2009, each of the Big Three credit-rating companies (Fitch, Standard and Poor's, and Moody's) downgraded Greece's credit rating. At the dawn of the third millennium's second decade, the new Greek miracle was shattered.

On February 9, 2010, Greece's Parliament passed the first package of austerity measures. Those measures, an attempt to make a dent in the national deficit, downsized the notoriously large Greek civil service, froze the salaries of government workers, and sharply cut their bonuses and work-related travel expenses. Since then, three bailout packages, or "memoranda of understanding" (MoUs), have been struck between Greece and the country's creditors: in May 2010, March 2012, and August 2015. Those MoUs have required the implementation of countless further austerity measures, and the effects have been harsh. For the past half decade, the official unemployment rate in Greece has hovered around 25 percent. The rate is about 50 percent among the young, and throughout the population underemployment is much higher. The country is therefore experiencing a massive brain drain at a time when it needs its best and brightest at home. There has also been a drastic increase in suicide rates and a precipitous reduction of basic health services. In a report titled "Children of the Recession," UNICEF calculated that more than 40 percent of Greek children were living in poverty in 2012, up from 23 percent in the precrisis year of 2008.[1] That statistic alone is perhaps an indicator of what prominent economists and political scientists such as Paul Krugman and Mark Blyth have, over the past few years, argued with increasing frustration: that austerity programs of this sort not only disproportionately affect the most vulnerable but also, from a pure economics perspective, simply do not work.

In his 2013 *Austerity: History of a Dangerous Idea,* Blyth defines austerity as "a form of voluntary deflation in which the economy adjusts through the reduction of wages, prices, and public spending to restore competitiveness, which is (supposedly) best achieved by cutting the state's budget, debts, and deficits."[2] Yet in Greece, as elsewhere, austerity has not succeeded at guiding the country out of debt. Instead, Blyth argues, "Deploying austerity in less than . . . ideal conditions has helped propel Spain and Greece to the brink of economic and political collapse and impoverished millions of people throughout the rest of Southern Europe. This is not 'blown out of proportion rhetoric.' It is a fact."[3] If this kind of austerity simply does not result in the economic rebounding its advocates say it is aimed at, then why have Greece's creditors been so insistent on imposing it?

Like many others, Blyth has underscored how austerity in Greece has become just as much an "ethical" matter as an economic one—"a morality tale of saints and sinners."[4] For many, the policy is synonymous with a strategy of tough love: its aim is to teach spending-happy, corrupt, and indolent Greeks how to tighten their belts and live within their means. One consequence, if not exactly a cause, of Greek austerity that fits well with Blyth's "morality tale" is impossible to quantify but easy enough to detect in Western coverage of the crisis: Greece's creditors seem to be suggesting that the abstract debt to Greece is no longer valid. One scholar has posed a question that hews to the bone of the embarrassment on both sides: "Could it be, then, that by reversing the asymmetry of debt / credit, the debt of Western creditors to Greece can now be cancelled out?"[5] In other words, does the current Greek monetary debt effectively erase the abstract classical debt that both Greece and Western countries had long been happy to agree was owed to Greece? Signs that international patience with the idea of that debt was wearing thin had already begun to appear in 1990, when the International Olympic Committee, whose members were rumored to have been annoyed at Greece's insistence on its "historic right" to host the centennial games in 1996, chose Atlanta over Athens. Is this most recent taunting of the Greeks another, and much crueler, way for the West to unburden itself of any sense that the symbolic debt must actually be repaid?

Ever since the crisis in Greece became a major international news story, certain media have implicitly disavowed any notion of classical debt by denying the existence of any real link between the Greeks of today and the Greeks of antiquity. In the early nineteenth century, as Greece edged toward independence, European and American supporters of the revolution thrilled at the thought that contemporary Greeks were, in a sense, living relics of antiquity; their advocacy for the cause stressed the Greek people's cultural and even genetic continuity from ancient times. Today, by contrast, articles and headlines emphasize the distance between living and ancient Greeks and ridicule that rupture. This kind of coverage in many ways reprises the views of early European travelers to Greece. George Wheler, in his 1682 travelogue *A Journey into Greece,* called attention to the land's status as a cautionary tale against unrest at home in England.[6] More recently Western politicians and news outlets have again positioned Greece as a fable against the dangers of profligacy and corruption. Just like the early European travelers, they underscore how far the Greeks have fallen since ancient times. Ultimately this analysis also insinuates the weakness of Greek claims to belong in the European West whose leaders and members often see themselves as ancient Greece's (and especially classical Athens's) most rightful civilizational heirs. As we will see, precisely because the country of Greece has an informal colonial legacy that is so abstract—and largely invisible to and unacknowledged by the West—Greeks today seem to remain acceptable targets of humor that in most other cases would be repudiated for obvious underlying bigotry.

Nevertheless, the Western media's reporting on Greece is in many ways a natural, if disheartening, extension of Europe's legacy of interference in the country, a story we have glimpsed in Chapters 3, 4, and 5. Anyone who accepts the premise that Greece is a "failure" today should probably also concede that it is largely the failure of a host of old philhellenic ideals. Over the past two centuries, those ideals took different forms, ranging from King Otto's dream of restoring Athens to its Periclean grandeur to the United States and Britain's insistence on saving the cradle of democracy from the threat of Soviet communism. It is also true that certain Greek leaders worked hard, especially during the prosperous first decade of the twenty-first century, to proclaim just the opposite: that the country was proof of the monumental success of two centuries of nation building. In the end, the antiquity-infused spectacles of the 2004 Olympics and the 2009 opening of the New Acropolis Museum only made Greeks more vulnerable to the cartoons, op-eds, and quips that lampooned them as the unworthy descendants of their illustrious ancestors—or not really descendants at all.

CROOKS IN THE EURO FAMILY

The February 22, 2010, issue of the German magazine *Focus,* published less than two weeks after the Greek Parliament introduced the first set of austerity measures, is an infamous case in point. That week the magazine was dedicated to the Greek debt crisis, and the tone and spirit of its coverage worked hard to add insult to injury. The cover featured a digitally doctored image of the Venus de Milo, one of the most iconic sculptures to have survived from Greek antiquity. Discovered in 1820 by a peasant farmer on the Greek island of Milos, the Venus de Milo is a marble statue of the goddess Aphrodite (Venus in Latin) and one of the most popular attractions in Paris's Louvre Museum. Today this Venus is most famous for what she is missing: her arms (a lyric of "Love Is Just around the Corner," a popular song recorded by the likes of Bing Crosby and Kenny Rogers, goes: "Now Venus de Milo was noted for her charm. But strictly between us, you're cuter than Venus, and what's more you've got arms"). On the cover of *Focus,* the statue was draped in a Greek flag. She was also restored with right arm intact and frozen in an obscene gesture, presumably meant to represent Greece's attitude toward its creditors. The text on the cover read "Crooks in the Euro Family" (Betrüger in der Eurofamilie) and was accompanied by this irate subheading: "Will GREECE cheat us of our money—and what about Spain, Portugal, Italy?" (Bringt uns GRIECHENLAND um unser Geld—und was ist mit Spanien, Portugal, Italien?).

The content of the magazine was even harsher than its cover. Stories inside emphasized how the Greeks had been swindling the rest of Europe with their typically corrupt creative accounting practices. An article titled "2000 Years of Decline" reviewed the familiar list of the ancient Greeks' achievements: philosophy, democracy, mythology, and so on.[7] Usually these kinds of lists are standard in formulations of the West's symbolic debt to Greece, but this time any idea of abstract indebtedness was conspicuously absent. Instead, the article posed this old chestnut of a question: "But who are their descendants, anyway?" For the answer, it suggested (in vaguely tongue-in-cheek tone) that the reader need look no further than the thesis of Jacob Fallmerayer, who, n the 1830s, had ignited scandal in Greece with his claim that, genetically speaking, contemporary Greeks were much more Slav than Socrates (see Chapter 5). Fallmerayer's idea still makes good sense, the *Focus* article explained, given that the "modern Greeks prove their dissimilarity to their ancestors almost daily." It then went on to dismiss Greece for its utter lack of contemporary relevance or achievement: "The country that gave rise to Socrates and Plato, Myron and Phidias, Pindar and Sophocles, Pythagoras and Thucydides, today has no significant poets, composers, artists or philosophers." Many European travelers to Greece in the seventeenth and eighteenth centuries had made similar observations, which revealed only their own ignorance. The journalists at *Focus* demonstrated similar contempt for contemporary Greek culture simply by stating that there is practically no such thing. In a way, their claims went even further than Fallmerayer's ever had: the magazine not only pronounced the Greeks unworthy of their ancestors but also implied that they had deceitfully co-opted antiquity as a pillar of their national identity. The upshot? Greeks today have no real claim to the true legacy of classical Athens: Europe and European civilization.

The issue gained notoriety immediately in Greece, where, unsurprisingly, the reaction was one of indignation and uproar. Protests erupted in Athens, and a Greek consumer group (INKA) called for a boycott of German products. It also responded with its own ethnically charged statement, telling Reuters that "the falsification of a statue of Greek history, beauty and civilization, from a time when there [in Germany] they were eating bananas on trees is impermissible and unforgivable" (in Greek the saying goes, "We were building Parthenons while they were eating acorns").

Within months of the *Focus* issue, Greece became insolvent. In April 2010, national borrowing reached a record high, and by the end of the month Standard and Poor's had downgraded Greece's credit rating to junk status. On April 23, Prime Minister George Papandreou officially requested a bailout from the European Union and the International Monetary Fund. At an IMF meeting on April 28, German chancellor Angela Merkel admitted that Europe might have made a mistake by admitting Greece into the Eurozone. In Greece, meanwhile, a new movement called *Seisachtheia* began to take shape. The name was owed to a radical reform of the Athenian constitution by the lawmaker Solon in the sixth century BCE. Solon's *seisachtheia*, literally a "shaking off of debts," was aimed at widespread debt relief for the lower classes of Athens. Under the old regime, Athenians unable to repay their debts had effectively become slaves to their creditors—a system of ancient serfdom. Solon's *seisachtheia* legislation canceled preexisting debts, freed the debt slaves, and restored their property. Now, the principle came to enjoy new popularity in a Greece suffering under the weight of austerity measures and desperate to shake them off.

In October 2010, Eurozone leaders reached an agreement on a loan package of 100 billion euros for Greece, coupled with a debt write-off of 50 percent. The terms of the agreement required still-deeper austerity. In response to large-scale protests against the new measures, on October 31 Prime Minister Papandreou proposed putting the terms of the bailout to the Greek people. In a *Foreign Policy* piece laden with classical references, Nick Malkoutzis, deputy editor of the English edition of the Greek newspaper *Kathimerini*, called the proposed referendum a "hemlock ballot." This was an allusion to the death of Socrates, who in 399 BCE was convicted by his fellow Athenians of impiety and corrupting the youth. Socrates was sentenced to death by suicide and was forced to commit it by drinking a cup of poison hemlock. Malkoutzis emphasized how vulnerable Papandreou had made himself by calling for the vote, a potentially "suicidal" move.[8] Leaders in Europe were certainly furious at the idea, which also sent shock waves through the financial markets. Buckling under intense pressure from his country's European creditors, Papandreou called off the referendum on November 3. Exactly one week later, on November 10, he resigned.

The day after the referendum was canceled, the Greek author George Zarkadakis wrote a caustic op-ed in the *Washington Post* titled "Modern Greece's Real Problem? Ancient Greece."[9] In it, Zarkadakis bitterly recalled how the *Focus* article had characterized the modern Greeks as "indolent sloths, cheats and liars, masters of corruption, unworthy descendants of their glorious Hellenic past." He also pilloried Europe more generally for having attempted, right from the birth of the Greek nation, to fashion the country in an ancient image designed by Europe for the purposes of its own vanity. Greeks, Zarkadakis observed, are in many ways "the imperfect reflection that the West imagined for itself." The irony of the *Focus* feature (and the line of thought it represented) was that Greece today had almost nothing to do with the Greece of antiquity: "If anything," Zarkadakis declared, "it is a failed German project." During the decades of King Otto's reign, Greece was "invented as a backdrop to contemporary European art and imagination, a historical precursor of many Disneylands to come." In the end, the pressure put on Greeks to play the part of good Europeans and prove themselves worthy descendants of their ancestors caused them to cave too quickly to the demands to call off the referendum.

Zarkadakis's opinion piece marked a plea for Europe, the West, and the world at large to let go of the old fantasy of Greek antiquity, or at least the idea that the modern state of Greece has anything to do with it. Other such calls have been made in recent years. Those who issue them repeatedly stress that today's Greeks, unlike their dead, buried, and impossibly idealized ancestors, are flesh-and-blood people with very real and modern problems. But they are also still citizens of a country whose entire modernization program was guided by a dream of white marble temples and Athenian democrats. Coverage of Greece's crisis has only reaffirmed how reluctant the West is to forget that dream—or, at least, to forgive the Greeks for the failure of that dream's realization. The popular overplay of tired classical metaphors and images has served as an important, if painful, reminder that all the anxieties that attended Greece's emergence as an independent country have not gone away. Today, both Greece and its creditors—many of them citizens of countries that have long claimed a debt to Greece—are being forced to rethink what place an idealized ancient past has in the present-day world. That question has no single answer, but exploring a different one might help explain its urgency. Just why did that issue of *Focus* hit such a nerve?

THE COLONY THAT WASN'T

On July 24, 1974, Greece's seven-year period of military dictatorship, known as the Junta, came to an end, and on December 8, the people of Greece formally reestablished their country as a democracy. They did so, fittingly, by means of a democratic vote, now known as the Greek Republic Referendum. A staggering 75.6 percent of voters turned out (to put this into perspective, 62.5 percent of eligible Greek voters participated in the July 2015 Greek Bailout Referendum, and 72 percent of British voters cast ballots in the June 2016 Brexit Referendum). In 1974, the margin of victory in the referendum was also large: 69 percent of Greek voters cast a "yes" ballot for democracy ("no" was a de facto vote to reinstate the monarchy). King Constantine II, who had been living in exile in England during the years of the Junta, bowed to the authority of the people's decision. In classical Athens, as in twentieth-century

Greece, coups and periods of oligarchy and foreign rule overturned democracy on more occasions than modern-day enthusiasts of Athenian democracy would like to remember. When the results of the 1974 Republic Referendum ushered in democracy's triumphant return, they also brought celebrations of a sort that the ancient monuments of the Acropolis had seen many times before.

The next year the airwaves were saturated with news about the arrest and high-profile, televised trials of the architects of the Junta, which were often seen as the Greek equivalent of the Nuremberg trials. Amid the great hopes for Greece's democratic future, the Greek journalist, television personality, and writer Nikos Dimou published a short book with a provocative title, *On the Unhappiness of Being Greek*. In 2014, the publishing house Patakis issued the thirty-second edition of the book; since its publication, it has been translated into a number of languages (including Chinese), spent a brief spell as a best seller in Germany, and earned countless accolades in periodicals on multiple continents. *On the Unhappiness of Being Greek* is a collection of 193 aphorisms arranged under thematic chapter titles, such as "Economy," "Religion," "Sex," and "Intellect." One of the first chapters is titled " 'N.I.C.' or Comparison in Time and Space." N.I.C. is Dimou's abbreviation for what he calls National Inferiority Complexes. Here is a sampling of the declarations that he makes about the Greek people's supposed national psychoses:

49 Any race descended from the ancient Greeks would be automatically unhappy. Unless it could either forget them or surpass them.[10]

55 The more we pride ourselves on our ancestors (without knowing them), the more anxious we are about ourselves.

61 Whenever a Greek talks of "Europe," he automatically excludes Greece. Whenever a foreigner talks of Europe, it's unthinkable for us that he should not include Greece.

63 It is a fact—whatever we may say—that we do not feel European. We feel like "outsiders." And worst of all is that it bothers and rankles us so when we're told this . . .

65 At the root of Greek unhappiness are the two National Inferiority Complexes. The one in time—with the ancient Greeks. The other in space—with the "Europeans." Unjustified complexes perhaps—but no less real for that.

None of these observations, of course, is particularly revelatory or groundbreaking; public debate rooted in similar worries predated the birth of the modern Greek state. But the success of the book is a significant barometer of public interest in these issues, both in Greece and worldwide. When I asked a friend of mine, a Greek author and political analyst who had recently interviewed Dimou, whether the book was worth reading, he wrote back that "the book might be of some interest since it was a bestseller, which shows that there was a public interest in this thrashing." A thrashing, that is, of Greeks by a Greek.

Some of the world certainly seems to take a peculiar form of satisfaction, even schadenfreude, in seeing how badly off Greece is today. It is a commonplace that ancient Greeks were the founding fathers of Western civilization and its hallmark values of democracy, rationality, and empiricism, but the public in countries where that claim is popular seems to revel in watching the modern country suffer under that legacy's impossible burden. Given the history of Greece's relationship with Europe, it is almost impossible to imagine that Greece could ever have not developed the complexes that Dimou describes. The long line of Western champions of Greek antiquity, a line that peaked with the nineteenth-century philhellenes, was remarkably effective at linking the nation of Greece in the Western mind with a whitewashed view of classical, especially Athenian, antiquity.

Greece gained independence thanks in large part to the intervention of Europe's Great Powers. For roughly a century and a half after independence, it was ruled by a succession of European monarchs. Yet, despite the many proud and prominent displays that Greece has made of its classical past—a largely Europeanized version of it—the country's relationship with Europe has always been uneasy. The nations that aided the revolutionaries' cause ultimately did little to support the Kingdom of Greece after they presided over its birth. Philhellenism died out quickly as a political movement; in London the Greek Committee collapsed under a loan scandal even before the Greek War of Independence was won. From its inception, the Kingdom of Greece effectively became a client state of Europe. The success of the Junta seemed only to confirm Europe's anxiety over Greece's fitness to join and in 1969 resulted in Greece's expulsion from the European Common Market. The country would not be readmitted until the first day of 1981, when the rest of Europe felt reassured that the era of the Junta was behind it for good.

Unsurprisingly, Greece's bid to join the Common Market rested largely on a campaign to emphasize the country's status as the birthplace of Western values. In Chapter 5, we saw that campaign on brilliant display in the *Acropolis Sound and Light Show,* with all its celebration of Athenian democracy in Periclean—or rather Anglo-American—terms. There we also heard about Constantine Karamanlis, whose many terms as both prime minister and president of Greece spanned the second half of the twentieth century, from 1955 to 1995. Karamanlis became famous for his role as a champion of Western values in opposition to communism and for his tireless advocacy of Greece's place at the West's table. His campaigning earned Greece its first "associate" membership in the European Common Market in 1961 (see Chapter 5), and his pro-Western stance played well to European audiences generally. In 1978, Karamanlis, then in his fourth term as prime minister, was awarded the Charlemagne Prize by the city of Aachen in West Germany. The award was established in the aftermath of World War II, and every year Aachen grants it to someone who has made an outstanding contribution to the ideal of European unity.

Karamanlis used his acceptance speech to make an appeal for the "Union of Europe." Stressing the common roots and common mission of all Europeans, he described European identity as a proud combination of Hellenic, Roman, and Christian values: "A synthesis to which the Greek spirit introduced the idea of freedom, truth, and beauty; the Roman spirit contributed the idea of the state and justice, and to which the Christian spirit gave faith and love."[11] Given his audience and the nature of the occasion, it was fitting, perhaps even to be expected, that Karamanlis dressed Greece's contribution to European identity in the language of European Hellenism. In 1819, amid the furor leading up to Greek independence, the British Romantic poet John Keats published his celebrated short poem "Ode on a Grecian Urn." The ode ends memorably with a lesson spoken by the urn itself: " 'Beauty is truth, truth beauty,'—that is all / Ye know on earth, and all ye need to know." In this context, Karamanlis's characterization of the Greek spirit as one defined by "freedom, truth, and beauty" hearkens back both to ideals of (philhellenic) Romanticism and to an ancient Greek idea about the essential difference between Greeks and "barbarians": that Greeks value freedom. In his *Washington Post* piece, Zarkadakis called Greeks "the imperfect reflection that the West imagined for itself." Karamanlis's speech, in projecting European identity through a filter of European classicism, essentially suggested the opposite. His country was n fact the perfect reflection of all that is best about the European West, and all that it continues to aspire to.

In more recent years, of course, that reflection has splintered. James Angelos, an author and reporter who has covered the Greek economic crisis extensively, describes Europe's view of Greece today as "bipolar." In a 2015 piece for *Politico* titled "Why on Earth Is Greece in the EU? Reverence for the Ancient Greeks Led to the Financial Crisis," Angelos argued that this bipolarity exists precisely because Europe believes that Greece "is both intrinsic to Europe and yet does not belong."[12] Greek history is no stranger to these kinds of ironies and impossibilities. Even in the late eighteenth and early nineteenth centuries, the philhellenism that gave birth to the Greek nation-state rested on a number of paradoxes and inconsistencies. Citizens of two of the world's great empires, Britain and France, hypocritically demanded Greece's liberation from foreign tyranny. They also prized Greek antiquity, paradoxically, as both mankind's innocent childhood and its moment of fullest maturity: an inimitable chapter of human history that nonetheless demanded imitation.

Europe's bipolar view of Greece has been described over the years within a whole variety of metaphors. In his short book *Modern Greece: What Everyone Needs to Know,* political scientist Stathis Kalyvas includes a brief section, a coda to his chapter on the Greek War of Independence, with this telling title: "What Explains the Love-Hate Relationship between the West and Greece?" Kalyvas reprises Dimou's psychological vocabulary when he describes the fraught relationship: "The link between ancient and modern Greece remains a sensitive issue today, as it is simultaneously a cornerstone of Greek national identity and an expression of the nation's pronounced insecurity."[13] In this unusual case, the "colonized" country (Greece) retains—and revels in—its bragging rights for having founded the civilization that the colonizer (the West) holds so dear. But even in making this observation, Kalyvas calls attention to another irregularity in the equation: no matter how tempted we are to speak of Greece with language and ideas borrowed from critiques of colonialism, Greece was never formally colonized by a European country. It might be more intuitive and even historically accurate to see the Ottomans as Greece's former colonizers, but the centuries of Turkish occupation do not constitute the colonial era that most beleaguers the country today.

In Chapter 3, we saw how early European travelers to Greece managed to implement a unique kind of colonial regime of their own, not over the land of Greece, but over Greek antiquity. Over the past two decades, a number of scholars have developed other models and metaphors to account for the prevalent (and justifiable) feeling in Greece that despite the absence of formal European colonization, the country continues to bear the scars and even open wounds of something that resembles the experience of other colonized nations. Largely inspired by his work in Greece, anthropologist Michael Herzfeld has developed the concept of "crypto-colonialism." By his definition, crypto-colonies are "living paradoxes: they are nominally independent, but that independence comes at the price of a sometimes humiliating form of effective dependence."[14] For Herzfeld, crypto-colonialism began in Greece when the country gained a form of political independence that immediately brought with it economic dependence on its European "liberators." Even today, the state continues to exist in the world as a crypto-colony. Ironically, given Europe's tradition of claiming a symbolic debt to Greece, the country is sometimes also described as a debt colony of the European Union, a body of which it is, paradoxically, also a full member.

Many accounts of Greece's more abstract colonization openly confront the racial anxiety that this peculiar colonial legacy left behind. In an 1893 essay titled "Easter Chanter" published in the newspaper

Akropolis, author Alexandros Papadiamantis (often seen as the "Greek Dostoyevsky") wrote of the "Greek nation, the enslaved nation, but the free one no less."[15] The Greek cultural historian Vangelis Calotychos has even compared the Greeks' conflicted self-image with W. E. B. Du Bois's formulation in the early twentieth century of the concept of the African American "double consciousness." In *The Souls of Black Folk,* Du Bois wrote of the African American's "sense of always looking at oneself through the eyes of others."[16] Since the Enlightenment dawned on Europe, Greeks too have found themselves backed into a corner in which they must be constantly and painfully alert to the way they are viewed by others, especially the European West. Yet Calotychos is also careful to explain that the Greek case is an "ironic inversion" of the African American experience that Du Bois described. The European fantasy of Hellenism forces Greeks to confront, again in Calotychos's words, "the racial impurity of not living up to the West's image."[17] To secure Western support for the cause of independence, some Greeks strove to give Europe the vision of Greece that it longed for. This, in turn, created the country's legacy of self-colonization, a phenomenon that scholar Artemis Leontis influentially articulated when she wrote, "It could really be argued that modern Greece endured a 'colonization of the mind.'"[18]

From the beginning, the Greek revolutionaries' strategy of playing to the European ideal of Greece had the potential only for short-term success. As Adamantios Koraïs knew very well, the generation of Pericles could never be resurrected. For that reason, he advocated *Katharevousa,* a "purified" form of the Greek language, as a compromise between Ancient and Demotic Greek. During the War of Independence, the Great Powers heeded the Greeks' pleas for support, but ever since the country's creation, Greeks have been forced to view themselves not just through Europe's eyes but through Europe's disappointed eyes.

Today in Greek tourist areas, it is even a commonplace for any perceived disruption—crime, disorder, or dilapidation of buildings—to be met with the self-policing question "What will the tourists think?"[19] Naturally, many blame Europe for what the country has become. The twentieth-century writer Panagiotis Kondylis went so far as to declare that Greece today is really a toilet constructed by philhellenes on top of the ruins of an ancient temple. Citing that provocative image, political scientist Ilias Papagiannopoulos remarks that it is a commonplace of contemporary Greek philosophers to approach modern Greece "as a giant historical pollution." Within the framework of Greek philosophical polemic, blame for the country's grotesque transformation is nearly always assigned elsewhere: the culprits are viewed as "not in reality 'us,' but some others, either these are Philhellenes or they are precisely neo-Hellenes—but they are not Greek and they do not deserve to be called as such."[20]

The legacy of classical antiquity is, of course, hardly the only element of Greek identity or of European-Greek relations that is real, complex, or worth discussing. In emphasizing how Greece has repeatedly used its moments in the international spotlight to present a "classical" face to the world—the side of itself that most pleases and impresses Western audiences—this book has largely neglected the long and complex history of resistance within Greece to European models and fantasies of Hellenism. That resistance began early in the history of the modern nation-state—or arguably even earlier—when many Greek thinkers actively rejected the European Hellenism born of the European Enlightenment and recast Greek identity as a complex fusion of multiple and diverse cultural traditions.

Those different visions have emphasized different strands of Greekness and even other obsessions with other epochs of antiquity (such as the "Minoan"). Above all, those other fantasies of Greekness speak to the Eastern, Byzantine, Orthodox identity—in Greek, *Romiosini,* "Romaicness"—that produces so much anxiety in Westerners' strained attempts to locate the boundaries of their own civilization. Some outsiders have, to be sure, also been fascinated by that other dimension of Greek identity. In the nineteenth century, widely traveled British soldier and author Patrick Leigh Fermor described a tension between "Hellenism" and "Romaism" that he perceived within Greek society as the "Helleno-Romaic Dilemma." He illustrated his theory with two lists of contrasting "characteristics, allegiances and symbols." For Fermor, the *Romios* was characterized by belief in the concrete, the real, by distrust of the law, and by his "looking on Greece as outside Europe." The *Hellene,* by contrast, favored theory over practice, worshipped the ideal, and loved the "remote past" (i.e., antiquity); he was characterized by his "adoption of Western customs, abhorrence of Romaic orientalism," and looked "on Greece as a part of Europe." "All Greeks," Fermor wrote, "are an amalgam, in varying degrees[,] of both" identities, which "contradict and complete each other."[21] His formulation of this "dilemma" has been influential in Anglophone discussions of Greece, but it is also schematic and caricatured: one cultural scholar has recently emphasized that the idea of "cultural dualism" that Fermor's thesis represents "obscures ambivalence and hybridization."[22] *Romiosini* nevertheless also has a long history as one kind of alternative Greek ideal. In an essay titled *"Romios and Romiosini,"* Kostis Palamas, a leading Greek poet of the nineteenth and twentieth centuries, declared, "[We are] Hellenes to dupe the world, but really we're *Romioi.*"[23]

Despite all the intricacies and overlaps of Greekness, Hellenism, Hellenicity, and *Romiosini,* international media continue to make relentless use of classical clichés. Even within Greece, Greek attempts to define or recast the national discourse have, as one scholar puts it, "never succeeded in disengaging the internalized circuit of Philhellenic desire"; this is "Philhellenism's punishment," which "consists precisely in imbuing the Neohellenic imaginary with the presence of an irretrievable but permanent ancestry."[24] Philhellenism continues its punishing course today in Western news outlets, especially (and not coincidentally) in its oldest great outposts in Europe and the United States. When many of those countries' pundits and politicians talk about Greece, they still have in their minds some image that derives as much from nineteenth-century interpretations of Winckelmann's Greek ideal as from the efforts made during the Cold War to equate the political structures of ancient Athens with Anglo-American liberal democratic ideals.

That kind of framework has the capacity to give rise to one of two perspectives. The first, as captured by both the early European travelers and the *Focus* special issue, again emphasizes rupture with the past and holds that Greeks are unworthy descendants (or, as Fallmerayer proposed, not even the descendants) of their ancient ancestors. Naturally, this view ignores the conundrum of its logic, a paradox we have now encountered at many points: if classical antiquity was so exceptional, how can today's Greeks (or anyone, for that matter) be expected to repeat that achievement? Irritation with the Greeks for failing to do so in truth reflects the West's displaced frustration at the failure of the wider European project, envisioned by the likes of Voltaire, of "reviving Athens." The other perspective, another oft-repeated refrain, uses the same premise—that Western civilization was born in ancient Athens—but draws the opposite conclusion. Precisely because the Greeks are the descendants of those illustrious ancestors, Europe and the West continue to owe Greece for clearing the path for European civilization. This view continues to accept the notion that Europe and the West owe Greece a symbolic debt.

With all this in mind, let us take a closer look at the proliferation of classical imagery and metaphors that the media have used in coverage of the Greek economic crisis.

REVENGE OF THE PHILHELLENES

In November 2011, shortly after Prime Minister George Papandreou called off his Bailout Referendum, controversy and protest flared in Greece around yet another new set of austerity measures. That month, the American comedy show *Saturday Night Live* aired a sketch that imagined the gods meeting on Mount Olympus to discuss the economic crisis. With requisite beard, garland, and regal staff, Zeus calls the summit to order: "I, Zeus, King of the Gods, have summoned you all to Mount Olympus because, somehow, the Greek economy has collapsed!" The gods react to the news with shock and uproar, and Zeus continues to address them:

> I know! No, I know! I was as surprised as you are! I mean, after all, the Greeks are widely known as a hard-working, industrious people—you know, a people willing to labor week in and week out, three days a week, one hour a day until the age of 45. But today, we Gods must come to their aid. So, quick—let us hear from the Greek God of Finance! [*the gods look around*] Wait . . . there is a Greek God of Finance, right? There has to be! Surely, someone has been looking after the economy all these years!

This provocative opening establishes the premise and tone for the rest of the sketch. There is no Greek god of finance; the crisis, Zeus learns, is to be blamed on Dionysus, the "party god." At the end, salvation finally comes in the guise of Klaus, the "German god of prudence and austerity." He offers a bailout to the gods on the condition that they make cutbacks, which Zeus snortingly refuses: "No way! Sorry, Klaus. Now, either you give us the money, or we take ALL of Europe down with us. I mean, we started democracy, we can end it." The sketch closes on the image of a spinning newspaper. It bears the headline: "Greece Gets Bailout: Vows to Spend it Unwisely."[25]

In my experience, this sketch is a useful tool for introducing students to Greek mythology. It almost always gets laughs, and its cringeworthy humor appropriately reflects the raciness of the ancient stories about the Olympian gods. It is also smart about identifying and satirizing a number of pervasive and perplexing hallmarks of Greek myth. For instance, why was there more than one god of war? Why did the gods have so many affairs, often with their own relatives, and in many cases disguised as some sort of animal? Showing the skit to classes is an effective way of capturing students' attention and orienting them to some of Greek mythology's characteristic themes and narrative structures. I have used it as a teaching tool ever since it first aired, but in the summer of 2015, when Alexis Tsipras's Bailout Referendum was making headline news, I encountered some surprising reactions. In a class discussion, some students observed that the sketch does a good job of calling attention to the fiscal recklessness and feeble decision making inherent in Greek culture. A few criticized the bit for its ethnic stereotyping, but others were amused by how it retrojected the "poor work ethic" of today's Greeks onto the ancient gods. A handful had been unaware that anything was amiss in Greece (or with the global economy more generally). For those students, representatives of an important slice of *Saturday Night Live*'s key demographic (eighteen- to forty-nine-year-olds), this was the first introduction to a major news story that, by then, was already more than half a decade old.

As remote as the sketch might seem from Percy Shelley or Lord Byron, it is a good representative of philhellenism's enduring punishment—handiwork still visible everywhere in the Western media, in headlines and cartoons from newspapers, magazines, and television. Thanks to philhellenic efforts to equate contemporary Greece with an ancient, classical legacy, references to Greek politics constantly rely on formulaic satire that assumes that the public will vaguely recognize certain ancient names, buildings, and artworks. Greece today is endlessly taunted as an Achilles's heel or a modern-day Icarus who has flown too close to the sun. Greek promises of fiscal belt-tightening have been compared countless times to a deceiving Trojan horse ("Beware of Greeks Bearing Bonds," warned a *Vanity Fair* article headline in October 2010). In the summer of 2015, the cliché that the crisis in Greece is like an "ancient Greek tragedy" even became the target of one of Elias Groll's "Bad Metaphor Watch" columns in the online news magazine *Foreign Policy*.[26] Ever since that crisis first came to international attention, innumerable political cartoons, graphics, and magazine covers have used some of the most recognizable images of Greek antiquity—the Parthenon, ancient Greek vases, comedy and tragedy masks, images of heroes, and (white) marble statues—as frames for Greece's present woes. Some pieces even use the same classical idiom to take what appears to be a more supportive stance toward the country: they represent its leaders as (tragic) ancient Greek heroes, called to battle the metaphorical monsters—the European Union and various financial institutions—that hold Greece's fate in their hands.

Against the popular tide, the cartoons that seem to take a more compassionate view by likening modern Greeks to ancient heroes rely more on an assumption that some glimmer of continuity exists between ancient and modern Greece. These kinds of images became especially popular after January 2015, when a tense election brought a relatively new political party, Syriza (an acronym for a phrase that means Coalition of the Radical Left), to power in Greece. With the bold young politician Alexis Tsipras at its helm, Syriza ran on a platform that promised to restore Greek dignity and to end the devastating austerity measures that, since the beginning of the decade, have brought more suffering with each new bailout agreement. On February 6, 2015, the cover of the American edition of *The Week* featured Tsipras as Prometheus, the Titan of ancient Greek mythology who betrayed the gods by revealing the divine secret of fire to mankind. As punishment, Zeus ordered some of the other gods to bind Prometheus to a cliff in the Caucasus. Every day an eagle pecked out his liver, but every night it grew back; each new day for Prometheus thus brought the same torture. The cover of *The Week* appeared at a moment when optimism was running high in Greece that Tsipras, his brassy new finance minister, Yanis Varoufakis, and Syriza would stand up to the European institutions and free Greece from the metaphorical fetters of endless and overpowering austerity measures.

But even images of ancient heroes can sometimes turn their symbolic power against the Greeks. One of the most famous cases of a classically themed cover appeared on a May 2012 issue of the *Economist,* which called Greece "Europe's Achilles heel." The *Economist* has a special penchant for these kinds of classical puns. In another case, from three years later, an installment in the magazine's weekly "Charlemagne" column on European politics ran accompanied by a Peter Schrank cartoon of Tsipras as Achilles. While the 2012 cover imagined Europe as that hero, the mightiest Greek to fight in the Trojan War, the new Tsipras-Achilles stood for Greece, where leaders' imprudent negotiating tactics were proving as good as an arrow shot in their own heel. "After more than three months of fruitless negotiations with Mr Varoufakis," the columnist wrote, "the reserves of Philhellenism among Greece's partners have run utterly dry. 'They are living in cloud-cuckoo land,' says one Brussels official."[27]

One can only wonder what it would mean if the "reserves of Philhellenism" were plentiful among Greece's creditors. The observation suggests that philhellenism is synonymous in Europe with a benign charity toward Greece, charity that the country does not really deserve. *Cloud-cuckoo-land,* on the other hand, is a phrase typically used (usually dismissively) to describe a fantasy state or impossible utopian society. People who think that they live in cloud-cuckoo-land are optimistic naïfs who do not understand how things really work. The phrase originated as the name of the fantasy city constructed in the clouds in Aristophanes's ancient comedy *The Birds* (the city is called *Nephelokokkygia* in Greek, from *nephele,* "cloud," and *kokkyx,* "cuckoo"); thus, whether or not the anonymous Brussels official knew it, he or she was scornfully casting Greek leaders in the role of absurd ancient Greek comic characters.

The column appeared in one of the West's most respected and influential media outlets, and it is a prime example of a piece that works in the service of Europe's ongoing symbolic colonization of Greece. This arsenal of instantly recognizable classical references allows the West, in the words of scholar Dimitris Tziovas, to "express their frustration at Greece's modern inhabitants, who have supposedly diminished or humiliated the ancient gods and heroes." Such metaphors imply that "the modern Greeks have wasted their symbolic capital and dishonored their heritage." The upshot is that the Greeks "do not deserve their classical past, which can therefore be appropriated by the West on moral and economic grounds."[28]

In some cases, media personalities even don the mantle of the early European travelers by pointing out how their grasp of classical civilization is superior to that of the "locals"—the Greeks themselves. In

February 2015, a lighthearted segment ran on the popular satirical news show *Last Week Tonight with John Oliver,* which is broadcast in North America on the premium cable channel HBO. This particular episode aired not long after Syriza came to power and Yanis Varoufakis took the helm of the country's debt negotiations. Oliver's shtick lampooned Varoufakis primarily for an infelicitous use of an allusion to Greek mythology. Calling Greece "a country in and of ruins," he noted how, at a recent press conference about a loan extension, Varoufakis had "tried to reassure people in the Greekest possible way." He then rolled footage of Varoufakis explaining to journalists that "sometimes, like Ulysses, you need to tie yourself on the mast in order to get where you're going and to avoid the Sirens. We intend to do this."[29] Varoufakis often uses such references (as we will see in a moment), but on this installment of *Last Week Tonight* Oliver tried to show how the strategy had backfired. When the clip ends, Oliver roars with mock exasperation that Varoufakis's remarks are not "reassuring, for two reasons: First, everybody in Ulysses' crew dies in that story, and Ithaca falls to absolute shit in his absence." Oliver's sarcasm amounted to an umpteenth version of the argument that holds that because of their superior knowledge, Westerners, especially the British, have stronger claims than the Greeks to the inheritance of Greek antiquity.

That argument was formulated nowhere so clearly as in the report issued in 1816 by the British House of Commons' select committee on Lord Elgin's marbles, which pronounced that "no country can be better adapted than our own to afford an honourable asylum to these monuments of the school of *Phidias,* and of the administration of *Pericles*" (see Chapter 4). Oliver's critique of Varoufakis thus painted a familiar picture: the Greek might attempt to invoke the classical past, but the Englishman really knows best. Oliver was clearly going for laughs and may not have been aware of the deep history behind his stance (he also may not have cared). Yet imagine the uproar that would ensue if a mainstream British television host haughtily mocked a politician from India for an infelicitous reference to an ancient Sanskrit epic, or if an *Economist* columnist punctuated a critique of Latin American politics with insinuations that the Peruvian people are shoddy excuses for Incas. What James Angelos called the West's bipolar stance toward Greece—the idea that ancient Greece belongs to the West, even if today's Greek people do not—has had the strange effect of keeping the Greeks fair game for the kind of jokes that in other cases simply would not be tolerated. Even *Focus* magazine called the Greeks "crooks in the Euro family." And after all, if you cannot tease your own family members, who can?

GREECE IS RUINED

In an October 2013 article in the *Journal of Modern Greek Studies,* archeologist Lauren Talalay offered one of the first academic analyses of the onslaught of classically themed political cartoons prompted by the Greek crisis. Drawing on images published between 2010 and 2012, she argued that there is "much more at stake in these cartoons than meets the eye" because these far-from-innocuous images actually reflect and reproduce deeply embedded Western notions of Hellenism's ancient successes and modern failures. In essence, they are the latest manifestation of the West's long-standing accusation that the Greeks have disgraced their ancient patrimony. In her article, Talalay also cited a revealing personal correspondence with British cartoonist and artist Patrick Blower, in which Blower offered an account of the countries that he and his cartoonist colleagues are most inclined to satirize: "USA top of the list. . . . Scotland punches well above its weight; France, England, Germany, Spain, Italy, etc. are an embarrassment of

"Greek Myth / Greek Math," July 2, 2015, cartoon by Steve Sack of the *Minneapolis (MN) Star Tribune.*

riches. Unanimous agreement, though, that Greece is a veritable feast. Thank God for Homer and our civilization's collective reliance on the Classics."[30]

Many of the cartoons, magazine covers, and even Internet memes aimed at satirizing the Greek debt crisis have especially relied on the public's ability to recognize the Athenian Acropolis as the symbolic heart of Greece. In May 2010, the *Economist* ran a cover story titled "Acropolis Now: Europe's Debt Crisis Spins out of Control"; in May 2012, the cover of *Der Spiegel* featured a fractured column and a broken euro coin with the text "Acropolis Adieu! Why Greece Needs to Leave the Euro" (Warum Griechenland jetzt den Euro verlassen muss). A number of images picture the Acropolis with a "for sale" sign. In May 2012, not long before the Athens Stock Exchange made a historic dip below five hundred points, another cartoon by Peter Schrank in the British *Independent* linked Greece's financial woes with the initial public offering of shares in Facebook. Standing in front of the Parthenon (for sale by "one careless owner"), one man suggests to another, "Maybe we should call Mark Zuckerberg." The Acropolis-for-sale images proved especially biting in part because certain European leaders have actually floated the idea that Greece should start selling off its ruins and other heritage sites (as well as small islands—Greece has thousands of them, although only 227 are inhabited) to help pay down its debt. In a 2010 interview with the German newspaper *Bild,* two German politicians, Frank Schäffler and Josef Schlarmann, maintained that Greece has a responsibility to its creditors to sell off its assets—companies, buildings, and islands. The article's sensational headline was even more inflammatory than the politicians' statements: "Sell Your Islands, You Bankrupt Greeks . . . and the Acropolis Along with Them!" (Verkauft doch eure Inseln, ihr Pleite-Griechen . . . und die Akropolis gleich mit!).[31]

In the early nineteenth century, the declaration of Greek independence heralded a new view of the importance of Greece's monuments, ruins, sculptures, and other material artifacts. These physical traces of antiquity were pressed into service as proof of the connection between the modern Greek people and their ancestors and even as justification for the existence of an independent Greek state (see Chapter 5). In the light of the role that monuments and ruins played in the work of Greek nation building, it is clear why calls for Greece to sell off its heritage—especially calls made by German politicians and the German media—cut so deep. The Greek national discourse often regards antiquities as possessed of their own life force: the Erechtheion caryatids in the New Acropolis Museum are imagined as still weeping at night for their missing sister in London. That force is supposed to

"Greek Ruins," May 16, 2012, cartoon by Rick McKee in the *Augusta (GA) Chronicle.*

connect all Greeks across the millennia. In analyses of the controversy surrounding the repatriation of the Parthenon Marbles, Yannis Hamilakis has repeatedly emphasized how the missing marbles "today stand as the exiled and imprisoned members of the national body. . . . Seen in that light, the marbles are not representations of ancestors, they *are* the ancestors."[32] According to this logic, even sardonic demands that Greeks sell off more of their heritage essentially ask the Greek people to do the same violence to themselves and their ancestors that the likes of Lord Elgin wrought. To reprise Hamilakis's metaphor, such demands call for further dismemberment of the "national body."

Dozens of cartoons have also used Greece's fame for its ancient ruins as a way of poking fun at the shambles of its modern economy, the country's newest debris. They tend to follow a fixed template: images

"It's a Fixer-Upper," July 15, 2015, cartoon by Gary Varvel in the *Indianapolis (IN) Star.*

of crumbling banks and beat-up ATM machines appear under titles along the lines of "Greece's New Ruins." Many of them depict tourists in front of tumbledown buildings and surrounded by broken pieces of marble. One example by American cartoonist Rick McKee features a typical dialogue: a tourist, camera in hand, declares, "I love the ancient Greek ruins." A woman beside him explains: "This was a bank yesterday."

In the summer of 2015, an anonymous Internet meme even envisioned a new phase in the restoration of the Acropolis's iconic Erechtheion. It depicted Angela Merkel in service as the missing caryatid (dressed in some unflattering swimwear), struggling to help prop up the Erechtheion's iconic porch—and, by extension, Greece and its collapsed economy. A handful of cartoons have also substituted

Merkel's image for other iconic statues from Greek antiquity. One example from relatively early in the crisis was by Bulgarian cartoonist Christo Komarnitski. It configured the German chancellor as the lost cult statue of Athena Parthenos, the colossal masterpiece by Pheidias, the sculptor of Pericles's fifth-century-BCE building program, that once stood inside the Parthenon. Amid tumbling columns, Merkel emerges as a triumphant Athena. The characteristic Gorgon head on her shield has been replaced by a snake in the shape of the euro currency sign: the European Union has here trumped and triumphed over both classical Athens and modern Greece.

Amid the vogue for accounts of new Greek ruins, the downfall of Greece as a modern-day cautionary tale is easy enough to construct.

"The Euro Parthenon," with Angela Merkel as Phidias's Athens in the ancient Parthenon, February 2, 2012, cartoon by Christo Komarnitski.

In 1682, George Wheler saw the plight of Greece as a sad case study of what might have happened to England had Oliver Cromwell's revolution enjoyed longer-term success. In his dedication to King Charles II, Wheler reflected, "When I consider the deplorable Condition of that once Glorious Nation, I cannot but adore the mercy of God to our own."[33] In July 2015, after the people of Greece overwhelmingly voted for the end of austerity in the Bailout Referendum, American conservative radio host Rush Limbaugh explicitly warned listeners of his show *This Is America* that the present state of Greece might well offer a glimpse at the United States' future. Limbaugh used part of his airtime that day to present a series of "facts" about the Greek mentality toward debt and social warfare. He claimed that on one Greek island alone, eight hundred people declare themselves blind for the free ride of government assistance. Limbaugh distilled the referendum as follows: "The people of Greece were asked to vote on cutting back social services and all kinds of crazy welfare state things, and they said F-no. F-you. F-no we're not cutting back a thing."[34]

Limbaugh's vision of Greece matches well with the typical media stereotypes, which cast Greeks as lazy, corrupt, tax-evading layabouts—an image perfectly captured in a May 2010 image by Slovak cartoonist Martin "Shooty" Sutovec. Limbaugh's anecdote, though, was from a 2015 book by James Angelos, *The Full Catastrophe: Travels among the New Greek Ruins*. Angelos's book guides the reader through crisis-stricken Greece, beginning with the island of Zakynthos, where 2 percent of the people allegedly claim to be blind. Angelos was deeply aware of austerity's catastrophic effects on the country. Yet despite his sensitivity to modern Greece's "problem" of ancient Greece (the topic of his previously mentioned *Politico* piece), in *The Full Catastrophe* he keeps the contrast between classical and contemporary Greece in sharp relief. Five of his seven chapters begin with quotations from famous ancient

"Greek Banquet," May 3, 2010, cartoon by "Shooty" (Martin Sutovec), syndicated by Cagle Cartoons.

Greek literary works and highlight the disparity between the land and its people's present and past.

Angelos's book in fact belongs to a small but emergent new subgenre of Greek travel literature, much of which reinforces, even if unintentionally, ethnic stereotypes about Greek corruption and laziness. A couple of years into the crisis, companies even began to offer luxury "crisis tours" of Athens and other spots in Greece. Publicity for a recent "Greece and the Euro" tour offered by the company Political Tours, which promises "travel beyond the headlines," advertised stops at Syntagma Square (a frequent site of political demonstrations), the municipality of Perama ("An example of frivolous spending and its results"), and empty sporting structures built at lavish expense for the 2004 Olympics.[35] This kind of tourism, dubbed *thanatotourism* (*thanatos* is a Greek word for "death") by some, is hardly new or even particularly rare. Intrepid, wealthy travelers can also book tours of former

first century, to whom does Greek antiquity belong? To which Greeks do citizens of the West supposedly owe a classical debt? Who are the debt's creditors, and just what is the nature of the repayment obligation? Certainly not ten euros for every "therefore."

SOFOKLIS AND SOPHOCLES

Those questions are difficult to separate from still further ones that are now being raised by the changing face of Greek society. In recent decades, the country's interwoven processes of modernization and globalization have given rise to greater population diversity, which in turn has led to debates about who is truly Greek—debates that only intensified with the refugee crisis. The Greek government's official data on "resident population citizenship" from 2011 (the most recent year available) tallied the country's legal permanent resident population as 91.6 percent Greek, 1.8 percent from the European Union, and 6.5 percent from "other countries" (the Greek government does not collect official data on race or ethnicity).[2] The 1991 figures, by contrast, had reckoned the entire legal immigrant population at just 1.6 percent.[3] None of these data count undocumented immigrants, and the 2011 numbers were compiled before hundreds of thousands of refugees arrived in Greece in 2015–2016 (many, though not all, of whom have since moved on or been sent back to Turkey). The statistics do, nevertheless, reflect the shifting demographics of twenty-first-century Greece and a diversity that poses challenges to one premise underlying the philhellenic conception of classical debt, formulated during the Greek War of Independence: that contemporary Greeks are descended from the Greeks of antiquity, a contention that Jacob Fallmerayer would later attempt to refute by arguing that modern Greeks are ethnically Slavic. New demographic realities do not risk similar wholesale dismissals of the

Greek population as "inauthentic" but have instead fostered internal divisions over the question of who within Greek society counts as Greek.

This point can be illustrated by the case of a Greek sporting celebrity. Greece is wild about basketball, and one of the most famous players of the past decades has been Sofoklis Schortsanitis. Schortsanitis, known as "Sofo" to his fans, has made a professional career on the Greek national team and with basketball franchises abroad (the Los Angeles Clippers even briefly flirted with signing him). He happens to be named after the most famous ancient Athenian tragedian, whose name in English is conventionally spelled Sophocles, the author of such celebrated plays as *Antigone* and *Oedipus the King*. Today the name Sophocles evokes all the glory of Greece's classical past in just three syllables. What most people might not expect, then, is that Sofoklis Schortsanitis is half Cameroonian.

Schortsanitis's father is Greek, but his mother is from Cameroon, where Schortsanitis was born and lived before moving to Greece as a child. But even though he has a Greek father, grew up in Greece, and speaks perfect Greek, that has not been enough to convince Ilias Panagiotaros, a leader of the extreme right-wing political party Golden Dawn, that he is Greek. Speaking on behalf of his party, in October 2012 Panagiotaros explained to the Greek television channel Extra 3: "We don't think that Schortsanitis, according to the criteria of the Hellenic race, is Greek. He's not Greek. Both of his parents would need to be Greek and belong to the European race. That's what we think. If you think that Schortsanitis is Greek, take him for your own party."[4]

The Golden Dawn is a group that would be very happy to see the myth of white ancient Greek statuary—and of thoroughly Caucasian ancient Greeks—perpetuated, especially as precedent for the Greeks'

Greek basketball player Sofoklis "Sofo" Schortsanitis in the uniform of the Greek national team.

essential "whiteness." Sofoklis Schortsanitis obviously does not fit the paradigm of the Greek ideal as formulated by Johann Winckelmann, an ideal that was treasured by Hitler and is now touted by members of the Golden Dawn. The many pages that Winckelmann dedicated to the nature of beauty in his 1764 *History of the Art of Antiquity* contain a clear account of the primacy of whiteness as a criterion for judging the beauty of a human body: "Since white is the color that reflects the most rays of light, and thus is most easily perceived, a beautiful body will be all the more beautiful the whiter it is." Although Winckelmann conceded that a "Moor can be beautiful when his facial features are beautiful," he explained that this is because beauty can come "in an unusual guise and in a color that in nature is displeasing" and is "thus different from agreeableness."[5] In her 2011 *A History of White People,* historian Nell

Irvin Painter traces how Winckelmann's formulations "elevated Rome's white marble copies of Greek statuary into emblems of beauty and created a new white aesthetic." That aesthetic, never informed by encounters with actual Greeks (Winckelmann never visited Greece), would come to "apply not only to works from antiquity, not only to Greek art, but to all of art and humanity."[6]

We have certainly encountered evidence in support of Painter's observation. The French writer Charles Maurras, for example, was dismayed at the "Oriental" appearance of the *korai* (archaic female statues) uncovered in 1886 during excavations on the Athenian Acropolis. Those statues severely disrupted his Caucasian fantasy of classical Athenians, which was surely shaped by Winckelmann's influence. Today, those statues are the darlings of the permanent collection at the New Acropolis Museum, but in a 1901 essay Maurras exclaimed: "If only someone would rid me of these Chinese girls!" Decades later, Winckelmann's characterization of the "Greek profile"—"the chief characteristic of a high beauty"—would come to underlie the Third Reich's understanding of the Aryan race: Hitler himself pronounced that "the Greek profile and that of the Caesars is that of the men of the North of ours, and I wager that I could find amongst our peasants two hundred heads of that type" (see Chapter 5). Winckelmann had idolized statues of young Greek athletes and faulted the art of ancient Egypt for having lent "a sort of Chinese cast to the Egyptian physique."[7] The thread that ties this line of thought to Ilias Panagiotaros's pronouncements is clear.

The Golden Dawn's position on Schortsanitis reveals a weakness at the foundation of the premise of classical debt, at least as it was constructed by nineteenth-century philhellenes and certain Greek revolutionary figures. When Westerners avow their civilization's debt to the descendants of the ancient Greeks, does their logic imply that they owe Sofo as much as they owe any modern offspring of Sophocles?

Percy Bysshe Shelley's pronouncement "We are all Greeks," formulated at the start of the Greek War of Independence, appears in one of the first attestations, the preface to his play *Hellas,* of Europe's metaphorical debt to Greece (see Chapter 4). In that preface, he expressed outrage over "the apathy of the rulers of the civilized world" to the plight of "the descendants of that nation to which they owe their civilization." He harped on the point of lineage: "The modern Greek," he insisted, "is the descendant of those glorious beings whom the imagination almost refuses to figure to itself as belonging to our kind, and he inherits much of their sensibility, their rapidity of conception, their enthusiasm, and their courage."[8]

The principle of modern Greek ethnic descent from ancient Greeks was born largely of European political and social thought in the late eighteenth and early nineteenth centuries. In Chapter 4, we saw just how radical a development the idea represented. Even in the late 1700s, European travelers complained that the Greeks called themselves Romiotes or even just simply "Romans." Within just half a century, the War of Independence saw Greece's modern inhabitants reinvented, with considerable philhellenic encouragement, as Hellenes. In hindsight, it may seem inevitable that the twin concepts of ancient Greek glory and Greek ethnic continuity would one day flower into an aggressive strain of nationalism.

Ever since the financial crisis began in Greece, Shelley's momentous declaration that "we are all Greeks" has nevertheless been resurrected as a battle cry of an international movement against austerity and in support of the Greek people. On one level, the phrase's new lease on life seems straightforward enough as an expression of sympathy and solidarity. Although it is nearly two centuries old, it also calls to mind a famous and much more recent statement that reporter Nicole Bacharan made on French news the evening of September 11, 2001:

"Ce soir," Bacharan momentously declared, "nous sommes tous Américains" (Tonight we are all Americans). The "We are all Greeks" Facebook page was created in 2012 and boasts more than 140,000 likes by users. Its banner advertises leftist politics with a saying attributed to the Argentine revolutionary Che Guevara ("Happy is he who gives without remembering and receives without forgetting").[9] It is understandable that those who support Greece today would adopt Shelley's old sound bite of British Romanticism as a kind of motto: there is no doubt that many of those who "liked" the Facebook page would be quick to express solidarity with Greeks who look like Schortsanitis, too. Yet it is also important to be mindful of the implications of the ideology at the root of Shelley's pronouncement, founded as it was on the assumption of ethnic continuity between the ancient and modern Greek people, on the concept of their common blood. When he wrote, "We are all Greeks," he meant that "we" who live in the Western "civilized world" are Greeks because the ancient Greeks gave us civilization, and we therefore (that's another ten euros) owe our support—financial, military, and otherwise—to their modern blood descendants.

GUARDS WORTHY OF HEROIC ANCESTORS

In Greece today, the West's white ideal of antiquity has manifested itself more generally in the persecution of immigrants. For some, shared heritage in classical antiquity is a criterion for true membership in the Greek nation (the *ethnos*). And for those deemed not to belong, antiquity's symbols can become powerful, intimidating weapons.

One particularly telling cartoon by the Greek political cartoonist Soloúp ran in May 2011 in the Greek weekly satirical newspaper *Pontiki*. It depicts two men pummeling two others. One of the men on the ground asks his assailants whether they are "Hrisavgistas," members of the Golden Dawn (Hrisi Avgi in Greek). One replies: "Yes, sort of like the Atenistas." The other explains what this means: "Volunteers who clean up the city" (Atenistas are volunteers who, since 2010, have been working to clean and beautify Athens by, for example, creating more public parks). What is most striking about this cartoon is that one of the Hrisavgistas is battering the men—immigrants, to judge by their darker skin color—with a marble column. In the light of the nineteenth-century efforts to "purify" the Acropolis of foreign barbarisms (see Chapter 5), it is all too tempting to interpret this cartoon as Soloúp's critique of a more modern and violent "purification" program, once again based on a classical, white Greek ideal.

Soloúp's image of extreme right-wing Greeks beating immigrants with a column is a chilling one, but the year after his cartoon ran, even the Greek government capitalized on the metaphor of

"Hrisavgistas," May 19, 2011, cartoon by Soloúp in *Pontiki*.

antiquity-as-weapon. In the summer of 2012, Greek police carried out a series of roundups of some 6,500 immigrants under the aegis of an operation code-named Xenios Zeus. In ancient Greek, *xenios* can mean "hospitable," and thus Xenios Zeus is "Zeus as protector of guests and strangers." One of the program's decriers stressed the odd choice of name, a phrase usually associated with the tourism industry: "Some critics thought it outrageous, offensive sarcasm, a direct and blatant provocation. Others thought it unintentionally ironic."[10] In a piece for the Greek news outlet *ThePressProject,* political analyst Konstantinos Poulis dryly sighed: "There's no point in fighting with the extreme Right over ideological handling of the past."[11] Like Soloúp's cartoon, the name of that anti-immigrant operation—an ironic English equivalent might be "Welcome Wagon"—points to a broader pattern in Greek xenophobic rhetoric and policy.

This sort of imagery, like the Golden Dawn itself, emerged largely in the context of the economic crisis, even before the arrival of refugees into Greece began to make world headlines. In August 2015, the United Nations High Commissioner for Refugees reported that the year's influx of refugees to Greece, some 124,000, already represented a 750 percent increase over the previous year.[12] In October, the count hit the half-million mark. The next year, between January 1 and April 21, 2016, more than 150,000 new refugees arrived.[13] Greece's already delicate position as the eastern frontier of Europe, both geographically and metaphorically, quickly served to cast it in an impossibly difficult role as the continent's guardhouse and gateway.

The refugee crisis clearly lurked in the background of a high-profile event conducted by a government official on September 30, 2015. That event carried an implicit anti-immigration message but was presented as a solemn memorial service for the anniversary of the Battle of Salamis. In 480 BCE, Greek forces led by the Athenian navy defeated the

Persians at Salamis, in a battle now often portrayed as a watershed moment in the rise of the West. The Athenians enshrined their success in the battle when they constructed the gateway of the Acropolis (the Propylaea) to frame the strait where it took place, and the Athenian memory of Salamis lay at the heart of the foremost attribute of the city's brand: "Athens saved Greece from barbarians." That aspect of the brand served as justification for the Athenian Empire and for the annual tribute that "allied" states paid to the city, nominally in return for protection against the threat of a future Persian invasion. Salamis thus contributed a great deal to Athens's formulation of the earliest classical debt: the debt that the rest of Greece owed to Athens.

Today, many members of the Greek Right see the Battle of Salamis as an ancient emblem of the country's ongoing commitment to defend itself against new kinds of foreign "invasions." At the Salamis ceremony in September 2015, Panos Kammenos, leader of the right-wing party Independent Greeks and Greece's minister of defense, paid his respects to the Greek ancestors who in 480 BCE defeated Xerxes and his army of invaders from the East. He walked to the edge of the sea over a specially strewn red carpet and placed a wreath on the water. As he did so, sailors in the Greek navy stood at attention. The event also featured a group of female extras, carefully arrayed to enhance the occasion's dignity. Some were outfitted in Greek national costume, but others were styled as ancient Greek women, all in white, bearing what one newspaper called "symbols of antiquity."[14]

In his formal remarks, Kammenos informed his fellow Greeks, "We celebrate today the naval battle which took place in September 480 BC in Salamis, not only as a historical event but also to honor the vast contribution to world history of the united Greek forces against the Persian invader." By way of conclusion, he declared, "It is our imperative commitment towards the heroes of our history and towards future

generations as well, to be watchful guards worthy of our heroic ancestors."[15] Before and during the Greek War of Independence, certain philhellenes had also made pilgrimages to Salamis and "invoked it as a
locus classicus of the 'salvation' of Western civilization."[16] Shelley's play
Hellas reenvisioned Aeschylus's tragedy *The Persians,* a play about
Xerxes's defeat at Salamis, as a prophecy of the triumph of Greece over
the Ottoman Empire. At his Salamis commemoration, Kammenos
pledged to support a bid to make Salamis the European Capital of
Culture in 2021. Many of the old philhellenes surely would have
approved.

In Greece, the arrival of refugees from Syria and other "Eastern"
countries intensified an atmosphere already thick with xenophobic
distrust and occasional outright racism. Hard feelings against immigrants and refugees are, of course, not unique to Greece, and both European countries and the United States have recently seen related
outbursts of nationalistically rooted bigotry. But while the refugee crisis
exposed and deepened divisions within Greece, it also added a great
deal of pressure to the country's already strained relationship with the
rest of Europe. Struggling to manage a financial and humanitarian
crisis of their people's own, Greek politicians insisted that other European countries do more both to curb the entry of refugees and to care
for those who had already managed to arrive. In February 2016, Prime
Minister Alexis Tsipras made a memorable statement of his position
that other European Union member states should assume more of
the burden. "What we refuse to do," he told Parliament, "is accept the
transformation of our country into a permanent warehouse of souls
and, at the same time, continue to act within the European Union and
at summits as if there's nothing wrong."[17] On a number of later occasions, Tsipras reaffirmed his wish that his country not become a "ware-

house of souls" *(apothiki psikhon)*. Ironically, that is exactly how the media began describing it.

Greece's handling of refugee arrivals fanned Europe's doubt about whether Greece really belongs in its number—a doubt first planted by the observations of early European travelers, who often remarked how the (Muslim) Ottoman Empire had (further) corrupted the character of the Greek people. Similar suspicions broke the surface again toward the end of 2015 as Europe's leaders once more entertained the possibility of revoking certain "privileges" associated with Greece's European status. This time the prospect was not one of a potential Grexit, the specter of which had dominated news cycles throughout the previous summer. Instead, the question centered on the future of Greece's participation in the Schengen area, the open border zone that, since the Schengen Agreement of 1985, has permitted free travel among twenty-six European member states. In the late fall of 2015, Slovakian prime minister Robert Fico voiced to London's *Financial Times* what many were thinking: that "it is high time" to eject Greece from the Schengen area. Fico also noted that all the leaders of the Schengen states were in private agreement on the point.[18]

For the second time in less than six months, Greece's European credentials had been publicly called into question by other European countries. Anthropologist Michael Herzfeld was one of the few public intellectuals who openly and rightfully cried racism. In a February 2016 article for *Foreign Policy*, he underscored the "exclusionary logic at the heart of not just the Schengen system, but also the European Union." He argued that because of that logic, the international refugee crisis "has also exposed Greece's tenuous cultural membership in that project." Herzfeld identified an insidious legacy of bigotry—a deep-seated prejudice against the fundamentally "Oriental" Greeks—at the heart of the threats to revoke the country's Schengen status. Acknowledging that most proponents of expelling Greece would vehemently deny racist motivations, he emphasized that the consequence of kicking Greece out of the club would nevertheless be clear: "The alleged birthplace of democracy will be treated as an anomaly, a foreign growth on the European body politic."[19]

Herzfeld's piece highlighted the hypocrisy of European leaders who saw Greece as the birthplace of Western democracy but also advocated putting an end to its membership in what *Focus* magazine memorably called the "Euro family." Generally, Greek antiquity has not played as prominent a role in the refugee crisis as it has in coverage of the financial one; the Greeks are not held culpable for the origins of this crisis, but only for its mishandling. Nonetheless, when refugee arrivals in Greece began to increase significantly in the first half of 2015, some political cartoonists also began to use icons of classical Greece to draw attention to the bitterness of Greece's "tale of two crises." Drawing particular inspiration from the conceit of the new "ruination" of Greece's economy and society (see Chapter 6), they reimagined that ruination in the context of the impossibly high demands on the country to receive hundreds of thousands of displaced people. On March 7, 2016, as heads of European Union member states worked to forge a deal that would allow them to send "all new irregular migrants" back to Turkey, Italian journalist and political cartoonist Vauro Senesi responded by envisioning a new role for the armless Venus de Milo. Senesi's cartoon, which ran in the Italian daily newspaper *Fatto Quotidiano,* portrayed the fragmented statue, not flipping the bird at her creditors (as she had on the cover of the February 22, 2010, issue of *Focus*), but doing her best to extend her arms to waves of refugees despite not having arms to extend. The text dripped with sad irony: "Migrants. In the Europe of walls only Greece has open arms." The controversial deal between the European Union and Turkey, denounced in many quarters as inhumane and illegal, was struck eleven days later, on March 18, 2016. It went into effect two days later, leaving tens of thousands of refugees in limbo, but still in Greece.

LOOK AFTER THE ANTIQUITIES!

Like many recent world events, the Greek Right's large-scale appropriation of antiquity, especially over the past decade, raises further questions about the nature of ownership of antiquity and antiquities. Who has the right to claim possession of antiquity or any particular relic of it? What does it mean to "own" the past, or even its material artifacts, and what rights and privileges do those who claim to be the past's true defenders believe that they gain? In the West, the history of heritage preservation is hardly unblemished, even by Western criteria. In some cases, the West's notion that it has a unique commitment to human heritage has proved to be exactly what leads to the destruction of artifacts.

The complicated question "Who owns antiquity?" can be illustrated by a small, rather out-of-the-way news story from July 2015. That month, in the full heat of Greece's hectic tourism season, a little article about a German tourist with a lot of chutzpah blew up Greek social media. The article first appeared on the news website of a radio station based on Crete (inotos.gr, 88.4 FM), but within hours it was picked up and reposted by dozens of Greek media outlets. Comment after comment left by outraged readers made clear that something bigger was brewing under the surface of this ultimately inconsequential incident. This is a translation of the piece, which never broke in non-Greek news outlets:

"THE ANTIQUITIES BELONG TO US!" THE AUDACITY OF A GERMAN TOURIST AT THE HERAKLION ARCHEOLOGICAL MUSEUM

July 26, 2015

It is well known that Germans have been more wary about coming to our country after the treatment our country received from Chancellor A. Merkel and Finance Minister W. Schäuble in the latest negotiations.

But there are also German tourists who make no hesitation about showing . . . their audacity at the first chance they get. One incident with a German tourist, uncovered today by inotos.gr, crossed every line and left employees at Heraklion's Archaeological Museum speechless.

It was one morning last week and the Archaeological Museum of Heraklion was packed. A German family was visiting our treasures. At a certain moment, the German father of our story approached a female guard at the museum and, in all seriousness (but also audacity, as we see it), told her: "look after the antiquities, because they belong to us and we want to make good use of them."

The guard was . . . astounded. Her surprise gave way to irritation, but unfortunately staff regulations did not allow her to respond to the German tourist.

Incidentally, according to information obtained by inotos.gr, tour guides confirm that the majority of German tourists avoid any kind of political or economic conversation and instead restrict their questions to topics of a historical and archeological nature.[20]

The anonymous author of the story knew well that the piece and the tourist's German nationality would hit a nerve with the Greek public.

Not long after the crisis began, certain German politicians had started to call on Greece to sell off the country's antiquities to help pay down the debt (see Chapter 6). In the summer the story ran—the same summer in which a video played in Athens metro stations calling on Germany to pay reparations for the Nazi occupation of Greece— German chancellor Angela Merkel and German finance minister Wolfgang Schäuble made daily headlines for their unwavering stance on Greece's debt obligations. Heraklion's archeological museum refuses to confirm the incident, but in a response to an official request for comment, it affirmed that it recognizes and respects the right of all its visitors to freedom of speech. One likely possibility is that the episode never happened as described. The previous summer had, after all, seen a similar story outed as a hoax: a stingy German couple supposedly sat for a good long while at the taverna Korali, in the port town of Evdilos on the island of Icaria, but ordered only a paltry five euros' worth of food and drink. That bit of "news" was first posted on social media by the popular Greek singer Matthaios Giannoulis (the self-avowed eyewitness). He included a photograph of the bill, which was later outed as having been doctored. This was, nevertheless, a hoax that appealed to Greek stereotypes about German stinginess and indifference to the plight of the Greek people: Giannoulis's account earned thousands of social media "likes."[21]

Whoever wrote the article about the German tourist at the museum added even more of the ingredients—German arrogance, prized antiquities, implied allusions to those antiquities' historical plundering and to foreign assumptions about Greeks' inability to "look after" them— that make for speedy sharing across social media. The story's instant notoriety also underscored the persistence of one Greek view of the nation's antiquities, with roots as deep as the War of Independence: that artifacts of ancient Greek civilization incontrovertibly belong to Greeks.

Yet the logo of the United Nations' world heritage organization, UNESCO, is based on an image of the Parthenon, which in one sense implies that the monument belongs to the whole world. UNESCO is the organization that designates "world heritage sites": sites of documented "outstanding universal value."[22] Seventeen of those 1,052 "properties" are located in Greece.[23] The Minoan palatial centers in Crete (Knossos, Phaistos, Malia, Zakros, and Kydonia) are not yet officially recognized by UNESCO but appear on its "tentative list." One of the criteria for designation is that a site "be directly or tangibly associated with events or living traditions, with ideas, or with beliefs, with artistic and literary works of outstanding universal significance."[24] The proposal for the Minoan Palatial Centers explains the sites' fulfillment of that requirement as follows: "The myths connected to the Minoan palaces (the Minotaur and the Labyrinth, Daedalus and Icarus, Theseus and Ariadne, etc.) exercised a great influence on mythology and the arts throughout the ancient world and remain a source of inspiration for world art, music and literature today."[25] Artifacts from the Minoan palatial centers are the stars of the Heraklion Museum. With UNESCO's rhetoric of world heritage and universal value in mind, let us perform a thought experiment. Imagine that the German tourist approached the Greek guard not in 2015 but at some point in the future, when the Minoan sites had been formally added to UNESCO's list. Imagine, too, that instead of saying, "Look after the antiquities because they belong to us," that tourist were to say, "Look after the antiquities because they belong to all of us." What if a Chinese tourist were to make the pronouncement, or an Egyptian or a Colombian or even an American? Would the watchdogs of UNESCO see that guard—or any other Greek—as entitled to take offense?

What, moreover, does it mean to "look after the antiquities"? In some cases, Westerners are eager to prove their commitment to do so even when they do not actually possess the antiquities that seem to need looking after. In the summer of 2015, the Islamic State set about systematically committing atrocities among the monuments of ancient Palmyra (recognized since 1980 as a UNESCO site). The events of Palmyra occurred in the context of a brutal chapter in the Syrian civil war, the conflict that brought so many refugees into Greece that summer. Yet the destruction of antiquities at Palmyra captured the attention and provoked the sadness of the West as few other human atrocities in the region did. That destruction continued into the autumn, and October saw ancient Palmyra's "triumphal arch," first built in the third century CE, leveled to the ground. Six months later, members of the British public responded by setting up a re-creation of the arch in London's Trafalgar Square. The London replica enjoyed a great deal of enthusiastic press, but other voices were sharply critical of the ideology that the installation also seemed to put on display.

One such critic was the art historian Mirjam Brusius. In a piece titled "The Middle East Heritage Debate Is Becoming Worryingly Colonial," Brusius argued that Western efforts to "remake" destroyed Middle Eastern antiquities are troubling because they show implicit subscription to the old line of thought that equates "'the Orient' with destruction and 'the West' with salvage."[26] That position, she wrote, can be traced back to "19th and 20th-century stances of imperialism, a context in which both archaeology as well as heritage concepts have their origins." Although the modern form of the concept may date to that period, we have also seen that its foundation was laid in the fifth century BCE, however unwittingly, by the Athenian response to the Persian Wars. During those wars, Greeks and Persians alike laid waste each other's sanctuaries; later, when the Athenians began to redevelop the Acropolis, they left rubble from earlier structures on view in new walls and temple foundations (see Chapter 2). Those visible reminders of defeat amounted to silent declarations of resilience, but they were also pronouncements that Athenians, unlike the barbarous Persians, were piously committed to preserving the material past.

In the light of the European West's pride in its commitment to preserve antiquities, recent criticisms of the Greek state for failing to look after its antiquities are an indication of the more general wariness that characterizes the relationship between Greece and Europe. In March 2016, Tom Nuttall, the "Charlemagne" columnist for the *Economist,* called on Italy and Greece both to step up investment in their heritage sites. He argued that part of the problem with Greece's approach to conservation is that "the state lays claim to total ownership of the past. . . . Private cultural initiatives, even those funded by Greeks, are often met with disdain."[27] The Greek state's assumption of responsibility for (and ownership of) antiquities shortly after its declaration of independence from the Ottoman Empire became a hallmark of its largely European-driven strategies of nation building. Now, however, the country has been cited for failing to protect its antiquities in the interests of all of Europe. To remedy the problem, Nuttall suggested that Greece should cooperate more closely with the European Union on matters of heritage management. The title of his piece, "The Necessity of Culture: Europe's Shared History Should Be Treasured, Not Ignored," is a good illustration of how preservation is valorized in the European West. Yet within that framework, the case of Greece is especially delicate because Greece's antiquity is so often cast as the first site of a collective European (Union) past.

One consequence of Western commitments to heritage has, ironically, been the destruction of antiquities. Ömür Harmanşah, an art historian and archeologist of the ancient Near East, has noted how the Islamic State—its members fully aware of the West's fetish for material antiquities—intentionally "choreographs" spectacles of artifact destruction, in part just to elicit reactions from Western audiences. Such spectacles, he points out, are orchestrated "in an attempt to allure their sympathizers and patrons, recruit further fanatics, humiliate local communities while annihilating their sense of heritage, and offend the humanitarian West."[28] The chilling implication? When citizens of the West share the Islamic State's videos on social media, buy up antiquities from the Islamic State's black market, and respond by generally foretelling the triumph of Western light over Eastern darkness, they are effectively following Islamic State orders. Harmanşah underscores that the Islamic State released videos of members destroying artifacts because its leaders knew that the message would spread quickly via likes and links on social media. Likewise, the story about the German tourist at the Heraklion Museum may well have been written because its author knew that it would be shared.

Over the past two centuries, Western enthusiasm just to acquire antiquities has led to the development of a complex black market for their trade. Illegally looted antiquities—many of which have no known archeological context and so are of little use to researchers—have made their way to some of the world's most prestigious museums. But even professional archeologists' desire to discover and excavate artifacts has come at a more obvious human cost. During the French Mandate of Syria and Lebanon, excavations began at Palmyra under Henri Seyrig, the French director of the Antiquities Service. Intent on clearing the ancient site of Palmyra for excavations and other archeological work, from 1929 to 1932 Seyrig oversaw the relocation of the entire village of Tadmur (as Palmyra is known in Arabic), which had been inconveniently built atop the ancient site. With the village (and villagers) removed, his team was free to begin excavation and *anastilosis,* the rebuilding of toppled ancient monuments. One guidebook to Syria written shortly before civil war broke out in 2011 noted that "many of the families still come on Fridays to picnic within the site close to their abandoned houses, school, mosques and churches."[29]

In Greece, both the Greek government and archeologists from foreign schools (in conjunction with the Greek government) have also been responsible for the destruction and appropriation of a startling amount of occupied buildings, all in the name of archeology, heritage, and preservation. In 1893, after a long period of negotiations, the French School at Athens was granted the right to begin systematic excavations at Delphi, the ancient sanctuary of Apollo and site of the Delphic oracle. Ancient Delphi had been built over in the Middle Ages, and the presence of an inhabited village among and atop the ruins was an impediment to archeological work. One consequence of the negotiations was the passage in Greece of an eminent-domain law dictating that private land containing antiquities may be expropriated by the state. Together, the French School and the Greek government arranged for the demolition of the houses of some three hundred local people, who had vocally and tenaciously attempted to resist forcible removal from their homes.

Thirty years later, the American School of Classical Studies in Athens negotiated permission to excavate the site of the Athenian Agora, the ancient city's marketplace at the foot of the Acropolis. At the time, refugee camps were being set up in Athens (and elsewhere in Greece) to house more than a million Christians who had recently been forced into Greece by the "exchange of populations" that concluded the Greco-Turkish War (the conflict that ended with the creation of the country of Turkey). The Greek Parliament voted not to assume responsibility for the Agora excavation because of the huge cost of expropriating land from so many people. Thus the American School, backed by the wallet of John D. Rockefeller, gained permission for the project and assumed responsibility for the destruction of some 365 inhabited houses spread over twenty-four acres. Shortly before the area of Vrissaki was flattened, a typewriter seller posted a sign in the window of his shop announcing, "Seeing as antiquities have existed for centuries underneath the buildings in our area . . . we are therefore being demolished."[30] Demolition of the houses, cafés, restaurants, and other businesses in Vrissaki, comprising three different neighborhoods, began in 1932, the same year in which the relocation of Palmyra's residents by the French Antiquities Service was completed.

Over the past couple of decades, major museums have come under intense scrutiny for their histories of acquiring antiquities through complex organized networks of looters and brokers. The Euphronios Krater, looted from an Etruscan tomb in 1971 and then smuggled out of Italy and sold to New York's Metropolitan Museum of Art, is just one of many notorious examples (the krater was repatriated to Italy in 2008). Such unprovenanced antiquities stand primarily as trophies to curators' continued desire to "possess" the ancient past. Artifacts have also been damaged by professional conservation efforts in museums. Before the construction of the New Acropolis Museum, one of the most popular arguments against the return of the Elgin Marbles was the alleged inability of the Greeks to conserve and display—to "look after"—them properly. Yet even these highly prized works, now nearly synonymous with the whole artistic achievement of classical Athens, have suffered at the hands of conservators. Not long after the museum acquired the marbles, controversy erupted over efforts to clean them. Michael Faraday, the scientist most famous for his breakthroughs in electromagnetics, was particularly upset by how they were being prepared for the molding process (molds allow casts, replicas of sculptures and friezes, to be made). In 1836, a committee was appointed to determine what evidence the sculptures still bore of their original bright-colored paint. In its report, the committee noted that in Faraday's opinion, corrosive cleaning chemicals (soap lye and caustic acids) had "removed every vestige of color that might have existed originally on the surface of the marble."[31] In other words, the already age-whitened marbles had been chemically "restored" to seem even whiter. A century later, in the 1930s, scandal erupted when the museum attempted to cover up another round of cleaning—in this case unauthorized—undertaken in advance of the marbles' transfer to the newly donated, purpose-built gallery where they are still displayed today.

At a two-day symposium held at the British Museum at the end of 1999, a team of Greek conservators and archeologists presented the findings of their investigations into the marbles' care and condition at the museum. Elisavet Papazoi, then Greek minister of culture, pronounced that the many instances of "barbarous cleaning" had erased valuable information, including not just paint but also original chisel marks.[32] The British Museum continues to insist that the story is much more complicated: officials admit that mistakes might have been made, but they urge that nineteenth- and early twentieth-century efforts at cleaning and restoration be viewed in their proper historical contexts.[33] In the June 2012 London debate about the Elgin Marbles, Stephen Fry proposed that in place of the marbles, the museum should install an exhibit about their history. As part of that exhibit, "you would see a period of two hundred years in which we curated them beautifully."[34] But as Papazoi's comments illustrate, not everyone would agree with Fry's claim about how well the sculptures have fared since the British government acquired them, or that the British Museum has always "curated them beautifully."

THE FUTURE OF THE CLASSICAL DEBT?

Ancient artifacts can be of just as much symbolic significance as the West's self-proclaimed debt to Greece. The famous case of the Elgin Marbles, with which this book began, is an especially rich and complex illustration of just how closely the two issues can be entwined. July 11, 2016, marked the two hundredth anniversary of the marbles' acquisition by the British government. In advance of the date, campaigners redoubled their efforts to persuade the British Museum to relinquish the marbles to Greece (the International Association for the Reunification of the Parthenon Sculptures boasts sixteen member organizations in as many different countries, from Britain to Brazil and from Canada to Cyprus).[35] In May, a 141-page legal document titled "The Case for the Return of the Parthenon Sculptures" was leaked to the *Guardian*.[36] The document had been prepared by a legal team that had recently investigated the validity of the Greek claims. It labeled the refusal of the trustees of the British Museum to negotiate with Greece (or even consider the claim seriously) "untenable" and argued that "international law has evolved to a position which recognises, as part of the sovereignty of a state, its right to reclaim unique cultural property of great historic significance which has been wrongfully taken in the past." Today that law "would entitle Greece to recover and reunite the Parthenon sculptures."[37]

On June 23, less than three weeks before the marbles' British bicentenary, the people of Britain voted by a hairline majority to exit the European Union. The figure of Boris Johnson happened to make for an intriguing link between the two sets of headlines. Johnson, now Britain's foreign secretary, was a prominent leader of his country's "Leave" campaign. He has also been insistent that the Elgin Marbles should stay. His history of involvement in the issue began long ago, when as an undergraduate he moderated the 1986 Oxford Union debate that pitted Melina Mercouri against Gavin Stamp. Nearly thirty years later, while mayor of London, he responded with characteristic bluntness to a public call by actor George Clooney for Britain to restore the Elgin Marbles: "Someone," Johnson commented, "urgently needs to restore George Clooney's marbles."[38] During his time as mayor, Johnson was an especially enthusiastic advocate for the study of Greek and Latin in British schools. In April 2016, he was even chosen to unveil the replica of Palmyra's triumphal arch in London's Trafalgar Square. Years earlier, as a member of Parliament, he had also expressed equal enthusiasm for Britain's colonial past. In a 2002 op-ed in London's *Spectator* (of which he was then the editor), he explained that "the best fate for Africa would be if the old colonial powers, or their citizens, scrambled once again in her direction."[39]

Johnson is not the first British figure whose views unite nationalism (and admiration for the British Empire) with insistence that the country hold on to the Elgin Marbles. The two positions have had a perceived link since the nineteenth century. In 1891, the Alexandrian Greek poet Constantine Cavafy published an essay titled "The Elgin Marbles" in the Athenian paper *Ethniki*. In it, he observed that for some members of the British public, retaining the marbles was tantamount to holding on to the nation's glory and its glorious empire. The essay was a response to a recent piece in the periodical *Nineteenth Century*, written by the magazine's editor. Cavafy summed up that editor's position as follows: "He vilifies Byron. He associates the carrying away of the marbles with the glorious victories of Nelson. He thinks that if the marbles are restored, Gibraltar, Malta, Cyprus, India must be given away also."[40] The June 2016 victory of the "Leave" campaign in Britain was widely read as a sign that nostalgia for the days of empire is still strong among certain segments of the British population. Of course, not everyone who is opposed to the marbles' reunification in Greece shares other views held by Boris Johnson, and certainly not the kind of views that he expressed in his 2002 *Spectator* piece. Nonetheless, the Elgin Marbles remain potent, storied symbols and tangible evidence of the success of at least one of Britain's former colonization efforts: the metaphorical colonization of Greek antiquity.

In Greece, one strain of the national conversation today is once again questioning what it would mean for the country to leave antiquity's legacy behind—not wholesale, for antiquity is inseparable from the history of the nation. Rather, the suggestion has been to cease bringing fanciful dreams of Greek classical antiquity to bear on the modern world. Konstantinos Poulis, a writer and political analyst, articulated one version of that suggestion in an episode of his popular Greek satirical show *Roundup (Anaskopisi)*. When, in 2015, it emerged that one of the conditions for a new bailout of Greece would be that the country promise to privatize more than 50 billion euros' worth of state assets, Poulis dedicated an episode of the show to a modest proposal: why not just sell the Acropolis? The episode was conceived as headlines in Germany snarkily called on Greece to sell off islands and antiquities alike and to send the proceeds to creditors. Poulis took the idea and ran with it. "A solution like this," he argued, "to pack up the rocks and send them to England, or to have the English come over here and buy them, will give Greece not just a financial boost but a moral and psychological one as well. It will be a sign of our present-day awesomeness: no longer will we have to swing from Pericles' balls just to get some respect."[41]

Poulis made an important point with his satire. For the Greeks "just to get some respect" in the European West, the specter of what they once were must always be present. When it is not, the public tends to react with a measure of surprise. Even as the media punish Greece for

Still from season 1, episode 10 ("Let's Sell the Acropolis!") of Konstantinos Poulis's satirical show *Anaskopisi,* produced and directed by Costas Efimeros of *ThePressProject.*

the modern failures of attempts to revive its ancient glory, they still demand that the country playact old tourism-board roles that rely on sea, sun, and ruins. But new cultural production is challenging that image. In 2016, Penguin released a collection of Greek poetry composed since the economic crisis broke out. The poems in the volume, *Austerity Measures: The New Greek Poetry,* were translated by literary scholar Karen Van Dyck. Referring, presumably, to a trope of ancient Greek myth, one reviewer observed that the volume contains "poems about metamorphosis (as you might expect from Greek writers)."[42] But Van Dyck herself was careful to point out how far these poems depart from the typical image of Greece. In the *Guardian,* she wrote, "Nothing here is as one might expect, even from the Greek poetry of the recent past." Why? For one thing, here there are "not many statues; not much myth, at least in the classical sense."[43] If Greece's experience of crisis is finally starting to have any positive effect at all, it may well be to dispel some very old commonplaces about the country's essential, unshakable identity.

That task will be difficult. Today there are still two robust strains of thought about classical debt: that the conceit is still valid, and that it is not. Those ideas can be mapped onto—even seen as radical outgrowths of—the two separate faces of the Athenian brand's last attribute:

Attribute 4.   Athens is the product of exceptional ancestors.
Attribute 4'.   Athens was much better in the past.

The first formulation of the attribute has its analogue in one camp's continued insistence on a symbolic debt that assumes the existence of a legitimate link between Greeks and their "exceptional ancestors." The second version, implied by those who deny the debt's (continued) existence, rejects the idea that there is any human connection between the country of Greece and the Greece that was so "much better in the past."

In following the history of the Western conceit of classical debt, this book has also followed the contours of a larger story: how the West claimed a dream of Greek antiquity for its own and then tried but apparently failed to fashion a new nation to conform to that dream. After the failure of the Greek Bailout Referendum, the cultural theorist Slavoj Žižek wrote an opinion piece that hewed to the bone of why attempts to realize such dreams often turn out so badly. However much European technocrats insist that austerity will lead to Greek economic growth in Greece, he argued, in reality, the Greek people are being forced to suffer for a European economic and political fantasy. He also quoted one of his favorite sayings, by the French philosopher Gilles Deleuze: "Si vous êtes pris dans le rêve de l'autre, vous êtes foutus" (If you're caught in someone else's dream, you're fucked).[44]

Deleuze's pronouncement could well apply to a whole host of someone else's dreams that have entangled Greece since its birth as a nation-state. Those dreams have contributed a great deal to the fraught and complex three-way relationship at the heart of the story here: among the West, classical antiquity, and modern Greece. Even today they give shape and urgency to the questions posed at the start of this book: How does a fantasy of ancient Greece reflect the values that are at the core of "Western civilization"? Who deserves to be counted as members of that civilization? Does Greece belong in today's Europe, or is it just the legacy of ancient Greece that belongs to the European West? These are questions that do not have definitive answers, which may well be an indicator that they are not, especially at this point, productive ones to be posing. But they are being posed, at least implicitly, and now perhaps in more difficult ways than ever. This book has aimed to fill in some of the historical background that helps explain why that is so.

The story we have seen here ultimately suggests that if Western countries do owe Greeks something symbolic today, it is not because liberal democracy (or philosophy or logic, or art or drama) on the Western model was invented in classical Athens. It is because those countries, with a great deal of Greek support, have long held Greece's people captive to a fantasy of their past and have repeatedly punished them for not living up to it.

Is there a better future for the concept of classical debt? Perhaps the concept would benefit from redefinition. Under new terms, the debt could cease to be seen as one that is owed to (certain) Greeks whose literal ancestors supposedly illuminated the path of Western civilization. Rather, it could be construed as a debt owed for the centuries of destruction that other people's dreams of the ancient past have wrought. Reenvisioned this way, the debt would be owed to Greeks—and to people from countless other places, too—by anyone willing to take it on.

In other words, the reconceived debt would be owed to everyone whose life has been worsened, or whose human value has been demeaned, at the hands of the West's Greek ideal. For far too long, dreams of the ancient past have been allowed to justify stances of bigotry, programs of "purification" (of all sorts), and blindness to the suffering of those who dwell in the present. The list of new creditors would include Shelley's Greeks, but also Sofoklis Schortsanitis, a Greek whose right to call himself a member of Greek society has been denied by people who look to antiquity to find precedents for their hate. Besides many others, the list would also encompass the hundreds of thousands of immigrants and refugees who have of late been metaphorically bludgeoned by antiquity and its symbols. This concept of debt might sound too loose and symbolic to right any wrongs or effect any practical change. Nevertheless, it is no more abstract—and no less rooted in antiquity—than the old "classical debt" whose history this book has traced.

Epilogue: A Note for Educators

ON THE AFTERNOON OF MAY 8, 2015, 110,000 high school students took the U.S. College Board's Advanced Placement Exam in European History. The exam covers European history from 1450 to the present, and twelve of the fourteen textbooks deemed by the College Board to meet the exam's "curricular requirements" have either "Western" or "The West" in their titles.[1] Those books often begin with surveys of ancient Egypt and Mesopotamia, but it is the civilization of ancient Greece that typically emerges as the most important forerunner of modern Europe.

As they prepared for the test, some of the students would have come across this passage from one of the approved textbooks:

Another way of appreciating the enduring importance of Greek civilization is to recall the essential vocabulary we have inherited from it: not only the word *democracy* but *politics, philosophy, theater, history.* How would we think without these concepts? The very notion of humanity comes to us from the Greeks.[2]

In *Teaching Global History: A Social Studies Approach,* education professor Alan J. Singer has noted that still today "social studies teachers may be presenting 'Greek myth' as history when they attribute the origin of 'Western Civilization' to ancient Greece."[3] Many books for advanced-placement courses and exams in European history and world history repeat, with varying degrees of nuance, platitudes like the ones quoted above. They stress the flowering of art and development of "realistic" sculpture in classical Athens; they also highlight the Greeks' supposed invention of "rational thought" ("Going beyond mythmaking," one explains, "the Greeks strove to understand the world in logical, rational terms").[4] But some students might rightly question, if a textbook claims that Greeks invented rational thought (let alone "the notion of humanity"), does that not imply that the Greeks' predecessors and contemporaries around the world were "irrational"? To return to Mircea Eliade's terms, many students are still being encouraged to see the ancient Greeks as having created "cosmos" amid chaos.

Approaches to the study of ancient Greek civilization at schools and universities have, in reality, grown far more attuned to the connectivity and multiculturalism of the ancient Mediterranean; they have also become much more tempered in their still-detectable praise of what used to be called the "Greek miracle." This heartening trend reflects the cross-pollination of ideas and approaches among scholars and educators at all levels. Within the academy, the past few decades have seen an explosion of interest in the cultural contacts between ancient Greeks, Egyptians, Persians, and others. In the early years of the twenty-first century, the field of classics also began to change radically with the introduction of "reception studies," a subfield dedicated to "the inquiry into how and why the texts, images and material cultures of Ancient Greece and Rome have been received, adapted, refigured, used and abused in later times and often other places."[5] These kinds of innovations have, happily, led to some university courses on, for example, the interactions (peaceful as well as martial) between ancient Greeks and Persians, and to others that set the *Bacchae* by Euripides side by side with the *Bacchae* of the Nigerian author Wole Soyinka, a play influenced by Greek as well as Yoruban traditions. Meanwhile, in secondary schools, newer editions of history textbooks are presenting more candid accounts of Athens's empire and democracy (and its limited direct influence on modern political structures); they are also franker about crucial points such as the extent of slavery in Greek—and not just Roman—antiquity.

There is, nevertheless, still room for improvement. What follows are three very brief suggestions for ways in which educators at all levels might continue the important work of introducing a more honest and realistic perspective to accounts of Greek antiquity.

1. *Acknowledge the considerable role played by ancient Athenian propaganda in constructing "Western" views of the city and its achievements.*

Another textbook often used by teachers of advanced-placement world history accounts for Pericles and "Periclean" Athens as follows:

> Under the leadership of Pericles, Athens became the most so-phisticated of the [Greek] poleis, with a vibrant community

of scientists, philosophers, poets, dramatists, artists, and architects. Little wonder, then, that in a moment of civic pride, Pericles boasted that Athens was "the education of Greece."[6]

According to Thucydides, Pericles made that claim in his funeral oration for the Athenians who had fallen in the first year of the Peloponnesian War. This version of an Athenian *epitaphios logos* makes exactly the same claim as the textbook: that Athens was the most "sophisticated" of all the Greek city-states. In Chapter 2, we saw how important the funeral orations (and the state funerals) were to the Athenians' formulation of their classical-era brand, but also that they were so over-the-top that even Athenians criticized them.

The problem is by no means limited to textbooks. In the fall of 2015, when the refugee crisis was at its peak in Greece, one classical scholar argued in the *Conversation* that ancient Athenian tragedies, such as Euripides's *Suppliants* and *Medea,* offer instructive explorations of ancient thought about refugees. Those plays explore the obligations, as well as risks and costs, of accepting refugees; they are also proof of how "Athens prided itself on welcoming the needy from other parts of the Greek world."[7] Yet on this point, too, Athenian representations can be misleading. At about the time at which Euripides wrote *Suppliants,* his city established a kind of "police station" at the entrance to the Acropolis, with "the clear aim of keeping undesirable suppliants away from the sanctuaries in the fortress."[8] Euripides's "refugee plays" might thus serve as an excellent prompt for classroom considerations of how a community, city, or nation's view of itself differs from its realities. In the United States, students might be especially encouraged to reflect on why it is that, in a country that styles itself as a "nation of immigrants," anti-immigrant sentiment also runs so strong.

2. *Encourage students to recognize how the notion of an ancient "Greek miracle" contributed to the predominant origin myth of "Western civilization."*

Many textbooks now highlight how limited enfranchisement was under the Athenian democracy: neither women nor slaves were allowed to participate in the political process. These books should also take care to point out that many of the ancient Greek thinkers most respected today were sharp critics of democracy. Plato's *Republic*, for example, stresses on many occasions that democracy leads to tyranny.[9] Such ancient criticisms contributed to the skepticism of the United States' "founding fathers" (many of whom were classically educated) about democracy; that skepticism in turn gave rise to their mixed constitution characterized by checks and balances. Educators would also do well to emphasize how Anglo-American Cold War ideology led to the myth that Athens was the cradle of Western liberal democracy—a model of democracy that from the start was tempered by wariness about granting too much "power to the people."

There is also room for more caution on the matter of ancient Greek art. Some textbooks point out that many ancient sculptures that today appear white have actually lost what was once vibrantly colored paint. Yet any introduction to the art of Greek antiquity should also be careful to stress that immensely destructive traditions of racial supremacy have been bolstered by the misconception that those statues, like the ancient Greeks themselves, were beautiful because they were "white."

Educators, especially those who use course materials with "Western Civilization" in their titles, should also stress that people from Western societies have been far from the only ones to engage with and seek to preserve aspects of Greek antiquity. Nor is Western cultural production unique in having drawn inspiration from ancient Greece. For this point, Evliya Çelebi's section on Athens in his *Book of Travels* could prove an illuminating text. In Chapter 3, we saw how Evliya, who was influenced by the Islamic inheritance of ancient Greek thought, had a view of seventeenth-century Athens that was on many points very different from that of the French and British travelers who were his contemporaries. Both views were nevertheless based on culturally determined fantasies about Athens and its antiquity. Evliya's memoir further illustrates that a history of admiration for Greek antiquity might be seen as more of a bridge than a barrier between "West" and "East."

3. Encourage students to consider alternative views of and approaches to heritage appreciation and management.

Climate-controlled museums and closely guarded archeological sites are not the only modes of "looking after" antiquities. The British Museum was famously touted by its former director Neil MacGregor as a "Museum of and for the World."[10] Museums of that scale are often seen as the positive ends that justify the doubtful means of the collectors we saw at work in Chapter 3, most of whom had no intention of ever putting their acquisitions on public display. This line of thought serves to reaffirm the long-held Western misperception of Eastern "indifference" toward antiquities. In her critique of the replica of ancient Palmyra's triumphal arch (constructed in London's Trafalgar Square in 2016), art historian Mirjam Brusius issued this important reminder and reality check for Western audiences: "Contrary to what the current debate implies, there [is] not a 'Middle East' or 'heritage' deemed valuable by everyone and thus in need of saving. The past is not a finite resource: the very definition of 'the past' is contestable."[11] Students should be encouraged to examine their assumptions about what an "antiquity" is and what determines its value. What is the distinction, for example, between an antiquity and an antique? Is there a difference between, say, using timber from an eighteenth-century barn to build a new farmhouse table and reusing an ancient inscription to pave a walkway? (Surely some people would think that this hypothetical barn should be restored rather than dismantled.) If there does seem to be a difference, what criteria are used to account for it? Students should be urged to consider how material heritage can also be acknowledged and cared for in ways that do not necessarily entail CCTV-monitored display cases.

Chapter 1 of this book mentioned a three-part National Geographic Society documentary titled *The Greeks,* which premiered in the United States on PBS in June 2016. The first line of that documentary introduces the show's subject with this pronouncement: "They rose from nothing . . . and changed everything." It may be a long time before filmmakers, headline writers, political cartoonists, and other commentators give up saying and implying just that. We can, however, far sooner accustom ourselves to hearing the claim with a more critical ear.

NOTES

1. CHAMPIONS OF THE WEST

1. Intelligence Squared, "About Intelligence Squared," http://www.intel ligencesquared.com/about-intelligence-squared.

2. "Cambridge Union Elgin Marbles Debate Results," *British Committee for the Reunification of the Elgin Marbles,* February 22, 2008, http://www.par thenonuk.com/2008-news-archive/228-cambridge-union-elgin-marbles -debate-results.

3. Greece.org, "Melina's Speech to the Oxford Union," http://www.greece .org/parthenon/marbles/speech.htm.

4. Intelligence Squared, "Send Them Back: The Parthenon Marbles Should Be Returned to Athens," filmed June 11, 2011, YouTube video, 46:38, posted June 22, 2012, https://www.youtube.com/watch?v=YE7DpRjDd-U.

5. Dan Bilefsky and Niki Kitsantonis, "Greek Civil Servants Strike over Aus- terity," *New York Times,* February 11, 2010, http://www.nytimes.com/2010 /02/11/world/europe/11greece.html. I thank Despina Lalaki for bringing this quotation to my attention.

6. Finbarr Barry Flood, "Between Cult and Culture: Bamiyan, Islamic Icon- oclasm, and the Museum," *Art Bulletin* 84 (2002): 641.

7. John Terry, "Why ISIS Isn't Medieval: It's Actually Viciously Modern," *Slate,* February 19, 2015, http://www.slate.com/articles/news_and_politics

/history/2015/02/isis_isn_t_medieval_its_revisionist_history_only
_claims_to_be_rooted_in.html.

8. Mircea Eliade, *The Sacred and the Profane: The Nature of Religion,* trans. Willard R. Trask (New York: Harper and Row, 1959), 29.

9. Samuel P. Huntington, *The Clash of Civilizations and the Remaking of World Order* (New York: Simon and Schuster, 1996), 46.

10. Ibid., 69–70.

11. David Gress, *From Plato to NATO: The Idea of the West and Its Opponents* (New York: Free Press, 1998), 1.

12. Quoted in Amanda Wrigley, *Greece on Air: Engagements with Ancient Greece on BBC Radio, 1920s–1960s* (Oxford: Oxford University Press, 2015), 147.

13. See especially Mary Lefkowitz, ed., *Not out of Africa: How Afrocentrism Became an Excuse to Teach Myth as History* (New York: New Republic and Basic Books), 1996.

14. PBS, "The Greeks," http://www.pbs.org/program/greeks.

15. G. H. Hardy, *A Mathematician's Apology* (Cambridge: Cambridge University Press, 1992), §8.

16. Rémi Brague, *Europe, la voie romaine* (Paris: Critérion, 1992; published in English as Rémi Brague, *Eccentric Culture: A Theory of Western Civilization,* trans. Samuel Lester [South Bend, IN: St. Augustine's Press, 2002]).

17. Charles Stewart, "Dreams of Treasure: Temporality, Historicization, and the Unconscious," in *Hellenisms: Culture, Identity, and Ethnicity from Antiquity to Modernity,* ed. Katerina Zacheria (Aldershot, UK: Ashgate, 2008), 279. Quoted in Dimitris Tziovas, "Introduction: Decolonizing Antiquity, Heritage Politics, and Performing the Past," in *Re-imagining the Past: Antiquity and Modern Greek Culture,* ed. Dimitris Tziovas (Oxford: Oxford University Press, 2014), 1.

18. Quoted in Mark Mazower, *Inside Hitler's Greece: The Experience of Occupation, 1941–1944* (1993; reprint, New Haven, CT: Yale University Press [Yale Nota Bene], 2001 [first published 1993]), 8.

19. Dan-el Padilla, "From Damocles to Socrates: The Classics in / of Hip-Hop," *Eidolon,* June 8, 2015, https://eidolon.pub/from-damocles-to-socrates -fbda6e685c26#.fxnvkvvq9. I thank Kathleen Larkin for the Jay-Z reference.

20. Karen Crouse, Doug Mills, and Chang W. Lee, "Michael Phelps' 14th Individual Gold Breaks Ancient Record," *New York Times,* August 11, 2016, http://www.nytimes.com/2016/08/12/sports/olympics/michael -phelps-200-im-ryan-lochte-leonidas.html; "Michael Phelps Spots Estranged Father Poseidon in Stands," *Onion,* August 11, 2016, http://www .theonion.com/article/michael-phelps-spots-estranged-father-poseidon -sta-53494.

21. Daniel Mendelsohn, "Unburied: Tamerlan Tsarnaev and the Lessons of Greek Tragedy," *New Yorker,* May 14, 2013.

22. "Ancient Greece: A Lasting Legacy: A Suggested 6th Grade Unit of Study: Gifted / Talented & Enrichment," *NYC Public Schools,* http://schools.nyc .gov/documents/teachandlearn/GT/G&T_2008_Greece_Unit_of_Study _FINALweb.pdf.

23. Pierre Briant, *Alexandre des Lumières: Fragments d'histoire européenne* (Paris: Gallimard, 2012; issued in English as *The First European: A History of Alexander in the Age of Empire,* trans. Nicholas Elliott [Cambridge, MA: Harvard University Press, 2016]).

24. I thank Sharmila Sen of Harvard University Press for this formulation.

25. Huntington, *Clash of Civilizations,* 139.

26. Giorgos Christides, "Could Europe Lose Greece to Russia?," *BBC News,* March 12, 2015, http://www.bbc.com/news/world-europe-31837660.

27. Huntington, *Clash of Civilizations,* 158.

28. Panagiotis A. Agapitos, "Byzantine Literature and Greek Philologists in the Nineteenth Century," *Classica et Mediaevalia* 43 (1992): 238.

29. Charles Diehl, "Byzantine Civilisation," in *The Cambridge Medieval History,* vol. 4, *The Eastern Roman Empire (717–1453),* general editor J. B. Bury

(Cambridge: Cambridge University Press, 1923), 774. I thank @Byzant Justice for the reference.

30. "European Luminaries Reflect on Euro: 'Seventeen Countries Were Far Too Many,'" *Spiegel Online,* September 11, 2012, http://www.spiegel.de /international/europe/spiegel-interview-with-helmut-schmidt-and -valery-giscard-d-estaing-a-855127.html.

31. Patricia Storace, *Dinner with Persephone* (New York: Pantheon Books, 1996), 8.

32. Niall Ferguson, *Civilization: The West and the Rest* (London: Penguin Books, 2011), 15.

2. HOW ATHENS BUILT ITS BRAND

1. "Cambridge Latin Course (North American Fourth Edition)," Cambridge University Press, http://education.cambridge.org/us/subject/classics /latin/cambridge-latin-course-(north-american-fourth-edition).

2. Athenaeus (third century CE), *Deipnosophists* 272c–d.

3. Paulin Ismard, *La démocratie contre les experts: Les esclaves publics en Grèce ancienne* (Paris: Éditions du Seuil, 2015). Issued in English as *Democracy's Slaves: A Political History of Ancient Greece,* trans. Jane Marie Todd (Cambridge, MA: Harvard University Press, 2017).

4. *Aeneid* 6.847–853.

5. E. N. Tigerstedt, *The Legend of Sparta in Classical Antiquity,* vol. 2 (Uppsala: Almqvist & Wiksell, 1974), 2.

6. Herodotus 5.105.

7. Samantha Martin McAuliffe and John K. Papadopoulos, "Framing Victory: Salamis, the Athenian Acropolis, and the Agora," *Journal of the Society of Architectural Historians* 71 (2012): 332–361.

8. Daniel Mendelsohn, "Deep Frieze: What Does the Parthenon Mean?," *New Yorker,* April 14, 2014.

9. Aristophanes, *Birds* 276–278.

10. Herodotus 5.102.

11. Rachel Kousser, "Destruction and Memory on the Athenian Acropolis," *Art Bulletin* 91 (2009): 264.

12. Aeschylus, *Persians* 1026.

13. Edith Hall, *Inventing the Barbarian: Greek Self-Definition through Tragedy* (Oxford: Oxford University Press, 1989). One of Hall's reviewers was right to note that the Orientalizing phenomena that she tends to ascribe vaguely to the "Greeks" are more specifically Athenian in origin: Malcolm Heath, "Inventing the Barbarian," *Classical Review* 41 (1991): 90–92.

14. Edith Hall, "Aeschylus' *Persians* via the Ottoman Empire to Saddam Hussein," in *Cultural Responses to the Persian Wars: Antiquity to the Third Millennium,* ed. Emma Bridges, Edith Hall, and P. J. Rhodes (Oxford: Oxford University Press, 2007), 169.

15. Barry Strauss, *The Battle of Salamis: The Naval Encounter That Saved Greece—and Western Civilization* (New York: Simon and Schuster, 2004).

16. Victor Davis Hanson, *Carnage and Culture: Landmark Battles in the Rise of Western Power* (New York: Doubleday, 2001).

17. See, for example, "Problems Facing N.A.T.O. Killed Ancient Greek Alliance," *Louisville (KY) Courier-Journal,* May 6, 1962, https://www.newspapers.com/newspage/109018111. See also Yannis Ragoussis, "Greece and NATO: A Long Lasting Relationship," *NATO Review,* 2012, http://www.nato.int/docu/review/2012/turkey-greece/greece-nato-partnership/en/index.htm.

18. Nathan Arrington, *Ashes, Images, and Memories: The Presence of the War Dead in Fifth-Century Athens* (Oxford: Oxford University Press, 2015), 113.

19. Thucydides 2.24.2–6, translation by Robert Crawley in Robert B. Strassler, *The Landmark Thucydides: A Comprehensive Guide to the Peloponnesian War* (New York: Free Press, 1996).

20. Thucydides 2.65.9.

21. Thucydides 2.40–41.

22. Thucydides 2.43.

23. Quoted in Amanda Wrigley, *Greece on Air: Engagements with Ancient Greece on BBC Radio, 1920s–1960s* (Oxford: Oxford University Press, 2015), 146.

24. Plato, *Menexenus* 234c–235c.

25. Isocrates, *On the Peace* 87.

26. Simon Goldhill, "The Great Dionysia and Civic Ideology," *Journal of Hellenic Studies* 120 (1987): 58–76.

27. Isocrates, *On the Peace* 82.

28. Euripides, *Erechtheus* fragment 360.8–12 Kannicht.

29. Plutarch, *Life of Alexander* 8.3 and *On the Fortune of Alexander* 5 = *Moralia* 328d.

30. Denis Feeney, *Beyond Greek: The Beginnings of Latin Literature* (Cambridge, MA: Harvard University Press, 2015).

31. Robin Rhodes, *Architecture and Meaning on the Athenian Acropolis* (Cambridge: Cambridge University Press, 1995), 92.

32. Plutarch, *Life of Pericles* 8.2.

33. Plutarch, *Life of Pericles* 12.2.

34. Plutarch, *Life of Pericles* 13.3.

35. Thucydides 1.10.

36. Inscription 2.69, lines 16–19 (ca. 116 BCE), in *Fouilles de Delphes*, vol. 3, *Épigraphie*, fasc. 2: *Inscriptions du Trésor des Athéniens* (Paris: Fontemoing, 1913).

37. Thucydides 1.23.4–6.

38. Thucydides 1.144.1.

39. Aristotle, *Constitution of the Athenians* 24.

40. Thucydides 3.36–49.

41. Aristophanes, *Frogs* 72.

42. Demosthenes, *On the Crown* 319.

43. Lycurgus, *Against Leocrates* 121.

3. COLONIZERS OF AN ANTIQUE LAND

1. K. E. Fleming, *The Muslim Bonaparte: Diplomacy and Orientalism in Ali Pasha's Greece* (Princeton, NJ: Princeton University Press, 2014), 13.

2. Cicero, *Letters to Quintus* 1.1.5. I thank Josh Pugh Ginn for the reference.

3. Dimitri Gutas, *Greek Thought, Arabic Culture: The Graeco-Arabic Translation Movement in Baghdad and Early ʿAbbāsid Society (2nd–4th / 8th–10th Centuries)* (London: Routledge, 1998), 93–95.

4. So argued the ninth-century Abbasid scholar and author al-Jahiz, as quoted by Franz Rosenthal in *The Classical Heritage in Islam*, trans. Emile Marmorstein and Jenny Marmorstein (London: Routledge, 1992), 18.

5. Robert Dankoff and Sooyong Kim, *An Ottoman Traveller: Selections from the Book of Travels of Evliya Çelebi* (London: Eland, 2010), 7.

6. Ibid., 278–279. All the following quotations from Evliya are from pages 280–285.

7. George Wheler, *A Journey into Greece . . . in the Company of Dr. Spon of Lyon* (London: William Caldeman et al., 1682), 332, 342.

8. Ibid., 337.

9. Ibid., 342.

10. Plutarch, *Moralia* 348b.

11. Wheler, *Journey into Greece*, 345.

12. Michael Harrigan, *Veiled Encounters: Representing the Orient in 17th-Century French Travel Literature* (Amsterdam: Rodopi, 2008), 129.

13. Wheler, *Journey into Greece*, 360, 352, and 364, respectively.

14. Patricia Fortini Brown's phrase throughout *Venice and Antiquity: The Venetian Sense of the Past* (New Haven, CT: Yale University Press, 1996).

15. Henri Omont, *Missions archéologiques françaises en Orient au XVIIe et XVIIIe siècles: Première partie* (Paris: Imprimerie Nationale, 1902), 616–617.

16. W. S. Lewis, ed., *The Yale Edition of Horace Walpole's Correspondence*, 48 vols. (New Haven, CT: Yale University Press, 1937–1983), 18:211.

17. Mark Crinson, *Empire Building: Orientalism and Victorian Architecture* (London: Routledge, 1996), 202.

18. Richard Chandler, *Travels in Asia Minor; or, An Account of a Tour Made at the Expense of the Society of Dilettanti*, 2nd ed. (London, 1775), ix.

19. Richard Chandler, *Travels in Greece: or, An Account of a Tour Made at the Expense of the Society of Dilettanti*, 2nd ed. (London, 1776), 131.

20. Ibid., 50.

21. Ibid., 51.

22. Ibid., 133–134.

23. Ibid., 136.

24. Chandler, *Travels in Asia Minor*, 39.

25. Thomas Roe, *The Negotiations of Sir Thomas Roe, in His Embassy to the Ottoman Porte, from the Year 1621 to 1628, Inclusive* (London: Samuel Richardson, 1740), 512, quoted by Benjamin Anderson in "An 'Alternative Discourse': Local Interpreters of Antiquities in the Ottoman Empire," *Journal of Field Archaeology* 40 (2015): 453.

26. Anastasia Stouraiti, "Collecting the Past: Greek Antiquaries and Archaeological Knowledge in the Venetian Empire," in *Re-imagining the Past: Antiquity and Modern Greek Culture*, ed. Dimitris Tziovas (Oxford: Oxford University Press, 2014), 29–46.

27. C. M. Woodhouse, *The Philhellenes* (Rutherford, NJ: Fairleigh Dickinson University Press, 1971), 27.

4. FROM STATE OF MIND TO NATION-STATE

1. This is the story as Melina Mercouri told it at the 1986 Elgin Marbles debate in Oxford: Greece.org, "Melina's Speech to the Oxford Union," http://www.greece.org/parthenon/marbles/speech.htm.

2. Artemis Leontis, *Topographies of Hellenism: Mapping the Homeland* (Ithaca, NY: Cornell University Press, 1995), 4.

3. K. E. Fleming, "The Paradoxes of Nationalism: Modern Greek Historiography and the Burden of the Past," *Bulletin of the Royal Institute for Inter-Faith Studies* 3, no. 2 (2001), http://riifs.org/old/review_articles/review_v3no2_fleming.htm (emphasis in original).

4. As translated in H. B. Nisbet, *German Aesthetic and Literary Criticism: Winckelmann, Lessing, Hamann, Herder, Schiller and Goethe* (Cambridge: Cambridge University Press, 1985), 33.

5. Constanze Güthenke, *Placing Modern Greece: The Dynamics of Romantic Hellenism, 1770–1840* (Oxford: Oxford University Press, 2008), 5 and passim.

6. Quoted in Robin Middleton, *Julien David Le Roy: The Ruins of the Most Beautiful Monuments of Greece* (Los Angeles: Getty Publications, 2004), 17.

7. Johann Joachim Winckelmann, *History of the Art of Antiquity,* trans. Harry Francis Malgrave (Los Angeles: Getty Publications, 2006), 304, 305, 312.

8. Katherine Harloe, *Winckelmann and the Invention of Antiquity* (Oxford: Oxford University Press, 2013).

9. Friedrich August Wolf, *Darstellung der Altertumswissenschaft* (Berlin: Realschulbuchhandlung, 1807), 16 (emphases in original).

10. Edith Hall, "Classics for the People—Why We Should All Learn from the Ancient Greeks," *Guardian,* June 20, 2015, http://www.theguardian.com/books/2015/jun/20/classics-for-the-people-ancient-greeks.

11. David E. Roessel, *In Byron's Shadow: Modern Greece in English and American Literature* (Oxford: Oxford University Press, 1997), 26–27.

12. Paschalis M. Kitromilides, *Enlightenment and Revolution: The Making of Modern Greece* (Cambridge, MA: Harvard University Press, 2013), 71.

13. Peter Walcot, *Greek Peasants, Ancient and Modern* (New York: Barnes and Noble, 1970); Margaret Alexiou, *The Ritual Lament in the Greek Tradition* (Cambridge: Cambridge University Press, 1974).

14. Eugene F. Miller, ed., *David Hume, Essays: Moral, Political, and Literary* (Indianapolis: Liberty Classics, 1985), 205–206.

15. Thomas W. Gallant, *The Edinburgh History of the Greeks, 1768 to 1913: The Long Nineteenth Century* (Edinburgh: Edinburgh University Press, 2015), 48.

16. Stathis Gourgouris, *Dream Nation: Enlightenment, Colonization, and the Idea of Modern Greece* (Stanford, CA: Stanford University Press, 1996), 97.

17. Greek Ministry of Education and Religious Affairs, General State Archives, "Rigas Feraios Map," http://www.gak.gr/frontoffice/portal.asp ?cpage=RESOURCE&cresrc=341&cnode=1&clang=1.

18. Vangelis Calotychos, *Modern Greece: A Cultural Poetics* (Oxford: Berg, 2003), 26.

19. Henry A. V. Post, *A Visit to Greece and Constantinople, in the Year 1827–8* (New York: Sleight and Robinson, 1830), 247.

20. *Report from the Select Committee of the House of Commons on the Earl of Elgin's Collection of Sculpted Marbles &c.* (London: W. Bulmer, 1816), 32.

21. Ibid., xxv (emphasis in original).

22. Edward Daniel Clarke, *Travels in Various Countries of Europe, Asia, and Africa, Part the Second: Greece, Egypt, and the Holy Land, Section the Second* (London: R. Watts, 1814), 484.

23. Fred. Sylv. North Douglas, *Essay on Certain Points of Resemblance between the Ancient and Modern Greeks,* 3rd corrected ed. (London, 1813), 85–86.

24. Lord Byron, *English Bards and Scotch Reviewers: A Satire* (London: James Cawthorn), 80 (lines 1009–1010).

25. Lord Byron, *Childe Harold's Pilgrimage* (London: John Murray, 1816), 67 (canto 2, stanza 13).

26. Ibid., 101 (canto 2, stanza 72).

27. Reported by Thomas Moore, *Letters and Journals of Lord Byron*, vol. 1 (London: J. and J. Harper, 1830), 255.

28. *Report from the Select Committee,* 4–5.

29. Ibid., 27 (emphasis in original).

30. Alexander Ypsilantis, "Address to the Greeks," *Niles' Weekly Register* (Baltimore), May 26, 1821, 206–207.

31. William St. Clair, *That Greece Might Still Be Free: The Philhellenes in the War of Independence* (Oxford: Oxford University Press, 1972; reprint, Cambridge: Open Book, 2008), 23–24.

32. Thomas Gordon, *History of the Greek Revolution*, vol. 1 (Edinburgh: Blackwood and Cadell, 1832), 183.

33. Percy Bysshe Shelley, *Hellas: A Lyrical Drama* (London: Charles and James Ollier, 1822), viii (emphasis in original).

34. Ibid., ix–x.

35. Byron, *Childe Harold's Pilgrimage*, 170.

36. Roderick Beaton, *Byron's War: Romantic Rebellion, Greek Revolution* (Cambridge: Cambridge University Press, 2013), 129.

37. Leicester Stanhope, *Greece, during Lord Byron's Residence in That Country, in 1823 and 1824* (Paris: A. and W. Galignam, 1825).

38. Edward Blaquiere, *Report on the Present State of the Greek Confederation, and on Its Claims to the Support of the Christian World: Read to the Greek Committee on Saturday, September 13, 1823* (London: G. and W. B. Whittaker, 1823), 28.

39. Daniel Webster, "Speech on the Greek Revolution," in *The Life, Speeches, and Memorials of Daniel Webster,* ed. Samuel Mosheim Smucker (Philadelphia: Duane Rulison, 1862), 306.

5. GREEK MIRACLE 2.0

1. Ernest Renan, *Recollections of My Youth,* trans. C. B. Pitman (London: Chapman and Hall, 1883), 151.

2. Miriam Leonard, *Socrates and the Jews: Hellenism and Hebraism from Moses Mendelssohn to Sigmund Freud* (Chicago: University of Chicago Press, 2013), 180.

3. Quoted by Ilias Arnaoutoglou, "'Διὰ δόξαν ἐκείνων καὶ κλέος τοῦ ἔθνους': The Philomousos Society of Athens and Antiquities," in *The Province Strikes Back: Imperial Dynamics in the Eastern Mediterranean,* ed.

Björn Fórse and Giovanni Salmieri, Papers and Monographs of the Finnish Institute at Athens 13 (Helsinki: Suomen Ateenan-instituutin säätiö, 2008), 124–125.

4. Yannis Hamilakis, *The Nation and Its Ruins: Antiquity, Archaeology, and National Imagination in Greece* (Oxford: Oxford University Press, 2007), 79.

5. William Miller, *Greek Life in Town and Country* (London: George Newnes, 1905), 184.

6. Quoted in Eleni Bastéa, *The Creation of Modern Athens: Planning the Myth* (Cambridge: Cambridge University Press, 2000), 102.

7. Hamilakis, *Nation and Its Ruins*, 88.

8. Eleni Hadjoudi-Tounta, *Adventures of the Acropolis Marbled Girls* (Athens: Agyra, 2012), 12 (English version of *Οι Καρυάτιδες μετράνε τα φεγγάρια* [Athens: Agyra, 2003]).

9. Ibid., 29.

10. Artemis Leontis, *Topographies of Hellenism: Mapping the Homeland* (Ithaca, NY: Cornell University Press, 1995), 74; the translation of the speech is after Richard Clogg, *A Short History of Modern Greece* (Cambridge: Cambridge University Press, 1979), 76.

11. Quoted in Richard Stoneman, *Land of Lost Gods: The Search for Classical Greece* (London: Hutchinson, 1987; reprint, London: Tauris Parke Paperbacks, 2010), 149.

12. École française d'Athènes, "Les circonstances d'une naissance," http://www.efa.gr/index.php/fr/ecole-francaise-athenes/histoire/1846-1870.

13. Charles Maurras, "Les musées d'Athènes (I)," *L'action française* 4 (1901): 894.

14. Greece.org, "Melina's Speech to the Oxford Union," http://www.greece.org/parthenon/marbles/speech.htm.

15. Gavin Stamp, "Keeping Our Marbles," *London Spectator*, December 10, 1983, 16.

16. Translated from the text as it appears in Eleftherios G. Skiadas, "Ολυμπιακές Διαδρομές: Η πρόταση του Παναγιώτη Σούτσου για την αναβίωση των Ολυμπιακών Αγώνων το 1834," *Μικρός Ρωμηός* (electronic journal of the Museum of the City of Athens), http://mikros-romios.gr /panagiotis-soytsos.

17. Basil Lanneau Gildersleeve, "My Sixty Days in Greece. I. The Olympic Games, Old and New," *Atlantic Monthly,* February 1897, 210, 211.

18. E. M. Butler, *The Tyranny of Greece over Germany: A Study of the Influence Exercised by Greek Art and Poetry over the Great German Writers of the Eighteenth, Nineteenth and Twentieth Centuries* (Cambridge: Cambridge University Press, 1935).

19. H. R. Trevor-Roper, ed., *Hitler's Table Talk: 1941–1944* (New York: Enigma Books, 2008), 220.

20. Johann Joachim Winckelmann, *History of the Art of Antiquity,* trans. Harry Francis Malgrave (Los Angeles: Getty Publications, 2006), 210.

21. Mark Mazower, *Inside Hitler's Greece: The Experience of Occupation, 1941–1944* (1993; reprint, New Haven, CT: Yale University Press [Yale Nota Bene], 2001), 157.

22. Despina Lalaki, "On the Social Construction of Hellenism: Cold War Narratives of Modernity, Development and Democracy for Greece," *Journal of Historical Sociology* 25 (2012): 553.

23. Ibid., 569–570.

24. C. M. Woodhouse, *Karamanlis: The Restorer of Greek Democracy* (Oxford: Clarendon Press, 1982), 266n11.

25. Richard Clogg, *A Concise History of Greece* (Cambridge: Cambridge University Press, 1992), 154.

26. Elizabeth Marlowe, "Cold War Illuminations of the Classical Past: 'The Sound and Light Show' on the Athenian Acropolis," *Art History* 24 (2001): 581.

27. Nicole Loraux, *The Invention of Athens: The Funeral Oration in the Classical City*, trans. Alan Sheridan (New York: Zone Books, 2006), 30–33.

28. Marlowe, "Cold War Illuminations," 581–582. Pericles's lines are drawn from Thucydides 2.37–41.

29. "Οι κρυφοί τεταρταυγουστιανοί. Γράφει ο Ιός," *TVXS*, August 5, 2013, http://tvxs.gr/news/egrapsan-eipan/oi-kryfoi-tetartaygoystianoi-grafei -o-ios.

30. Dimitris Plantzos, "Archaeology and Hellenic Identity, 1896–2004: The Frustrated Vision," in *A Singular Identity: Archaeology and the Hellenic Identity in the Twentieth Century*, ed. Dimitris Damaskos and Dimitris Plantzos (Athens: Benaki Museum, 2008), 18.

31. *George Seferis: Poems*, trans. Rex Warner (London: Bodley Head, 1960), 12.

32. Nobelprize.org, "The Noble Prize in Literature: 1963: Award Ceremony Speech," http://www.nobelprize.org/nobel_prizes/literature/laureates /1963/press.html.

33. George Seferis, "Some Notes on Modern Greek Tradition," Nobel lecture, December 11, 1963, http://www.nobelprize.org/nobel_prizes/literature /laureates/1963/seferis-lecture.html.

34. Greece.org, "Melina's Speech to the Oxford Union."

35. Paul Anastasi, "Olympics: Birthplace of Games Shocked and Angered," *New York Times*, September 19, 1990, http://www.nytimes.com/1990/09 /19/sports/olympics-birthplace-of-games-shocked-and-angered.html.

36. Vangelis Calotychos, *Modern Greece: A Cultural Poetics* (Oxford: Berg, 2003), 3.

37. Anastasi, "Olympics."

38. Stephen R. Weisman, "Atlanta Selected over Athens for the 1996 Olympics," *New York Times*, September 19, 1990, http://www.nytimes.com /1990/09/19/sports/atlanta-selected-over-athens-for-1996-olympics.html.

39. Athens 2004, "Phevos and Athena: The Two Mascots of the 2004 Olympic Games," available only via the *Wayback Machine,* web.archive.org/web /20060410065628/http://www.athens2004.com/en/OlympicMascots.

40. Plantzos, "Archaeology and Hellenic Identity," 12 (emphasis in original).

41. Matthew Campbell, "Vangelis Papathanassiou Fights Greek Gods of Demolition," November 26, 2007, http://www.greeknewsonline.com /vangelis-papathanassiou-fights-greek-gods-of-demolition.

6. CLASSICAL DEBT IN CRISIS

1. UNICEF, "Children of the Recession: The Impact of the Economic Crisis on Child Well-Being in Rich Countries," *Innocenti Report Card 12,* September 2014, 10, https://www.unicef-irc.org/publications/pdf/rc12-eng -web.pdf.

2. Mark Blyth, *Austerity: History of a Dangerous Idea* (Oxford: Oxford University Press, 2013), 2.

3. Ibid.

4. Quotation reported in Jennifer Szalai, "The Tough Love of Austerity," *New York Times Magazine,* August 4, 2015, http://www.nytimes.com/2015 /08/09/magazine/the-tough-love-of-austerity.html.

5. Yannis Hamilakis, "Some Debts Can Never Be Repaid: The Archaeopolitics of the Crisis," *Journal of Modern Greek Studies* 34 (2016): 239.

6. George Wheler, *A Journey into Greece . . . in the Company of Dr. Spon of Lyon* (London: William Caldeman et al., 1682), "Epistle Dedicatory."

7. Michael Klonovsky, "2000 Jahre Niedergang," *Focus,* February 22, 2010, http://www.focus.de/finanzen/news/staatsverschuldung/wirtschaft -2000-jahre-niedergang_aid_482500.html.

8. Nick Malkoutzis, "The Hemlock Ballot: Why the Greek Referendum Controversy Is a Tragedy in Slow Motion," *Foreign Policy,* November 2, 2011, http://foreignpolicy.com/2011/11/02/the-hemlock-ballot.

9. George Zarkadakis, "Modern Greece's Real Problem? Ancient Greece," *Washington Post,* November 4, 2011, https://www.washingtonpost.com /opinions/modern-greeces-real-problem-ancient-greece/2011/11/01 /gIQACSq9mM_story.html.

10. Nikos Dimou, *Η δυστυχία του να είσαι Έλληνας* (On the unhappiness of being Greek), trans. David Connolly (Alresford, UK: Zero Books, 2012). Connolly's translation of aphorism 49 takes a controversial liberty: he translates "Any race believing itself to be descended from the ancient Greeks." The Greek literally reads "Any race descended from the ancient Greeks," not "believing itself to be descended."

11. Constantine Karamanlis, "The Ideal of a United Europe," *Pro-Europa .org,* http://www.pro-europa.eu/index.php/en/library/the-struggle-for -the-union-of-europe/161-karamanlis,-konstantinos-the-ideal-of-a-united -europe.

12. James Angelos, "Why on Earth Is Greece in the EU? Reverence for the Ancient Greeks Led to the Modern Greek Crisis," *Politico,* June 22, 2015, http://www.politico.eu/article/why-is-greece-in-the-eu-grexit.

13. Stathis N. Kalyvas, *Modern Greece: What Everyone Needs to Know* (Oxford: Oxford University Press, 2015), 33–34.

14. Michael Herzfeld, "The Absent Presence: Discourses of Crypto-colonialism," *South Atlantic Quarterly* 101, no. 4 (2002): 900.

15. Mary Kitroeff, trans., "Alexandros Papadiamantis: *Easter Chanter,*" in *Modernism: Representations of National Culture,* ed. Ahmet Ersoy, Maciej Górny, and Vangelis Kechriotis (Budapest: Central European Press, 2012), 188.

16. W. E. B. Du Bois, *The Souls of Black Folk: Essays and Sketches,* 3rd ed. (Chicago: A. C. McClurg, 1903), 3.

17. Vangelis Calotychos, *Modern Greece: A Cultural Poetics* (Oxford: Berg, 2003), 47–53.

18. Artemis Leontis, *Topographies of Hellenism: Mapping the Homeland* (Ithaca, NY: Cornell University Press, 1995), 68n2. Leontis's phrase is inspired by postcolonial scholarship centered on Africa, such as Ngũgĩ wa Thiong'o's *Decolonising the Mind: The Politics of Language in African Literature* (London: J. Currey; Portsmouth, NH: Heinemann, 1986) and Chinweizu, Onwuchekwa Jemie, and Ihechukwu Madubuike's *Toward the Decolonization of African Literature* (Washington, DC: Howard University Press, 1983).

19. I thank Vassilis Varouhakis for making this point to me.

20. The Kondylis reference and quotation are from Ilias Papagiannopoulos, "'Much Earlier, Much Later, Today': Modern Greek Political Time and Christos Vakalopoulos," in *The Problem of Modern Greek Identity: From the Ecumene to the Nation-State,* ed. Georgios Steiris, Sotiris Mitralexis, and Georgios Arabatzis (Cambridge: Cambridge Scholars Publishing, 2016), 67.

21. Patrick Leigh Fermor, *Roumeli: Travels in Northern Greece* (New York: New York Review of Books, 2016), 113–115 (first published in London by John Murray in 1966).

22. Greek News Agenda, "Rethinking Greece: Dimitris Tziovas on the Greek Crisis & the Reinvention of Modern Greek Studies," March 20, 2016, http://www.greeknewsagenda.gr/index.php/rethinking-greece/5917-rethinking-greece-dimitris-tziovas.

23. "'Έλληνες για να ρίχνουμε στάκτη στα μάτια του κόσμου, πραγματικά 'Ρωμιοί.'" Kostis Palamas, *Ο Δωδεκάλογος του Γύφτου* (Athens: Hestia, 1907), 126.

24. Stathis Gourgouris, *Dream Nation: Enlightenment, Colonization, and the Institution of Modern Greece* (Stanford, CA: Stanford University Press, 1996), 152.

25. Hulu (video property of NBC), "Greek Gods," *Saturday Night Live,* November 5, 2011, Hulu video, 46:27, http://www.hulu.com/watch/297346.

26. Elias Groll, "Bad Metaphor Watch: The Tragedy of the Greek Crisis Edition," *Foreign Policy*, July 7, 2015, http://foreignpolicy.com/2015/07/07 /bad-metaphor-watch-the-tragedy-of-the-greek-crisis-edition.

27. Charlemagne [Tom Nuttall], "The Sorry Saga of Syriza," *Economist*, March 9, 2015, http://www.economist.com/node/21650600.

28. Dimitris Tziovas, "Introduction: Decolonizing Antiquity, Heritage Politics, and Performing the Past," in *Re-imagining the Past: Antiquity and Modern Greek Culture*, ed. Dimitris Tziovas (Oxford: Oxford University Press, 2014), 15–16.

29. Pappas Post (video property of HBO), "Last Week Tonight with John Oliver Pokes Fun at Yanis Varoufakis," filmed February 22, 2015, YouTube video, 3:12, posted February 23, 2015, https://www.youtube.com/watch ?v=_U4U7M4WOPU.

30. Cited in Lauren Talalay, "Drawing Conclusions: Greek Antiquity, the €conomic Crisis, and Political Cartoons," *Journal of Modern Greek Studies* 31 (2013): 250.

31. "Verkauft doch eure Inseln, ihr Pleite-Griechen . . . und die Akropolis gleich mit!," *Bild*, October 27, 2010, http://www.bild.de/politik/wirtschaft /griechenland-krise/regierung-athen-sparen-verkauft-inseln-pleite -akropolis-11692338.bild.html.

32. Yannis Hamilakis, *The Nation and Its Ruins: Antiquity, Archaeology, and National Imagination in Greece* (Oxford: Oxford University Press, 2007), 32 (emphasis in original).

33. Wheler, *Journey into Greece*, "Epistle Dedicatory."

34. *This Is America*, transcript of July 6, 2015, show, http://www.rushlimbaugh .com/daily/2015/07/06/this_is_america_2015.

35. Political Tours, "Greece and the Euro Tour," http://www.politicaltours .com/tours/tour-greece-the-euro.

36. Perron3, "Samaras Amfipolh," filmed August 12, 2014, YouTube video, 5:51, posted August 12, 2014, https://www.youtube.com/watch?v=cTpV5_vBd9c

37. As quoted in Nikolaos Zahariadis, *Essence of Political Manipulation: Emotion, Institutions and Greek Foreign Policy* (New York: Peter Lang, 2005), 122–123.

38. Yannis Hamilakis, "Archaeo-politics in Macedonia," *London Review of Books: LRB Blog*, January 22, 2015, http://www.lrb.co.uk/blog/2015/01/22/yannis-hamilakis/archaeo-politics-in-macedonia.

39. Hamilakis, "Some Debts Can Never Be Repaid," 254.

40. Alexis Tsipras, "On the Cusp of a Historic Change," *World Post*, January 5, 2015, http://www.huffingtonpost.com/alexis-tsipras/on-the-cusp-of-a-historic_b_6417124.html.

41. Hellenic Republic Prime Minister's Office, "Prime Minister Alexis Tsipras' Address Concerning the Referendum to Be Held on the 5th of July," June 27, 2015, http://primeminister.gr/english/2015/06/27/prime-minister-alexis-tsipras-address-concerning-the-referendum-to-be-held-on-the-5th-of-july.

42. Joanna Kakissis, "After the Fall: Greece's Former Prime Minister Assesses the State of His Nation," *Time*, May 1, 2012, http://content.time.com/time/world/article/0,8599,2113624,00.html.

43. Yanis Varoufakis, "Minister No More!," *Thoughts for a Post-2008 World* (blog), July 6, 2015, https://yanisvaroufakis.eu/2015/07/06/minister-no-more.

44. Yanis Varoufakis, "How I Became an Erratic Marxist," *Guardian*, February 18, 2015, http://www.theguardian.com/news/2015/feb/18/yanis-varoufakis-how-i-became-an-erratic-marxist.

45. Yanis Varoufakis, *The Global Minotaur: America, the True Origins of the Financial Crisis and the Future of the World Economy*, 2nd ed. (London: Zed Books, 2015), 25 (the subtitle was updated for the book's second edition).

46. Yanis Varoufakis, "The Eurozone, the Ant, and the Grasshopper," *Channel 4 News* video, posted February 12, 2012, http://www.channel4.com/news/the-eurozone-the-ant-and-the-grasshopper.

47. TED.com, "Yanis Varoufakis: Why Capitalism Will Eat Democracy," transcript of a December 2015 TEDGlobal talk presented in Geneva, https://www.ted.com/talks/yanis_varoufakis_capitalism_will_eat _democracy_unless_we_speak_up.

48. Yanis Varoufakis, "So, Why Did the Crash of 2008 Happen? A First Glimpse of the Global Minotaur," *Thoughts for a Post-2008 World* (blog), January 15, 2011, https://yanisvaroufakis.eu/2011/01/15/so-why-did-the -crash-of-2008-happen-a-first-glimpse-of-the-global-minotaur.

49. Michael Kimmelman, "Elgin Marble Monument in a New Light," *New York Times*, June 23, 2009, http://www.nytimes.com/2009/06/24/arts /design/24abroad.html.

7. WE ARE ALL GREEKS?

1. Fiachra Gibbons, "Jean-Luc Godard: 'Film Is Over. What to Do?,'" *Guardian*, July 12, 2011, http://www.theguardian.com/film/2011/jul/12 /jean-luc-godard-film-socialisme.

2. Hellenic Statistical Authority (ΕΛΣΤΑΤ), "2011 Population and Housing Census: Demographic Characteristics," http://www.statistics.gr/en /statistics/-/publication/SAM03.

3. Hellenic Statistical Authority (ΕΛΣΤΑΤ), "Demographic Characteristics / 1991 (#16: Πληθυσμός Ελληνικής και ξένης υπηκοότητας με διάκριση του συνόλου των χωρών της Ευρωπαϊκής Ένωσης, κατά φύλο και ομάδες ηλικιών. Σύνολο Ελλάδος)," http://www.statistics.gr /el/statistics/-/publication/SAM03/1991.

4. "Χρυσή Αυγή: Ο Σχορτσιανίτης δεν είναι Έλληνας," *TVXS*, October 26, 2012, http://tvxs.gr/news/ellada/xrysi-aygi-o-sxortsianitis-den-einai -ellinas.

5. Johann Joachim Winckelmann, *History of the Art of Antiquity*, trans Harry Francis Malgrave (Los Angeles: Getty Publications, 2006), 195.

6. Nell Irvin Painter, *A History of White People* (New York: W. W. Norton, 2010), 61.

7. Winckelmann, *History of the Art of Antiquity*, 210, 128.

8. Percy Bysshe Shelley, *Hellas: A Lyrical Drama* (London: Charles and James Ollier, 1822), ix.

9. "We Are All Greeks" Facebook page, https://www.facebook.com /Eimaste.Oloi.Ellhnes.

10. Yannis Hamilakis, "Hospitable Zeus," *London Review of Books Blog*, August 8, 2012, http://www.lrb.co.uk/blog/2012/08/08/yannis-hamilakis /hospitable-zeus.

11. "Δεν ωφελεί να ανταγωνιζόμαστε με την ακροδεξιά στην ιδεολογική διαχείριση του παρελθόντος." Konstantinos Poulis, "Ο Ξένιος Ζευς, ο Άδωνις και η αρχαιογνωσία," *ThePressProject*, September 3, 2012, http://www.thepressproject.gr/article/27001.

12. UNHCR: The UN Refugee Agency, "Number of Refugees and Migrants Arriving in Greece Soars 750 Per Cent over 2014," August 7, 2015, http://www.unhcr.org/55c4d1fc2.html.

13. UNHCR: The UN Refugee Agency, "Greece Data Snapshot 23 April 2016," https://data.unhcr.org/mediterranean/download.php?id=1095.

14. "Σαλαμίνα: Ο Π. Καμμένος, το κόκκινο χαλί σε παλέτες και τα δόρατα," *In.gr*, September 30, 2015, http://news.in.gr/greece/article/?aid =1500029548.

15. Hellenic Republic Ministry of National Defense, "Defense Minister Panos Kammenos Attends the Commemoration of the Naval Battle of Salamis," 2015, http://www.mod.mil.gr/mod/en/content/show/36/A86890. The first quotation is Yannis Hamilakis's more accurate translation of Kammenos's Greek-language speech and appears in "Some Debts Can Never Be Repaid: The Archaeo-politics of the Crisis," *Journal of Modern Greek Studies* 34 (October 2016): 230.

16. Gonda Van Steen, *Liberating Hellenism from the Ottoman Empire: Comte de Marcellus and the Last of the Classics* (New York: Palgrave, 2010), 115. Van Steen is here referring to the case of the French diplomat and traveler Lodoïs de Martin du Tyrac, Comte de Marcellus.

17. "Migrant Crisis: Greece Will Not Be Turned into a 'Warehouse of Souls,' Says Tsipras," *Euronews,* February 25, 2016, http://www.euronews.com /2016/02/25/migrant-crisis-greece-will-not-be-turned-into-a-warehouse -of-souls-says-tsipras.

18. Alex Barker, Duncan Robinson, and Kerin Hope, "Greece Warned EU Will Reimpose Border Controls," *Financial Times,* December 1, 2015, http://www.ft.com/intl/cms/s/0/463dc7a0-982b-11e5-9228-87e603d47bdc .html#axzz47V2Ozoi6.

19. Michael Herzfeld, "Welcome to Greece (but Not to Europe)," *Foreign Policy,* February 25, 2016, http://foreignpolicy.com/2016/02/25/welcome -to-greece-but-not-to-europe-schengen-racism.

20. "'Τα αρχαία μας ανήκουν'! Το θράσος γερμανού τουρίστα στο Αρχαιολογικό Μουσείο Ηρακλείου," *inotos.gr,* July 26, 2015, http://www .inotos.gr/archives/208678.

21. One account of the story and the hoax: "Τι παρήγγειλε τελικά το ζευγάρι Γερμανών σε ταβέρνα στην Ικαρία;" *LiFO,* July 7, 2014, http:// www.lifo.gr/team/bitsandpieces/49894.

22. UNESCO, "The Criteria for Selection," http://whc.unesco.org/en/criteria.

23. UNESCO, "World Heritage List," http://whc.unesco.org/en/list.

24. UNESCO, "The Criteria for Selection," http://whc.unesco.org/en/criteria.

25. UNESCO, "Minoan Palatial Centres (Knossos, Phaistos, Malia, Zakros, Kydonia)," http://whc.unesco.org/en/tentativelists/5860.

26. Mirjam Brusius, "The Middle East Heritage Debate Is Becoming Worryingly Colonial," *Conversation,* April 25, 2016, http://theconversation .com/the-middle-east-heritage-debate-is-becoming-worryingly-colonial -57679.

27. Charlemagne [Tom Nuttall], "The Necessity of Culture: Europe's Shared History Should Be Treasured, Not Ignored," *Economist*, May 12, 2016, http://www.economist.com/news/europe/21694541-europes-shared-history-should-be-treasured-not-ignored-necessity-culture.

28. Ömür Harmanşah, "ISIS, Heritage, and the Spectacles of Destruction in the Global Media," *Near Eastern Archaeology* 78 (2015): 175.

29. Diana Darke, *Syria*, 2nd ed., Bradt Travel Guides (Guilford, CT: Globe Pequot Press, 2010), 114.

30. *Μηχανή του Χρόνου*, "Άγνωστες ιστορίες της παλιάς Αθήνας," YouTube video, 56:04, posted December 15, 2014, https://www.youtube.com/watch?v=1FclXKp7oaE. An image of the notice appears from 11:48 to 12:02.

31. Quoted in Thomas L. Donaldson, "Report of the Committee Appointed to Examine the Elgin Marbles," *Civil Engineer and Architect's Journal* 5 (1842): 249.

32. "Museum Admits 'Scandal' of Elgin Marbles," *BBC News*, December 1, 1999, http://news.bbc.co.uk/2/hi/uk/543077.stm.

33. Ian Jenkins, *Cleaning and Controversy: The Parthenon Sculptures, 1811–1939*, British Museum Occasional Paper 146 (London: British Museum, 2001). Available on the British Museum website as "The 1930s Cleaning of the Parthenon Sculptures in the British Museum," https://www.britishmuseum.org/about_us/news_and_press/statements/parthenon_sculptures/1930s_cleaning.aspx.

34. Intelligence Squared, "Send Them Back: The Parthenon Marbles Should Be Returned to Athens," filmed June 11, 2011, YouTube video, 46:38, posted June 22, 2012, https://www.youtube.com/watch?v=YE7DpRjDd-U.

35. International Association for the Reunification of the Parthenon Sculptures, http://www.parthenoninternational.org.

36. Helena Smith, "Greece Looks to International Justice to Regain Parthenon Marbles from UK," *Guardian*, May 8, 2016 (the online article

includes the link to the leaked document), https://www.theguardian .com/artanddesign/2016/may/08/greece-international-justice-regain -parthenon-marbles-uk.

37. "The Case for the Return of the Parthenon Sculptures," 5–6, link in Smith, "Greece Looks to International Justice."

38. Padraic Flanagan, " 'Someone Needs to Restore Your Marbles': Boris Johnson Reacts to Clooney's Elgin Marbles Comment," *Telegraph,* February 12, 2014, http://www.telegraph.co.uk/culture/film/10634710 /Someone-needs-to-restore-your-marbles-Boris-Johnson-reacts-to -Clooneys-Elgin-Marbles-comment.html.

39. Boris Johnson, "The Boris Archive: Africa Is a Mess, but We Can't Blame Colonialism" (reprint of an article originally published by Johnson in the *London Spectator* on February 2, 2002), *Spectator Blog,* July 14, 2016, http://blogs.spectator.co.uk/2016/07/boris-archive-africa-mess-cant -blame-colonialism.

40. *C. P. Cavafy: Selected Prose Works,* trans. Peter Jeffreys (Ann Arbor: University of Michigan Press, 2010), 21–22.

41. *ThePressProject,* "Review: Let's Sell the Acropolis," YouTube video, 19:10, posted October 15, 2015, https://www.youtube.com/watch?v=3k STtkuAOyA.

42. Kate Hellaway, *"Austerity Measures: The New Greek Poetry—Review,"* *Guardian,* April 3, 2016, https://www.theguardian.com/books/2016 /apr/03/austerity-measures-new-greek-poetry-review-karen-van -dyck.

43. Karen Van Dyck, "The New Greek Poetry," *Guardian,* March 25, 2016, http://www.theguardian.com/books/2016/mar/25/new-greek-poetry -karen-van-dyck.

44. Slavoj Žižek, "How Alexis Tsipras and Syriza Outmaneuvered Angela Merkel and the Eurocrats," *In These Times,* January 23, 2015

http://inthesetimes.com/article/18229/slavoj-zizek-syriza-tsipras -merkel.

EPILOGUE

1. College Board, "AP European History: Example Textbook List," http:// www.collegeboard.com/html/apcourseaudit/courses/european_history _textbook_list.html.

2. Joshua Cole and Carol Symes, *Western Civilizations: Their History and Their Culture,* 18th ed. (London: W. W. Norton, 2003), 108–109.

3. Alan J. Singer, *Teaching Global History: A Social Studies Approach* (New York : Routledge, 2011), 78.

4. John P. McKay et al., *A History of World Societies,* 9th ed. (Boston: Bedford / St Martin's, 2011), 114.

5. Classical Reception Studies Network, "Welcome to CRSN," http://www .open.ac.uk/arts/research/crsn.

6. Jerry Bentley, Herbert Ziegler, and Heather Streets Salter, *Traditions and Encounters: A Global Perspective on the Past,* 3rd ed. (Boston: McGraw-Hill, 2006), 237.

7. Laura Swift, "If Only We Could Ask Euripides about the Refugees," *Conversation,* October 2, 2015, http://theconversation.com/if-only-we-could -ask-euripides-about-refugees-48352.

8. Ulrich Sinn, "Greek Sanctuaries as Places of Refuge," in *Greek Sanctuaries: New Approaches,* ed. Nanno Marinatos and Robin Hägg (London: Routledge, 1993), 73.

9. A brief BBC article by historian Paul Cartledge provides a handy and engaging overview of democracy's ancient Greek critics: Paul Cartledge, "Critics and Critiques of Ancient Greek Democracy," *BBC History,* February 17, 2011, http://www.bbc.co.uk/history/ancient/greeks/greek critics_01.shtml.

10. Neil MacGregor, "The British Museum: A Museum for the World," *British Museum Blog,* November 12, 2015, https://blog.britishmuseum .org/2015/11/12/the-british-museum-a-museum-for-the-world.

11. Mirjam Brusius, "The Middle East Heritage Debate Is Becoming Worryingly Colonial," *The Conversation,* April 25, 2016, http://theconversation .com/the-middle-east-heritage-debate-is-becoming-worryingly-colonial -57679.

FURTHER READING

The following paragraphs contain suggestions for further reading in English and are intended to complement (and in some cases emphasize) the sources listed in each chapter's notes.

GENERAL AND INTRODUCTORY

Good general introductions to the history of modern Greece include Richard Clogg's *A Concise History of Greece*, 3rd rev. ed. (Cambridge: Cambridge University Press, 2013) and Thomas W. Gallant's *Modern Greece* (London: Arnold, 2001). Gallant is also general editor of *The Edinburgh History of the Greeks*, an ongoing project to document, in ten volumes, Greek history from antiquity to the present (Edinburgh: Edinburgh University Press, 2014–; three volumes have appeared to date). *Modern Greece: What Everyone Needs to Know* by the political scientist Stathis N. Kalyvas (Oxford: Oxford University Press, 2015) is an indispensable pocket guide to the historical background of the modern Greek financial crisis.

For Greek antiquity's importance to the history of modern Greece, two especially wide-ranging sources are Yannis Hamilakis's *The Nation and Its Ruins: Antiquity, Archaeology, and National Imagination in Greece* (Oxford: Oxford University Press, 2007) and the set of essays collected in Dimitris Tziovas's edited volume *Re-imagining the Past: Antiquity and Modern Greek Culture* (Oxford: Oxford University Press, 2014).

CHAPTER 1

Two insightful articles on the complexity of ideologies behind the recent destruction of antiquities in the Middle East and beyond are Finbarr Barry Flood's "Between Cult and Culture: Bamiyan, Islamic Iconoclasm, and the Museum," *Art Bulletin* 84 (2002): 641–659, and Ömür Harmanşah's "ISIS, Heritage, and the Spectacles of Destruction in the Global Media," *Near Eastern Archaeology* 78 (2015): 170–177. Nicos Christodoulakis's *Germany's War Debt to Greece: A Burden Unsettled* (New York: Palgrave, 2014) examines the Greek case that Germany should pay reparations for the Nazi occupation during World War II.

Endless sources illustrate the presence of ancient Greece in modern popular culture. Besides the recent titles named in Chapter 1, two that attempt to account for Greek antiquity's continued relevance for modernity are Charlotte Higgins's *It's All Greek to Me* (London: Short Books, 2008; New York: Harper-Collins, 2010) and Thomas Cahill's *Sailing the Wine-Dark Sea: Why the Greeks Matter* (New York: Nan A. Talese / Doubleday, 2003). Mary Beard and Daniel Mendelsohn are critics who consistently and eloquently bring Greek and Roman antiquity to bear on modernity; good introductions to their work include Beard's *Confronting the Classics: Traditions, Adventures, and Innovations* (London: Profile Books; New York: W. W. Norton, 2013) and Mendelsohn's *Waiting for the Barbarians: Essays from the Classics to Pop Culture* (New York: New York Review of Books, 2012).

Samuel P. Huntington debuted his "clash of civilizations" thesis in his article "The Clash of Civilizations?" (*Foreign Affairs*, Summer 1993). The article marked a response to arguments put forth by Francis Fukuyama, his former student, in *The End of History and the Last Man* (New York: Macmillan, 1992). There were many responses out of Greece to Huntington's work; philosopher Christos Yannaras's *Orthodoxy and the West: Hellenic Self-Identity in the Modern Age* (Brookline, MA: Holy Cross Orthodox Press, 2006) is one of the few that has been translated into English. More recently, in *Civilization: The West and the Rest* (New York: Penguin Press; London: Allen Lane, 2011), Niall Ferguson has attempted, with characteristic provocativeness, to define and describe Western civilization and to account for what he sees as its current decline.

CHAPTER 2

Josiah Ober's *The Rise and Fall of Classical Greece* (Princeton, NJ: Princeton University Press, 2015) offers an interpretation of the "miracle" (or "efflorescence") of classical Greece; it has been both acclaimed and critiqued. In *Democracy: A Life* (Oxford: Oxford University Press, 2016), Paul Cartledge traces the rise of democracy in Athens (and elsewhere in Greece), as well as the influence of Greek democracy—by no means direct or simple—on the modern constitutions of the United States, Britain, and France.

One standard narrative of the Athenian Empire is P. J. Rhodes's *The Athenian Empire* (Oxford: Clarendon Press, 1985). Polly Low's edited volume *The Athenian Empire* (Edinburgh: Edinburgh University Press, 2008) collects key scholarship on the subject. In *Inventing the Barbarian: Greek Self-Definition through Tragedy* (Oxford: Clarendon Press, 1989), Edith Hall influentially argues that the Athenian view of non-Greeks was chauvinistic and inspired immense cultural production. In *Athens and Persians in the Fifth Century B.C.: A Study in Cultural Receptivity* (Cambridge: Cambridge University Press, 1997), Margaret Miller emphasizes the significant "foreign" influence on classical Athenian culture. Kostas Vlassopoulos's more recent *Greeks and Barbarians* (Cambridge: Cambridge University Press, 2013) uses the premise of an ancient "globalized" Mediterranean to explore Greek interactions with non-Greeks in antiquity.

The definitive study of the Athenian institution of the funeral oration (the *epitaphios logos*) is Nicole Loraux's *The Invention of Athens: The Funeral Oration in the Classical City* (New York: Zone Books, 2006), Alan Sheridan's translation of Loraux's original *L'invention d'Athènes: Histoire de l'oraison funèbre dans la "cité classique"* (Paris: Mouton, 1981). Simon Goldhill's "The Great Dionysia and Civic Ideology," *Journal of Hellenic Studies* 107 (1987): 58–76, is a foundational English-language study of Athenian drama's context in the imperial city; that essay was collected with others on the relationship among Athenian drama, politics, and society in John J. Winkler and Froma I. Zeitlin's *Nothing to Do with Dionysus? Athenian Drama in Its Social Context* (Princeton, NJ: Princeton University Press, 1990). Robin Rhodes's *Architecture and Meaning on the Athenian Acropolis* (Cambridge: Cambridge University Press, 1995) accounts for the entire Acropolis as an "integrated architectural concept" and is a good introduction to the Periclean building program and its imperial history and politics.

CHAPTER 3

Dimitris Gutas's *Greek Thought, Arabic Culture* (London: Routledge, 1998) offers an excellent account of the Abbasid translation movement in Baghdad. Michael D. Reeve's chapter "Classical Scholarship" in the *Cambridge Companion to Renaissance Humanism,* edited by Jill Kraye (Cambridge: Cambridge University Press, 1996), is a brief but informative overview of the "rediscovery" of classical learning (and of ancient Greek texts) during the European Renaissance. Mary Beard's *The Parthenon,* rev. ed. (Cambridge, MA: Harvard University Press, 2010), fills out the history of the Athenian Acropolis in the long period that the cinematic sequence of this chapter hurtles through. Molly Greene's *The Edinburgh History of the Greeks, 1453–1774: The Ottoman Empire* (Edinburgh: Edinburgh University Press, 2015) offers a rich overview of Greece in the years when travelers from Europe began to visit in increasing numbers.

The bibliography on early travelers to Greece is immense. Robin Dankoff's *An Ottoman Mentality: The World of Evliya Çelebi* (Leiden: Brill, 2004) sheds light on the context and author of Çelebi's *Book of Travels.* Two engaging accounts of early European travelers are David Constantine's *Early Greek Travellers and the Hellenic Ideal* (Cambridge: Cambridge University Press, 1984; reprinted in London by Tauris Parke Paperbacks in 2011 as *In the Footsteps of the Gods*) and Richard Stoneman's *Land of Lost Gods: The Search for Classical Greece* (London: Hutchinson, 1987; reprint, London: Tauris Parke Paperbacks, 2010). Richard Eisner's *Travelers to an Antique Land: The History and Literature of Travel to Greece* (Ann Arbor: University of Michigan Press, 1991) traces the tradition of European travel writing about Greece from its beginnings into the twentieth century. The "Travelogues" project of the Aikaterini Laskaridis foundation is an especially rich resource for primary texts (and drawings and photographs) by travelers to Greek lands from the fifteenth to the twentieth century (http://eng.travelogues.gr). In *Homer's Turk: How Classics Shaped Ideas of the East* (Cambridge, MA: Harvard University Press, 2013) Jerry Turner explores how classical texts often shaped Western travelers' ideas about the East

On antiquities collecting in the early modern period, see especially Ruth Guilding's *Owning the Past: Why the British Collected Antique Sculpture, 1640–1840* (New Haven, CT: Yale University Press, 2014). Jason M. Kelly's *The Society of Dilettanti: Archaeology and Identity in the British Enlightenment* (New Haven, CT: Yale University Press, 2009) situates the society in its historical and social contexts. Benjamin Anderson's "'An Alternative Discourse': Local Interpreters of Antiquities in the Ottoman Empire," *Journal of Field Archaeology* 40 (2015): 450–460, marks an important attempt to recover some of the lost voices of the early travelers' era.

CHAPTER 4

E. M. Butler's *The Tyranny of Greece over Germany* (Cambridge: Cambridge University Press, 1935) is a classic study of German Hellenism; it is outdated in approach but a testament to the topic's importance in the first part of the twentieth century, especially during the rise of the Third Reich. More recently, Suzanne L. Marchand considers the "institution" of German philhellenism in *Down from Olympus: Archaeology and Philhellenism in Germany, 1750–1970* (Princeton, NJ: Princeton University Press, 1996), while Katherine Harloe's *Winckelmann and the Invention of Antiquity* (Oxford: Oxford University Press, 2013) offers an important reappraisal of Johann Joachim Winckelmann that focuses on the early reception and influence of his work (Friedrich August Wolf features here, too).

Thomas W. Gallant includes an overview of the Greek War of Independence in his *The Edinburgh History of the Greeks, 1768 to 1913: The Long Nineteenth Century* (Edinburgh: Edinburgh University Press, 2015). Lucien J. Frary's *Russia and the Making of Modern Greek Identity, 1821–1844* (Oxford: Oxford University Press, 2015) is excellent on Russia's role in the Greek independence movement. Paschalis M. Kitromilides's *Enlightenment and Revolution: The Making of Modern Greece* (Cambridge, MA: Harvard University Press, 2013) and Stathis Gourgouris's *Dream Nation: Enlightenment, Colonization, and the Institution of Modern Greece* (Stanford, CA: Stanford University Press, 1996) are studies of the Greek Enlightenment and the intellectual context of the Greek War of Independence. Peter Mackridge's *Language and National Identity in Greece,*

1766–1976 (Oxford: Oxford University Press, 2009) is an interpretive history of the Greek "language question."

A foundational work on Lord Elgin's acquisition of the Parthenon Marbles (and the controversy that quickly ensued) is *Lord Elgin and the Marbles* (London: Oxford University Press, 1967; 3rd rev. ed., 1998) by William St. Clair. St. Clair also authored *That Greece Might Still Be Free: The Philhellenes in the War of Independence* (Oxford: Oxford University Press, 1972; reprint, Cambridge: Open Book, 2008). Roderick Beaton's *Byron's War: Romantic Rebellion, Greek Revolution* (Cambridge: Cambridge University Press, 2013) is a meticulous account of the Greek War of Independence and, above all, of Lord Byron's role in it. Unsurprisingly, the "independence loans" have lately been much discussed in Greece; in English, legal scholar Michael Waibel discusses those loans and their significance for later Greek debt in "Echoes of History: The International Financial Commission in Greece," in *A Debt Restructuring Mechanism for Sovereigns: Do We Need a Legal Procedure?*, edited by Christoph G. Paulus (Munich: C. H. Beck, 2014). In Greek, Giorgos Romaios has provided an extensive account of the country's history of sovereign debt problems and crises in *Η Ελλάδα των δανείων και των χρεοκοπιών* (Athens: Patakis, 2012).

CHAPTER 5

Yannis Hamilakis's *The Nation and Its Ruins: Antiquity, Archaeology, and National Imagination in Greece* (Oxford: Oxford University Press, 2007) is an indispensable study of the relationship between antiquity and Greek history in the period discussed in this chapter. So too are Vangelis Calotychos's *Modern Greece: A Cultural Poetics* (Oxford: Berg, 2003) and Artemis Leontis's *Topographies of Hellenism: Mapping the Homeland* (Ithaca, NY: Cornell University Press, 1995).

The Creation of Modern Athens: Planning the Myth (Cambridge: Cambridge University Press, 2000) by architectural historian Eleni Bastéa is a fascinating study of the nineteenth-century planning of Athens and of antiquity's role in it. David Randall's *1896: The First Modern Olympics* (London: Blacktoad, 2011; available only as an e-book) is an informative and enjoyable read, as is the American classicist Basil Lanneau Gildersleeve's eyewitness account "My Sixty Days in Greece. I. The Olympic Games, Old and New," in the February 1897 issue of the *Atlantic Monthly*.

Mark Mazower's *Inside Hitler's Greece: The Experience of Occupation, 1941–1944* (1993; reprint, New Haven, CT: Yale University Press [Yale Nota Bene], 2001) is an excellent book by one of the most important historians of modern Greece, and it acknowledges the influence of Hellenism on Hitler and the German troops who occupied Athens. Gonda Van Steen's *Theatre of the Condemned: Classical Tragedy on Greek Prison Islands* (Oxford: Oxford University Press, 2011) is a fascinating account of performances of Athenian tragedy by prisoners during the Greek civil war. Robert Frazier's *Anglo-American Relations with Greece: The Coming of the Cold War, 1942–1947* (New York: St. Martin's, 1991) investigates Greece's role in the development of policies that led to the Truman Doctrine. Sociologist and historian Despina Lalaki's work is important for understanding the role played by Cold War politics in the recasting of Athens as the birthplace of (Western liberal) democracy; her "On the Social Construction of Hellenism: Cold War Narratives of Modernity, Development and Democracy for Greece," *Journal of Historical Sociology* 25 (2012): 552–577, is a good place to start. A volume on the American archeologist Carl Blegen also opens a window onto the entwinements of archeology and ideology in the mid-twentieth century: *Carl W. Blegen: Personal and Archaeological Narratives,* edited by Natalia Vogeikoff-Brogan, Jack L. Davis, and Vasiliki Florou (Atlanta, GA: Lockwood Press, 2015). Roderick Beaton's biography of George Seferis, *Waiting for the Angel* (New Haven, CT: Yale University Press, 2003), is the best English-language account of the poet's life.

A Singular Identity: Archaeology and the Hellenic Identity in the Twentieth Century, edited by Dimitris Damaskos and Dimitris Plantzos (Athens: Benaki Museum, 2008), contains valuable interpretations of the 1896 and 2004 Athens Olympic Games. Dimitris Papaioannou's opening and closing ceremonies at the 2004 Olympics are easy to find on YouTube. Bernard Tschumi Architects published *The New Acropolis Museum* (New York: Skira Rizzoli, 2009) to mark the museum's opening.

CHAPTER 6

The essays collected in Kevin Featherstone's edited volume *Europe in Modern Greek History* (London: Hurst, 2014) offer a range of perspectives; Greece's current finance minister, Euclid Tsakalotos, is among the contributors.

The Problem of Modern Greek Identity, edited by Georgios Steiris, Sotiris Mitralexis, and Georgios Arabatzis (Cambridge: Cambridge Scholars Publishing, 2016), confronts many of the questions about Greek identity that are raised in this chapter. Michael Herzfeld influentially outlined his theory of "crypto-colonialism" in "The Absent Presence: Discourses of Crypto-colonialism," *South Atlantic Quarterly* 101 (2002): 899–926.

Accounts of the Greek financial crisis are plentiful in print and on the Internet; journalist Paul Mason's 2015 gripping three-part documentary #*This IsACoup,* which focuses on the events of the summer of 2015, is available on his YouTube channel @PaulMasonNews. Important articles on the use of classical imagery in representations of the crisis include Lauren Talalay's "Drawing Conclusions: Greek Antiquity, the €conomic Crisis, and Political Cartoons," *Journal of Modern Greek Studies* 31 (2013): 249–274, and Yannis Hamilakis's "Some Debts Can Never Be Repaid: The Archaeo-politics of the Crisis," *Journal of Modern Greek Studies* 34 (2016): 227–264. Hamilakis's piece includes meditations on the notion of the West's symbolic debt to Greece (and "symbolic debt" generally) and an extensive account of the "archaeo-politics" of the recent excavations at Amphipolis. It is also richly illustrated with representative political cartoons and includes an extensive up-to-date bibliography.

CHAPTER 7

Sofia Vasilopoulou and Daphne Halikiopoulou's *The Golden Dawn's "Nationalist Solution": Explaining the Rise of the Far Right in Greece* (New York: Palgrave, 2015) is an informative, if disturbing, account of the new Greek extreme Right. Denise McCoskey's book *Race,* in Oxford University Press's Antiquity and Its Legacy series (Oxford: Oxford University Press, 2012), and Nell Irvin Painter's *A History of White People* (New York: W. W. Norton, 2010) both explore the influence of Greek antiquity on later understandings of race; Dave Bindman's *Ape to Apollo: Aesthetics and the Idea of Race in the 18th Century* (Ithaca, NY: Cornell University Press, 2002) is dedicated to Winckelmann's era.

The articles by Flood and Harmanşah mentioned in the section on further reading for Chapter 1 are again relevant here. Peter Watson and Cecilia Todeschini's *The Medici Conspiracy: The Illicit Journey of Looted Antiquities, from Italy's Tomb Raiders to the World's Greatest Museums* (New York: BBS PublicAffairs,

2006) is a particularly informative book about the global illegal trade in antiquities and reads as a thrilling detective story. Erin Thompson's *Possession: The Curious History of Private Collectors from Antiquity to the Present* (New Haven, CT: Yale University Press, 2016), by a professor of "art crime," begins in Rome and ends in the modern Middle East.

A 2013 special issue of *Hesperia: The Journal of the American School of Classical Studies at Athens* (80, no. 2, edited by Jack L. Davis and Natalia Vogeikoff-Brogan) titled "Philhellenism, Philanthropy, or Political Convenience? American Archaeology in Greece" addresses darker aspects of the school's history in Greece. Yannis Hamilakis's article in the issue, "Double Colonization: The Story of the Excavations of the Athenian Agora (1924–1931)" (pages 153–177), discusses the leveling of Vrissaki. Derek Gillman's *The Idea of Cultural Heritage,* rev. ed. (Cambridge: Cambridge University Press, 2006), is a good account of the major issues in heritage definition and management; it includes discussions of both the Elgin Marbles and Afghanistan's Bamiyan Buddhas. Although Jeanette Greenfield's *The Return of Cultural Treasures,* 3rd rev. ed. (Cambridge: Cambridge University Press, 2007), is now a little out of date, it is still a useful handbook on repatriation debates.

ILLUSTRATION CREDITS

96 *Travelogues: Travellers' Views,* Collection of the Aikaterini Laskaridis Foundation Library, Pireaus, Greece

110 bpk Bildagentur / Klassik Stiftung, Weimar, Germany / Art Resource, NY

113 Scala / Museo Pio Clementino / Art Resource, NY

127 De Agostini Picture Library / A. Dagli Orti / Bridgeman Images

154 Private Collection / The Stapleton Collection / Bridgeman Images

156 bpk Bildagentur / Bayerische Staatsgemaeldesammlungen, Munich, Germany / Art Resource, NY

157 Dimboukas at English Wikipedia / Wikimedia Commons (CC BY-SA 3.0)

166 Photograph by Dimitrios Constantin, ca. 1865 (detail) / ELIA-MIET Photographic Archive / Hellenic Literary and Historical Archive– Cultural Foundation of the National Bank of Greece

192 *Klepsydra,* Opening Ceremony, 2004 Summer Olympic Games, Athens. Conceived, visualized and directed by Dimitris Papaioannou. Screenshot by Johanna Hanink.

222 © 2015 Steve Sack / *The Minneapolis Star Tribune* / Cagle Cartoons, Inc.

224 © 2012 Rick McKee / *The Augusta Chronicle* / Cagle Cartoons, Inc.

225 © 2015 Gary Varvel / *The Indianapolis Star* / Creators Syndicate, Inc.

226 © 2012 Christo Komarnitski, Bulgaria / Cagle Cartoons, Inc.

228 © 2012 Martin Sutovec, Slovakia / Cagle Cartoons, Inc.

245 Reuters / Ivan Milutinovic

249 © 2011 Soloúp (Antonis Nikolopoulos) / *Pontiki* (May 19, 2011)

268 *Anaskopisi,* "Let's Sell the Acropolis!" S01, E10 (*ThePressProject,* July 28, 2015). Screenshot by Johanna Hanink.

INDEX